The
Cigar

CARMINE GALANTE, MAFIA TERROR

The Cigar

Frank Dimatteo &
Michael Benson

CITADEL PRESS
Kensington Publishing Corp.
www.kensingtonbooks

CITADEL PRESS BOOKS are published by

Kensington Publishing Corp.
119 West 40th Street
New York, NY 10018

All Kensington titles, imprints, and distributed lines are available at special quantity discounts for bulk purchases for sales promotions, premiums, fund-raising, educational, or institutional use. Special book excerpts or customized printings can also be created to fit specific needs. For details, write or phone the office of the Kensington sales manager: Kensington Publishing Corp., 119 West 40th Street, New York, NY 10018, attn: Sales Department; phone 1-800-221-2647.

CITADEL PRESS and the Citadel logo are Reg. U.S. Pat. & TM Off.

ISBN: 978-0-8065-4237-9

First Citadel hardcover printing: April 2023

10 9 8 7 6 5 4 3 2 1

Printed in the United States of America

Library of Congress Control Number: 2022948705

ISBN: 978-0-8065-4239-3 (e-book)

To Louie the Syrian
for what he told me after the meet
—Frank Dimatteo

Those who call the police are fools or cowards. Those who need police protection are both. If you are attacked, do not give the name of your attacker. Once you recover, you will want to avenge the attack yourself. A wounded man should say to his assailant: "If I live, I will kill you. If I die, you are forgiven."

—The Code of Omerta

CONTENTS

The Glare of a Killer

NEW YORK POLICE DETECTIVE Ralph Salerno was on the job for decades, working the rackets, and he'd seen his share of the underworld. Some of it seemed just like everything else, guys trying to get over, maybe just the other side of the street.

And then again some of it was sick.

Evil.

Salerno considered himself an expert on mobsters. He'd known dozens of them, he said. Knew them A to Z. But Salerno had only met two gangsters personally who, when he looked them in the eye, he decided he wouldn't want them to be mad at him.

Aniello Dellacroce of the Gambinos was one.

Carmine Galante, a Bonanno through and through, was the other.

"They had bad eyes. I mean they had the eyes of killers. You could see how frightening they were, the frigid glare of a killer," Salerno said.

Organized crime is known for its nasty fucks, but no fuck was nastier than Carmine "Lilo" Galante. "Lilo" means "cigar" in Castellammare. Only the people he liked could call him Lilo. If he was in a bad mood, only the people he liked could live.

He had that dead-eyed stare, and Detective Salerno wasn't the only one to notice it. He had it when he ate, when he spoke, and when he killed. I met him twice. He had it both times.

There might be a little glint in his eyes when he killed, but it

1

didn't last for long. His eyes were ice hard, and they terrified both Galante's fellow mobsters, and the cops who were supposed to bring him to justice.

Galante had a lot of numbers. He was identified as New York State DCI Number 137561X. He was known as New York Police Department (NYPD) Number B66994. His FBI number was 119 495. His Social Security number was 071-12-0666, which appropriately contained the devil's number.

His kills were cold as ice. How many? They were uncountable.

Galante once shot a kid, a little girl. All right, it was an accident, he was aiming for a cop, and it was only a flesh wound in the thigh, but . . . he shot a kid. One story has him throwing a plate of boiling spaghetti in a pretty girl's face, that was on purpose—if it happened. It might've. He didn't grow into his evil self. By all accounts, he was born evil, bad to the bone from birth.

He made his millions selling that most insidious of substances, the babonia—heroin, dope—*narcotics*, as it was called by the Law. He fed his coffers uncaring of the blight that it put on entire neighborhoods. Fuck 'em. Ca-fucking-ching. That's all Galante thought.

That is, if he thought.

He never showed much sign of intellect, at least none that could be measured by professional shrinks and the like. He seemed to consist of raw ruthlessness, nuts in a psycho-killer sort of way, which made customers much less aggressive when it came time to do business with him.

He told people how it was going to be and that was how it was.

He didn't look like the sort of guy who would become powerful. He was five five, squat, and later in life thoroughly bald. But when you were near him, you could feel it, raw danger crackling around him like so much static electricity.

Sure, he was a psychopath. He didn't give a shit about anything but himself. And he was a true sadist, a man whose only joy was dishing out the hurt, dishing out the death. Plus, he was narcissistic. His hunger for power was legendary, and apparently without limit.

As had his hero Joe Bonanno before him, Galante dreamed of ruling the global underworld—*capo di tutti capi*—and could never be subservient.

He needed to win every time. He fixed games so that he couldn't lose—small games like cards, and some of the largest games there were, games like global drug trafficking. The world he could conquer, but New York City was another matter. It was New York and Lucky Luciano's five-family system that did him in.

Power, no matter its size, is never bulletproof. And, in the end, Carmine Galante got what he deserved, mob-dom's all-time number-one hit—dead on a Bushwick patio with his omnipresent cigar, his last *lilo*, still in his mouth.

CHAPTER ONE

New York City, 1910

ON FEBRUARY 21, 1910, a free concert held in the Normal College auditorium on New York's Park Avenue resulted in a near riot when four thousand people showed up at the two-thousand-seat venue. Desperate for free entertainment, some broke windows to crawl in.

Later that day, in a separate incident, a New York policeman named John Kelly was fired after striking an eleven-year-old and an eight-year-old with his nightstick. Kelly said they had it coming and lost his badge.

Two streetcars ran into each other at the corner of 34th Street and Third Avenue in Manhattan, injuring two people.

In Philadelphia, five hundred people were arrested for rioting over a trolley strike.

In Williamsburg, Brooklyn, an insane man named James Brady escaped from Eastern District Hospital and ran around like the maniac he was, frightening people until he was captured and returned to his padded cell.

The top news story of the day was the rare hurricane that was whipping across Great Britain, affecting the United Kingdom and shipping routes in the Atlantic.

Riots, ill-tempered cops, runaway streetcars, escaped lunatics, and hurricanes aside, the biggest storm of the day was the angry infant being birthed in a Lower East Side tenement.

According to the Manhattan Bureau of Vital Statistics, one Camillo Galante was born in a Manhattan tenement building, a charred-brick cold-water flat at 27 Stanton Street. He was issued by the City of New York Birth Certificate #10302.

Carmine Galante's mother, the former Vincenza Russo, was twenty-five years old. The baby boy was the Galantes' second child. Throughout his life, the gangster known as Carmine Galante claimed this was he. Him. It said Camillo on the birth certificate, but he was Carmine. So the fuck what? Paperwork. None of this mattered to an Italian family struggling to get by in the New World. What difference did it make? Spelling was the least of his troubles.

You can't count on an Italian man to spell his name the same way every time. My dad routinely changed the spelling of our name. "It throws 'em off," he said.

Spelling aside, the details of Carmine Galante's birth were for years considered suspect—at least by members of law enforcement looking to get rid of him. There was the wrong first name thing, and more. He was born on the Lower East Side yet lived in East Harlem, East 101st Street, between First and Second avenues. Other than various jails, Carmine never had another address than the tenement on 101st until he got married, and even after that the building's connection to the rackets lived on, apparently. (During the spring of 1958, the first-floor apartment in that building was raided by New York police and evidence of a numbers racket was seized. Lookouts, runners, and collectors were arrested. A 1958 police investigation into Galante's background, done as part of a parole violation probe, found "evidence" that Galante's parents had moved to America when Carmine was already four years old. If there had been anything in this, one would figure, Galante would have been deported, which never happened. As fate would have it, Galante *was* once deported, but it was *to* the United States rather than *from*.)

The neighborhood of Galante's birth is now called Little Italy. Back then, if you said something happened in "Little Italy," you were referring to the Uptown hood now known as East Harlem, which as far as we can tell was where Galante lived from the time he was an infant.

Italian organized crime in America in 1910 was known as the Black Hand. Simultaneous to Galante's birth, Italian mobsters were being scooped up left and right by New York cops and Secret Service agents. By the time they were done, there were twenty gangsters in the Tombs, charged with passing "queer money," money printed by the Black Hand rather than the U.S. Mint.

Black Hand's counterfeit bills often went unnoticed because of the quality of paper they were printed on. If you looked close, the engraving was poor, but the paper felt right and they soaked the bills in coffee to make them look as if they'd been passed from hand to hand many times.

The feds spent eight months investigating these guys who had been flooding New York City with bogus two-dollar (then far more common in circulation than now) and five-dollar bills. The bust was big, and the men caged in the Tombs, all Italian, were small-time—passers of the bills, rather than printers. The hope was that the minions could be used to get to the big fish.

Turned out that dealing with these schlubs was easy. Several spoke up and told the same story. They picked up the bundles of counterfeit money at a grocery store at 235 East 97th Street, then Little Italy. Secret Service agents watched the store and went undercover to purchase some of the phony bills. That resulted in another nine arrests and more deals being cut with prosecutors.

In the meantime, the feds caught word that large shipments of paper and ink were being delivered to Highland Station, on the west bank of the Hudson River opposite Poughkeepsie. The paper was going into a house there, but by the time the feds raided an innocent family had moved in. There might've been new residents, but the telltale ink stains remained. The printing press was gone, and the occupants seemed to genuinely know nothing about it.

The feds eventually got their men, raiding a joint in Bay Ridge, Brooklyn, and nabbing Ignazio Lupo and Giuseppe Palermo, upper-echelon men in the Black Hand. For the Law, Lupo was quite a catch. Lupo, aka Ignazio Saietta, aka Lupo the Wolf, terrorized the Italian section of Harlem from 1890 to 1920. Lupo had a "horse stable" on East 107th Street. Stables were common before automobiles took over. When police got around to raiding the Wolf's stable it was found to be equine-free but did contain sixty decomposing gangsters hung on meat hooks.

The Wolf's mistake was broadening his horizons instead of sticking with the thing he was good at—which was stealing, killing, and lending money, not necessarily in that order. Instead, the Wolf went into counterfeiting and got caught. He was sentenced to thirty years behind bars but only served a dozen because President Warren G. Harding commuted his sentence. It's good to have friends in high places.

(When it came time for the new generation of hoodlums, the so-called Young Turks, to take over the streets, Lupo wasn't iced like the other elders, known at the time as Mustache Petes. He gracefully stepped aside, giving up all of his rackets except for one small policy bank in Brooklyn so he could make a living, and lived to be almost seventy, maybe not so old in life expectancy, but ancient in Life expectancy. An only slightly fictionalized version of Lupo the Wolf appeared in a Damon Runyon story, where he cohabitated in the world of Broadway Eddie, Nicely-Nicely, and Nathan Detroit.)

Cops busting the counterfeiters learned that the brains of the gang was Giuseppe Morello, aka the Clutch Hand, aka the Fox, a boss who was also the son of a boss, who'd first met the Wolf when they both tried to run saloons out of the same building, 8 Prince Street. Eventually, Morello became Lupo's brother-in-law. He was nabbed in the Bay Ridge raid as well.

Authorities learned that Morello and Lupo were both wanted men back in Italy—Lupo for murder, Palermo for forgery. Lupo was a suspect in a famous murder in New York, too, the Barrel Murder, in which a man who knew too much named Benedetta Madonia was found disassembled in a barrel in 1903.

Morello ended up serving six months on the counterfeiting charge. The resulting void on the street led to war between Morello and his "replacement" Salvatore "Toto" D'Aquila. When Morello was released, he and D'Aquila had a meeting. Instead of divvying up the power, both wanted it all. Morello and his hoods walked out of the meeting and war was declared, which turned out to be a big mistake. Morello's effectiveness had eroded during his time away, and he found himself outgunned. D'Aquila's killers were everywhere. Morello's men were decimated.

Italian organized crime was growing by the day, but at the time of Galante's birth most of the gangs were Irish. When baby Galante was only a few months old, a William H. Green, a twenty-seven-year-old dockworker—and a cop's son—was a "party to" the murder of Patrick Gaffney in a Second Avenue saloon. The triggerman was William "Skiboo" Gilbride, a member of the Gashouse Gang. Skiboo's brother "Gangs" Gilbride was indicted in the murder but never charged. Green skated when he agreed to testify against Skiboo.

So, as you can see, regardless of his name—Camillo, Carmine, whatever—baby boy Galante had been born into a world where immigrant men and the sons of immigrant men in America had two choices, a lifetime of backbreaking work or joining a gang. One offered drudgery and crippling pain. The other offered danger and potential glory, potential riches.

It was an easy choice.

CHAPTER TWO
The Boys from Castellammare

IN ORDER TO UNDERSTAND Carmine Galante, you've got to go way back, to nineteenth-century Sicily, where the secret society known as the Mafia began protecting citizens from the corrupt government—in exchange for a fee, of course. Sicily was a tough place—a tough place to live in and a tough place to farm. The soil was poor and the climate harsh.

The natives, mostly poor, felt helpless. The Mafia was a private government, just as corrupt as the other. They organized individual criminals into gangs. After a time the gangs united and worked together, not without a beef now and again, of course. The result was an organization, the Mafia, that was hugely powerful. Late in the nineteenth century, Sicilian Mafiosi came to America and set up operations. In America, the people first became aware of the Mafia's existence in 1890, with the hit on New Orleans Police Superintendent David Hennessy.

Back in Sicily, one of the Mafia's largest and most scenic strongholds was Castellammare del Golfo, and that was where Galante's people came from.

Carmine Galante's father was born in Castellammare del Golfo, which means "Sea Fortress on the Gulf," a town in the Trapani Province of Sicily. He was Vincenzo "James" Galante, a fisherman, whose scarred and calloused hands had had enough of mending nets. The town was beautiful, but the work was hard.

The village was built near the former site of the city of Segesta where lived an indigenous Sicilian people known as the Elymi. The city dated back as far as 2,000 BC, and the Greeks claimed it was founded by traveling Greeks from Troy. Around the time of Christ's birth, the city was the site of a mint. Because of this, impressive fortifications were built to keep out invaders.

Near the village of Castellammare were the ruins of the Greek temple at Segesta, thirty-six marble columns, originally built in the fifth century A.D. when Sicily was drawn into hostilities between Carthage, Athens, and Sparta.

During the early 1900s, the ruins were beautiful, a place where the color of the columns, fourteen on each side and six along the facades, changed depending on where the sun was in the sky. Even today, the ruins are far more complete than most other examples of ancient Greek architecture.

Castellammare del Golfo was built atop a bluff overlooking a crystal green gulf in westernmost Sicily. The fortress in the town's name was an actual castle that predated the town but came to serve as a centerpiece for waterfront commerce. Today it remains a fishing town, but most of its money is made in the tourist industry. Its twenty miles of white-sanded beaches are a vacation destination for beautiful people from around the world.

But that's not what Castellammare is best known for. Not even close. It is best known as the birthplace of many famous mobsters.

Among the goodfellas who came from Castellammare del Golfo were:

Joseph "Don Peppino" Bonanno, who came to America to set up operations for his old man. Joey Bananas wasn't like other bosses in America. He was old-fashioned and loved when his men called him Father.

My mom insists that no American men ever kissed another man's ring, no matter how Italian they were. Well, Bonanno was never really an American man, despite spending most of his life here. Bonanno might have gotten his ring good and kissed in his day.

Whereas many members of organized crime, upper echelon included, read very little—comic books maybe, or the sports page in the *Daily News*—Bonanno read poetry and philosophy and could quote the prophets of antiquity.

He hated the fact that Americans had taken the word "Mafia" to be synonymous with gangsterism when he knew the Mafia was something more important than that, something sacred, a link with the traditions and the honor of the Old World. But American thugs were ruining it, and as Bonanno grew until middle age and beyond he felt himself growing increasingly anachronistic.

He was also different in that he distinguished power from money, preferring the former. Of course, one came with the other, but we're talking about the man's focus. He had dreams of a one-man Commission with him being the One Man.

The Commission eventually had mercy on him, because of his heritage and sociopathic dignity. They spared his life but stripped him of power and sent him into exile. Galante was always faithful to Bonanno, and he—*Castellammarese!*—would try until his dying day to gain control of the family Bonanno lost.

John Tartamella, the man who most had Bonanno's ear—a wise old man who was the Bonanno Family consigliere for three decades, a leader in the AFL barbers' union eventually expelled by the Italian-American Labor Council for being too radical, a man with a strategic sense of humor who could diffuse tense situations with a bright quip and used his good humor during sit-downs to prevent little beefs from growing into something that might hurt business.

Vito "The King" Bonventre, arrested and released in 1921 as leader of a sette known as the Good Killers. (A sette is a brotherhood of professional killers. The most famous sette in the United States was Murder, Inc.) Other members of the Good Killers included Stefano Magaddino (whom we'll soon meet), Francesco Puma, Giuseppe Lombardi, Mariano (no relation) Galante, and Bartolomeo Di Gregorio. Bonventre always publicly claimed he was legit, said he was a retired baker. He lived for almost another decade until he became one of the first casualties of the Castellammarese War.

On the morning of July 15, 1930, Bonventre had just left his home at 69 Orient Avenue in East Williamsburg, Brooklyn, and was about to enter his garage behind his house when he was shotgunned twice in the chest and died instantly.

Two men were seen escaping from the scene in an automobile that had been waiting nearby. A third man was behind the wheel. Bonventre's son Anthony heard the shots and was the first to reach his fallen father.

A patrolman from the Herbert Street station called an ambulance, but there was nothing the medics could do. Neighbors told police, in a soft whisper, that they were afraid of Bonventre because he was rumored to be a member of the Mafia and involved in Black Hand activities. Bonventre operated a garage in Williamsburg, at North 8th and Havemeyer Streets that had been raided in 1928 because it contained a large quantity of bootleg booze.

Stefano Magaddino, aka The Undertaker. In 1916, a street hood by the name of Camillo Caizzo of New York City whacked Magaddino's brother Pietro. Five years later, on July 31, 1921, Stefano avenged his brother when he dispatched Caizzo in a hit involving the prolifically deadly gunman Bartolo Fontano, near Asbury Park, New Jersey.

Magaddino and Fontano were arrested and thrown into the same dank Jersey cell, where they engaged in exhausting fisticuffs, each thinking the other had burned him. Magaddino had a death grip on Fontano's throat when cops interceded. Magaddino turned on the cops, who without hesitation beat Magaddino into unconsciousness.

As soon as Magaddino was out on bail, he fled, splitting for Buffalo, New York. There Magaddino set down roots and established himself as a top hood of western New York. While operating a legit-imate funeral parlor called the Magaddino Memorial Chapel, many of his other interests were merely camouflaged speakeasies.

Magaddino wasn't afraid to take out a guy who was in his way, as he proved in 1944 when he and the Papalias—Antonio and Johnny—caused Rocco Perri to disappear and took over Perri's slice of the pie.

There were a couple of attempts on Magaddino's life, first in 1936 when a bomb went off, killing his sister but not him, and then twenty-two years later when someone tossed a live hand grenade through his kitchen window that failed to explode.

Magaddino went on to become boss of Buffalo, a piece of turf that yawned into the Midwest of the United States and to Canada, earning him a seat at the Commission table. Despite his power, he shunned fame and stayed behind the scenes.

Salvatore Maranzano, who is given credit for instigating the Castellammarese War, a war that ended when Lucky Luciano had him whacked and set up the Five Family system. But that's the end of the story. Maranzano went to Buffalo to be part of Magaddino's crew. There he was arrested in 1925 on weapons charges—the up-shot being the police didn't consider him American enough (Maran-zano spoke no English) or of good enough character (the judge called him a thug) to possess a gun.

He later got in trouble for human trafficking but made his bundle bootlegging while pretending, his English now passable, to be a real estate broker. Maranzano built an empire but wanted more. It was his declaration of war on Joe "The Boss" Masseria that started the Castellammarese War in the first place.

Joe the Boss was being played by Lucky Luciano, played like a fiddle, who said that he'd whack Joe the Boss for Maranzano if Lu-ciano could be his second-in-command.

Maranzano jumped at that, never once thinking it odd that Lu-ciano was willing to be second-in-command to anyone. Masseria was offed by an all-star cast in Coney Island. Maranzano could feel the target on his back and tried to have Lucky Looch hit, but the would-be assassins ratted Maranzano out instead. After that, of course, he was toast.

On the Night of the Sicilian Vespers, September 10, 1931, four Jewish members of Murder, Inc., entered Maranzano's high-rise Park Avenue office and blew Maranzano away. Second-in-command! The guy didn't even get it was a joke.

(For more about the Jewish gangsters of Murder, Inc., and their heroic campaign against American Nazis during the Great Depression, be sure to read co-author Michael Benson's book *Gangsters vs. Nazis*. Those guys are also discussed doing their day job in our book *Lord High Executioner*, about Albert "The Mad Hatter" Anastasia.)

And **Sebastiano DiGaetano**, one of the original guys to come over on the boat, arriving in New York Harbor in 1898, already thirty-six years old, leaving behind a wife and daughter who didn't join him in Brooklyn until 1901.

DiGaetano made a living as a barber. His first known underworld activities came in 1910 when he was a prime suspect in the kidnapping-for-ransom of eight-year-old Giuseppe Longo and seven-year-old Michael Rizzo. The charges were dropped for lack of evidence.

DiGaetano was the guy who assumed power in what would become the Bonanno Family, when his boss Giuseppe Morello went down in the big counterfeiting bust of 1910, about the time Galante was born. DiGaetano went on to become an early, early crime boss, who ran Williamsburg, Brooklyn, until March 1912, when he disappeared off the face of the earth as if beamed up by aliens. His wife disappeared, too, which leads some to think he wasn't hit but rather quietly got on a boat back home to Castellammare. Either way, he was done on the streets of New York.

The so-called Castellammarese War was fought between the Masseria gang and the Maranzano gang during 1930 and '31, beginning with the whacking by Castellammarese hit men of Masseria enforcer Giuseppe Morello in East Harlem, and then two weeks later with the offing of Joseph Pinzolo in a Times Square office building.

Masseria struck back on October 23, 1930, when a Maranzano loyalist, the president of the Chicago Unione Sicilane, was hit. Back and forth it went. It was this organized-crime chaos that caused Lucky Luciano to set up the Five Family/Commission system in New York City—with the Bonannos—that is, Castellammare—getting one of the five.

The relationship between Vincenzo Galante, Carmine Galante's father, and the Bonanno Family is unknown, but it must have been a comfort to him when he came to America, a strange land with a strange language, and found that the Bonannos were there to protect the Castellammarese who'd come over on the boat. The Castellammarese in New York stuck together, so it is likely, almost certain, that Vincenzo Galante knew the Bonannos, had a business relationship with them, when he came to New York. If the Galantes were like many families in that town, they at times depended on the Bonannos and therefore would have owed the Bonannos favors. It is entirely possible that Carmine never had a choice as to what he'd do for a living. His dad was from Castellammare—he was going to work for the Bonannos.

You've got to get this: for an immigrant from Castellammare, the Bonannos were the *government*. In Castellammare del Golfo, the Bonannos had things sewn up tight. They owned land, cattle, and horses. It was necessary to have a patriarchal family to take care of the humble working folk. Joe Bonanno was not only the son of a godfather, but he was also the grandson of a godfather—the shiny boy, glowing with privilege, who came from the house on the hill. When that glow wore off, as it turned out, Joe would be the last to know.

The Castellammarese in New York knew nothing of the U.S. government—maybe Vincenzo Galante knew the name of the U.S. president, maybe not—and there was no reason to think the American system would help a poor immigrant. The Italian government had never seemed concerned with helping the poor people of Sicily. That was how governments were. They were comprised of rich guys taking care of the upper class. What's that got to do with Vincenzo Galante and his scarred fisherman's hands?

It had been the rough conditions in Sicily that spawned the formation of the Mafia to begin with. Throughout its history, conquering armies—Greeks, Phoenicians, Carthaginians, Romans, Vandals, Byzantines, Saracens, Normans, Angevins, Aragonese, Bourbons—had overrun it, and each in turn had poached the island's natural resources.

Vincenzo Galante and his wife came over on the boat in 1906—not in 1914 as the U.S. government briefly hoped. Carmine had two brothers—one older, Samuel, and one younger, Peter—and two sisters, Angelina (born 1918) and Josephine (born 1920). Samuel grew up to have a no-show job for the New York City Department of Sanitation.

The newcomers to America were often ambitious men with lots of energy, but they lacked everything else. They were usually broke and carrying their worldly belongings in a cardboard suitcase. If such an immigrant wanted to start a business, he would need a loan, start-up money, a loan that was impossible to get from American banks as they had no credit record or collateral.

Besides, the American bankers looked down their noses at Italians, thought of Italian immigrants as lesser and untrustworthy. The loan had to come from the boss. It was not uncommon a hundred years ago for the ruling mob in any neighborhood to be referred to as the "Italian Bank." So, any Sicilian who established himself in America almost inevitably owed a lifelong debt of gratitude to the controlling family. It was true that these start-up loans came with a larger interest than might've been offered by an American bank, but the rates were not as outrageous as one might find years later being offered to a degenerate gambler down on his luck in the parking lot at Belmont Park. And if a new businessman was late in his payments, that could be excused, as long as the guy did the boss a favor—or two.

For the Bonanno Family of Carmine Galante's youth, headquarters were in Williamsburg, Brooklyn, which was in the northern part of the borough, directly across the East River from Manhattan.

One of the first things the Bonanno clan did when they got to Brooklyn was set up the "Italian lottery," which was like Lotto today, only illegal because the government wasn't getting a cut. For a very small daily bet, there was the chance of making a small fortune. The law against "betting the numbers" was thought of, and rightfully so, as bogus. If you were a millionaire you could gamble in a casino or throw your money into a volatile stock market, but if you were poor and bet the numbers you were subject to arrest. Again, the Mafia as a government was preferable to the actual government in Gracie Mansion, Albany, or Washington, D.C.

Galante was not much of a student, and like many future hoods, he found school was cutting into his hanging-around-on-street-corners time. He attended Public School #79 on East 120th Street in Harlem, off and on because of a stint in reform school. After that, he went to a vocational school in Queens until the seventh grade, again with time off for time in a juvenile facility. He dropped out at age fifteen. So much for reading, writing, and arithmetic. He never gave a shit about any of that. On to the serious business of the streets. Already some of the guys who'd be with him always were at his side: his cousin Angelo "Moey" Presenzano and best friend, Giuseppe (Joseph) "Joey Beck" DiPalermo, three years Galante's elder, who managed to look simultaneously stretched and short.

The details of Galante's youth are sketchy. He no doubt got away with a lot, but we only know about the times he was caught and the times he hurt himself. In 1921, Galante was briefly hospitalized in Post Graduate Hospital in NYC with an injury to his head, suffered in an automobile accident. (Years later, experts would wonder if this blow to the skull had aggravated Galante's already-pronounced personality disorder.)

Later that same year, in another traffic mishap, Galante was hit by a car and broke his ankle. He was treated at St. Mark's Hospital. Galante, as you'll see, never had much luck when automobiles were involved.

From 1923 to 1926, during his early teens, he was "employed" at the Lubin Artificial Flower Company, located at 270 West Broadway in Lower Manhattan, in the same building as the International Sales and Export Company. At least that was what it said on paper. It wouldn't be long before the New York police discovered he was doing more than selling fake flowers.

CHAPTER THREE
Early Crimes

FEW CRIMINAL CAREERS BEGAN as early as Galante's. The old joke about future hoods shaking down kids for their lunch money, that was Galante. By the time he turned ten, he was already in reform school.

He was fourteen when he first got in trouble with the police, busted for shoplifting "trinkets" off a store counter. The items weren't even something he wanted. He was just practicing his stealing. And clearly he needed more practice, as he got caught. As a result of the bust, he was placed on probation for juvenile delinquency.

Like many future crime bosses, Galante had his own juvenile delinquent gang when he was a kid, terrorizing the streets of New York's Lower East Side at fourteen.

In the gang was Galante's most trusted friend, the previously mentioned Joey Beck, born in 1907, who would survive childhood and grow up to become the so-called dean of dope dealers. In a world of tough guys who were slightly squat, Beck looked like he'd been tortured for too long on the rack. He was elongated, with spidery arms and legs, fingers so long they looked like they should have an extra knuckle. His neck was creepy long, and his protruding Adam's apple bobbed when he talked. He led with his Adam's apple, like it was tugging the rest of him behind it.

He blinked rapidly behind the Coke-bottle lenses of his glasses and from a very early age had a chrome dome with only a fringe of hair across the back and sides, a bulbous bare head that shined like a spotlight.

Intellectually, Joey Beck was on Galante's level—which meant they never outgrew the schoolyard bully mentality. They knew how to terrify people, so good at it that they always got what they wanted—and what they wanted was money.

Beck's brother, seven years his junior, Peter "Petey Beck" Di-Palermo, was also a member of Galante's gang from the start.

When Galante and his pal Joey Beck quit school together at fifteen, the reason was to become full-time hoodlums. It was about that time that Galante began running errands for his criminal elders, endearing himself with the boys who made all the dough during Prohibition.

Beating people up was Galante's forte. While he was beating them up, he cleaned out their wallets. Some thugs would leave their victims enough for a token, so they could take the train home. Galante said fuck that. Let 'em walk—or limp. Or hop.

On December 12, 1925, at age fifteen, Galante first saw time inside jail. He gruffly pleaded guilty to petty larceny and assault, second degree, and went to the city penitentiary for a few months.

In 1926, at age sixteen, he first saw time inside a state prison. He was convicted of armed robbery, and on December 22 of that year he was sentenced to Sing Sing for two and a half to five years, minus the twenty-six days of jail time he spent awaiting trial.

There were other arrests during his teen years, but charges were always dismissed. Even when he was a kid, potential jurors and witnesses decided that contributing to Galante's legal woes was a very risky business.

By the time he turned twenty he was considered one of the mob's top enforcers.

* * *

On January 18, 1930, Galante was paroled to the Catholic Society—one year, ten months, and nine days shy of his maximum sentence. We can guess how he celebrated. A couple of weeks later he was treated for gonorrhea.

He was up to other shenanigans as well, and within weeks he'd again be in trouble with the Law, this time involving a dead cop.

CHAPTER FOUR
First Kill

BORN IN 1895, Patrolman Walter O. De Castillia was thirty-four years old in March 1930. He lived with his wife and child on 148th Street in Jamaica, Queens, and he worked mornings at the Poplar Street station in what is today known as the DUMBO section of Brooklyn, practically under the Manhattan Bridge, a place of shadows even at midday.

Then as now, many cops walked a beat in Manhattan and the outer boroughs and never unholstered their weapon. But De Castillia's career, all nine years of it, had been an active one. Before this fateful late-winter day, he had been involved in at least one shootout.

That occurred during the summer of 1929, when he and Patrolman Oscar Meyer—seriously, that was his name—pursued a holdup trio and ended up shooting it out with them in a cellar on Brooklyn's Adams Street. All three robbers were captured and sent up the river. Apparently, this shootout caused someone in the underworld to hold a grudge, as the incident came back to haunt De Castillia.

And so it was that on March 15, 1930, De Castillia again had to reach for his gun, but this time, just like a kid playing quickdraw, he came out second best.

De Castilla's job that morning was to guard the delivery of the $7,267 payroll of the Martin-Weinstein Shoe Company warehouse located at the corner of Washington and York Streets, just around the block from the station house.

It was a few minutes before noon, and the transfer was almost finished. Guards from the Mechanics Bank had delivered the money and taken it upstairs. De Castillia went up with the money. As the money sat on a desk, an executive of the company surreptitiously opened the safe.

At that moment, downstairs in the lobby, a group of hoods entered the front door like they owned the place and marched on short legs to the elevator.

It was Carmine Galante who shoved a pistol into the ribs of elevator operator Louis Semle and said, "Sixth floor—and make it snappy."

"OK, but there's a cop up there," Semle said.

"We know it, but we're going in anyway," Galante reportedly said. Maybe he just grunted.

The elevator rose like an hour hand, seemingly taking forever to get to the sixth floor. Finally, they arrived, came to a halt with a rude jerk, and Semle pulled the door open.

"Get the hell out of the way," Galante said, and Semle pressed himself thin as a pancake against the side of his diminutive domain.

On the sixth floor, the gunmen quickly scanned the scene. There were three men and two women there with the money, not counting the cop. One of the men was the messenger from the bank.

The women were there to distribute the payroll. They would carefully open the bundle of cash and place the appropriate number of bills in each labeled employee envelope. It was payday and it worked like clockwork.

De Castillia had just registered the invasion and turned his shoulders toward the elevator. Without a word of warning, the gunmen opened fire and riddled his body. The first bullet struck just as De Castillia reached his gun, but his service weapon remained holstered. He slumped for a moment before falling, his right hand still clumsily slapping at the handle of his gun, now slippery with blood.

Witnesses were amazed at the calmness of the killers. They looked for all the world like they were shooting mechanical ducks in a row at Coney Island, having fun with target practice even as they snuffed out a human soul.

Two women in the office (Minnie Weinstein and Lillian Duckert, both of Manhattan) began to scream and didn't stop. Annoyed by the shrill caterwaul, Galante was tempted to silence them the fast way but had mercy.

"Now, girlies, keep quiet and stick up your hands," he reportedly said.

The women obeyed, hands elevating so quickly that their breasts leaped, but one continued to whimper a little.

Then an odd thing happened. The gunmen never made a move for the money, which they must've known was there. They didn't flee in panic. They leisurely moved back to the elevator. One of the men fired one last shot that passed through a wooden partition, crossed a hallway, and embedded itself in framework. Galante grabbed Semle by the shirt and pulled him from the elevator.

"We'll go down alone," he said, and the elevator moved just as slowly on the way down. By the time the men were back to the ground floor, there was chaos. The shots and the screaming had brought everyone—both from inside the building and on the tightly packed block outside—running to see what happened.

Why didn't they take the money? It was right there on a table. All they had to do was grab it and take it with them. But they didn't care. This would lead investigators to believe that the payroll was never the idea.

Killing De Castillia was the idea.

This was a grudge hit, committed by men as cold as any ever known in Brooklyn—and that was saying something.

The men dashed from the elevator across the lobby and out into the street, into the faces of dozens of Martin-Weinstein employees and neighbors. The four men piled into a getaway car, driver already in place, and rattled on cobblestoned streets into the Brooklyn sunshine.

"Semle!" someone inside the building urgently said. "He didn't come down with his elevator."

Co-workers ran up the stairs, girding their loins for the worst. They breathed a sigh of relief when they found Semle terrified but unharmed. Not so for the targeted police officer.

De Castillia was dead of multiple gunshot wounds to the chest and abdomen.

Police Commissioner Grover A. Whelan appeared on the scene with his chest puffed out and took charge. First, he ordered that the "morgue wagon" be summoned, only to be told it was already on its way. This annoyed him.

"Let the police take care of their own dead," the commissioner said. He then ordered two patrolmen to act as a guard of honor to escort the body from the scene of the killing to the morgue. They were to always remain with the body until the completion of an autopsy, which would take place at Feeney's Morgue, as these were the days before county morgues, when autopsies were done in private mortuaries that doubled as coroners' offices.

Whelan then went to the De Castillia home on 148th Street in Jamaica, Queens. There he informed the widow—the former Helen Raynor of Richmond Hill, Queens—and nine-year-old son Everett that Dad wasn't coming home. Whelan knew it was a small comfort to Helen, a wife for sixteen years, but informed the family that De Castillia would be buried a hero and posthumously promoted to inspector.

The funeral for De Castillia was held at the family's church, Bethany Baptist Church in South Jamaica, with police chaplain William Ivie presiding. An escort of 125 police, including more than a dozen high-ranking cops, escorted the body from the church to a plot in a pasture called Tulip Grove in the Cemetery of the Evergreens, an agrarian illusion straddling the Brooklyn/Queens border.

When the widow returned to her hauntingly empty Jamaica home, she found a policeman there waiting for her with an envelope in his hand—$500 from the police relief fund to go toward funeral expenses.

She was also informed that, from then on, she'd be getting fifty bucks a week for one hundred weeks—fifty grand—or until she re-married, from the same fund.

Police, in the meantime, were taking a close look at De Castillia's career. He'd been a hero twice before, once after rescuing someone during a house fire and again when he took part in the high-profile arrests in the Adams Street cellar.

If this was a grudge killing rather than an attempted robbery, as it appeared, then something in the officer's past might lead them to the killers.

"This murder is another indication of the wanton disregard of the young gunmen of today for life and limb. They gave the officer no chance to defend himself," the commissioner said.

Reporters asked him if he thought the earlier shootout involving Patrolman De Castillia had anything to do with this killing, the com-missioner replied that he knew of no evidence connecting the two, but, judging from the lack of a robbery motive here the previous in-cident would have to be re-examined.

The commissioner added that his best bet remained that the rob-bers simply panicked and chickened out, choosing to run without the money instead of with it. Maybe they planned another job later in the day and hoped to have better luck there. This suggestion pleased no one. Grudge kill was so much sexier and considering the circumstances more feasible.

On March 20, day six of the investigation, police got what they hoped was a major break in the De Castillia murder. A lone cop ar-rested three gunmen outside the Bank of the Manhattan Company branch on Nostrand Avenue in Crown Heights, Brooklyn. Naturally, the hopes were that these were the same guys. The arrested men ranged in age between nineteen and twenty-three years old, one each hailing from Manhattan, Queens, and Brooklyn. The men in-sisted from the moment they surrendered that they had nothing to do with any cop killings.

The investigation heated up when one of the three men, Joseph

Machin, was identified by a witness named Jay Fierst, a Powell Street hosiery dealer, as the same guy who mugged him as he left the Belmont Avenue BMT subway station.

Fierst said that Machin had been one of three men and though he'd received quite a beating, he'd managed to hang on to his money. This meant that these guys were serial criminals, which they'd already admitted, confessing to robbing a pair of garages in the Bronx and Manhattan. But it didn't tie them into the cop's death.

The trio were also questioned about a pair of Bronx rubouts in February—Carmine Barelli, a ferrety thirty-four-year-old Bronx pimp, a "trader in white slaves," in the parlance of the day, and his enameled dance-hall goomara Mayme Smith Layton, both shot again and again in a parked car at 3:00 a.m. on Inwood Avenue, Valentine's Day, 1930, by four pros who ran away in four different directions. Mayme, it was said, was a dime-a-dance girl at both Dreamland in the Bronx and the Nut Club in Greenwich Village. The three men said they didn't know nothing about that.

The Galante murder of the cop on York Street was big news at the time and continued to resonate generations later, when the ninetieth anniversary of the hit was commemorated in the Big Apple tabloids. It remained the oldest "unsolved" cop killing in NYC history. That was because everyone knew who did it—they just couldn't prove it.

Stories had grown over the years, conspiracy theories hatched, and revisionism in full bloom. De Castillia's great-niece told a reporter that she'd heard it was a setup. The cop who was supposed to guard that payroll caught wind of what was up and called in sick, so poor Uncle Walter had to work on what was supposed to be a day off. Maybe it was true. There was no way to check. She had heard it again and again over the years. Uncle Walter was a clean cop, a man who could not be swayed, in a world where dirty cops were a dime a dozen.

Being a cop is still dangerous today, of course, but nothing like it was in 1930. The movies of the day, featuring rat-a-tat-tat cars tommy-gunning pedestrians in a montage of mob violence, well, they weren't that much of an exaggeration. Astoundingly, Walter De Castillia was the seventh of nineteen New York cops to be killed in 1930.

Nineteen!

From 1930 to 1935, Galante claimed to be employed as a sorter by the O'Brien Fish Company at 105 South Street. Of course, his dad had been a fisherman back in Castellammare. (Today that street is most famous for the South Street Seaport, a plaza of stores on what used to be a working pier.)

The fish company was legit to a point and even made the front page of a local tabloid when a fisherman brought in a four-pound Japanese fluke caught off the Connecticut shore, far, far, from home.

The company was legit but involved, it would seem. During Prohibition, the building housed a "Café" that was really a speakeasy. When seafood union czar William "Mack" McNamara was whacked in the spring of 1926, many arrests ensued; two of them—of Louis Guma and Joseph Lanzo—were at 105 South Street.

Police later theorized that the murder was done right there at 105 South. Mack was a well-known underworld character, once did a fourteen-year stretch, and now was chilled to room temperature, blackjacked on the head, blasted point-blank with hot lead in the left cheek, and limp on the floor.

Police were initially flummoxed over how the body got from where it was shot to where it was dumped, via a location where extraneous slugs were pumped into the corpse. They eventually figured that immediately following the shooting Mack's body was moved to an adjacent building *through a skylight*, then taken down into a cellar where an additional two shots were fired into the right temple to make sure it was dead. The body was dumped at dawn, at a location on Front Street only fifteen feet from the spot where Mack's friend and seafood czar predecessor Whitey Britt was hit.

A surprising number of market workers on their way to the morning shift stumbled over Mack's stiff before anyone said anything.

Officials determined that Mack had been slain about two hours before arriving on Front Street. Officials knew something else as well: seafood union czar was a dangerous position.

A few weeks after the De Castillia murder, on May 6, 1930, Galante was back doing high-profile crimes. On that day he was one of five gunmen who forced a manager and clerk to reach for the sky while $1,200 worth of the payroll was lifted from the safe of the Prudential Life Insurance Company on Pennsylvania Avenue in the Broadway Junction section of Brooklyn. Along with grabbing the cash, the thieves spent extra time with the female employees, grabbing earrings, bracelets, and rings.

A lot of troubled teenagers "age out" of their delinquent behaviors, but nobody thought that would happen to Galante. He was a lifer. So, no one blinked when twenty-year-old Galante was arrested on August 30, 1930, for an armed robbery at a restaurant.

Also arrested at that time were Michael Consolo, who later would work as Galante's bodyguard, and Galante's "Cousin Moey" who was pretty much always at Galante's side—and would be with Carmine Galante right up until the last minutes of Galante's life.

Galante thought he might be in big trouble; they were still asking him about that dead cop. He cooled off in the Kings County jail for a few months, but—*Castellammarese!*—high-priced lawyers beyond Galante's means eventually came to his defense and his troubles seemingly evaporated.

That autumn, on October 6, 1930, Galante spent the morning before Magistrate Leo Healy in Homicide Court, Brooklyn. The top: Walter O. De Castillia.

Witnesses?

Well, there were some, but they clammed.

Healy discharged Galante, lack of evidence.

Galante walked. Strutted. Like he was invulnerable. Bulletproof. Then he turned a corner, and boom, more trouble. He was on his way back to Manhattan from the Brooklyn courthouse when he was overtaken by an urgent squad of police cars making a racket with their high-pitched sirens and stopping traffic cold on the entrance to the Manhattan Bridge, only feet from the scene of the De Castillia murder.

Galante pulled over. Cop came to his window, which he cranked down an inch or two.

"What the fuck you guys want now?" Galante said.

The police were surprised at how dark Galante was, not just his character, which couldn't have been darker, but his deep, almost chocolate brown complexion.

"Out of the car, Carmine. We're taking you back to Brooklyn," a cop said.

Galante was informed on his way to a courthouse on New Jersey Avenue that he was to answer new charges involving the May 6 holdup of the Prudential Insurance Company's office on Pennsylvania Avenue.

Affidavits by investigating detectives James Conners and William King, both of the Miller Avenue station, were filed before Magistrate Jeanette G. Brill on October 6, and Galante was thrown back into the same cell that he'd left so joyously earlier in the day.

Again, Galante cooled off for a while, but he was back on the streets in time for Christmas.

CHAPTER FIVE

Holdup of the Lieberman Brewery

SILVER BELLS! AH, CHRISTMASTIME in the city. Colorful lights strung around town, Salvation Army Santas on street corners with a black kettle, and last-minute shoppers out hustling and bustling.

Williamsburg, Brooklyn, a busy area, but not as crowded as a few years earlier. For many Brooklynites, there was no money and Christmas was downsized. That's because it was the end of the first full year of the Great Depression and headlines were still stirring up fears of runs on banks. People in a country that had been heavily invested in stocks and bonds now, if they still had money, kept it in cash under their mattresses.

The country's economic woes didn't affect crooks quite as much. No stocks and bonds for them. It was a cash-only business, and their source of income remained the same. They stole. They fought for turf. And when they weren't stealing, they shot one another, sometimes up close, sometimes in drive-by fashion.

In Chicago that year two Christmas shoppers were wounded by machine-gun fire when they accidentally stepped between a mob target and a drive-by shooter.

In Williamsburg, there was also a Yuletide gunfight and again innocent bystanders were victims. This time, Carmine Galante was one of the guys pulling the trigger.

* * *

At about 1:00 p.m. on Christmas Eve, 1930, Galante, still shy of his twenty-first birthday, took part in a spectacular gun battle at the corner of Driggs Avenue and South 8th Street. (If you've been to Peter Luger's, you've been in the neighborhood. The shooting took place within sight of the Kings County Saving Bank's giant dome, now the Williamsburg Art & Historical Center.) It was the sort of exchange between cops and robbers that usually only happened in the movies, but this was real, as one poor little girl standing on the sidewalk with her mother was to learn.

By any standards it was pretty spectacular, but it wasn't even the first gunfight on Driggs Avenue that year. There was trouble during the spring of 1930 when one John Earl Robertson tried to knock off a speakeasy on Driggs by pretending to be a Prohibition agent on the take.

"Forty simoleons or I give you the pinch," Robertson said.

Someone called the cops, who raided the place. Robertson ran out into the street and was shot dead by police. Now it was months later, and an even larger shootout was to take place just down the avenue.

Carmine Galante was one of four men who had just stuck up the Lieberman Brewery on Forest Street in Bushwick, Brooklyn. The men, $4,000 richer, didn't immediately attempt to get away but instead broke open the back of a truck outside the brewery to snatch some free beer.

This turned out to be a big mistake. After stealing the beer, now slightly loaded down, they retreated to their getaway car, a green sedan, and were sitting in traffic at Driggs and South 8th when Detective Joseph Meenahan approached on foot.

Meenahan—a Brooklyn boy, born in Williamsburg, on the police force for nine years—initially took note of the four men because they appeared to be, in his words, "rifling a delivery truck." (With Galante was a twenty-three-year-old from Bensonhurst named Andrew Bucaro, aka Andy Curly, more about him later. The identities of the other two remain to this day unknown.) As Meenahan observed the men trying to get away, the sidewalks were humming with shoppers: men, women, and children who suddenly came under the dark category of "innocent bystanders."

"Hey, what are you guys doing there?" Meenahan called out in his best cop voice. He blew his police whistle, which was the best way to "call for backup" back then.

One of the men in the green sedan turned his head with a warning: "Just stay right where you are, buddy—or we will knock you off." The driver would have loved nothing better than to hit the gas, but there was gridlock, no place to go.

Meenahan continued his approach.

The sedan's doors opened, and the four men made a run for it.

"Halt," Meenahan said, and fired a single warning shot into the air.

Galante turned—"eat lead, copper"—and emptied his gun in Meenahan's general direction but fired wildly. One of his bullets struck six-year-old Shirley Hershowitz of Bedford Avenue in the thigh. The other men fired their guns as well.

Five of the bullets struck Meenahan. Well, sort of. Amazingly, four of them struck Meenahan's overcoat but not Meenahan. That must have been some coat. The fifth bullet struck him in the leg and embedded in his meaty thigh. Meenahan returned fire and struck Galante once.

We don't know if it was coincidence or in response to Meenahan's police whistle, but Sergeant Richard Flynn at that moment came cruising by in a patrol car and saw Meenahan in foot pursuit of the gunmen, with only the slightest indication that one of his legs had a bullet in it.

Flynn slowed to a stop and Meenahan jumped into the car. Traffic had started moving again. The four gunmen ran after the open back end of a moving truck. Three of them managed to climb into the back of the truck. The fourth, Galante, missed his step and fell to the street.

At least that was one version of the story, the New York police version.

In another, the FBI version, Galante's three companions made their getaway while Galante purposefully stayed behind to slow the progress of the police with his blazing gat.

Meenahan jumped out of Flynn's patrol car and grabbed the fallen gunman by the scruff of the neck. Both the captor and the captive had lead in them. The captive was taken to the Clymer Street station in Brooklyn and questioned. Meenahan, his adrenaline wearing off, realized he was in pain and was taken to a hospital to have the bullet dug from his thigh. If Galante was treated for his wound it wasn't reported.

Stitched up, Meenahan returned to Clymer Street to question his prisoner.

"Who are you?" Meenahan asked.

"Charles Bruno."

"Where you live?"

"Three-Thirty-Two East One-Oh-First Street."

Galante was pretending to be his own cousin, who lived across the street.

That lie didn't work for very long, only until the captured man was spotted by a police captain who'd already had a run-in with Galante.

The captain exclaimed, with a thick Irish accent, "That's not Charles Bruno. That's his cousin Carmine Galante and he lives with his old mother at Three-Twenty-Nine East One-Oh-First Street."

At some point following Galante's arrest, he was given a thorough once-over, and his scars and marks were documented. He had a small, round burn scar on the underside of his left forearm, a small diagonal scar on the second joint of his right thumb, a small diagonal scar on the left side of his forehead, and a round boil scar on the back of his neck.

On Christmas Day, little Shirley, daughter of a tailor, got her picture in the *Daily News*, lying in her bed in her home on Bedford Avenue, one leg out from under the covers to show off the bandage on her thigh where the bullet entered. The headline, in typical tabloid fashion, was (in all caps): "BULLET IS YULE GIFT."

Galante got his picture in the paper, too. He is shown looking downward and disgusted. His tie loosened and askew, hair ruffled. He's been through it. In stark contrast, he is surrounded by three plainclothes policemen, all in fedoras, all a good six inches taller than Galante, kempt and spit shined, calm and collected. Two of the policemen are holding pistols, both of which according to the caption were taken off Galante when he was searched.

Galante—as intellectually and emotionally dull as ever, a personality once described by a shrink as "indifferent"—stoically went back to prison immediately for parole violation and awaited his trial on the latest charges.

On January 8, 1931, Galante pleaded guilty and was sentenced by forty-one-year-old Judge Albert Conway in Kings County Court, a bespectacled man whose serious countenance more than a little resembled that of a young Woodrow Wilson.

The judge was a New York boy through and through, born in Brooklyn, attended Fordham in the Bronx, and was an alternate delegate to the 1928 Democratic National Convention and was a favorite of New York State governor (and future president), Franklin Delano Roosevelt, which helped his climb up the judicial ladder.

He was not expected to go easy on a lowlife like Carmine Galante—and he didn't. Judge Conway sentenced Galante to twelve and a half years in prison—minus thirteen days of jail time served while awaiting and during his trial.

"In addition, you will serve the delinquent time on a Sing Sing prison confinement from which you were released early," Judge Conway said.

Reporters did the math. Galante would become eligible for parole on Memorial Day, 1941. Galante went first to the state prison in Ossining—aka Sing Sing—overlooking the Hudson River and a short drive from New York City. When his delinquent time was through he was transferred to Hell Frozen Over, a prison up north known as Little Siberia.

* * *

There were a few ways to get ahead in organized crime. One, of course, was to be ruthless and kill everyone above you in the pecking order. Another was to be a trusted confidant of the boss. And the third was to do the right thing in pressure situations. Staying behind and shooting it out with the cop, allowing your colleagues to get away, well, that was the right thing. Galante had a rep now of having balls the size of grapefruits.

As it turned out, being sent upstate at that time was a stroke of luck, as Galante missed, and therefore survived, the Castellammarese War.

The identities of two of the Lieberman Brewery gunmen remained unknown, but we know that one of Galante's accomplices was Andrew "Andy Curly" Bucaro. We know because Detective Meenahan went through the big book of mug shots and found Curly in there. That's the guy, Meenahan said, and an APB was put out.

Bucaro was born in 1906 in New Jersey and had been in trouble before. That's how he got in the book. During the late winter of 1925, a teenaged Bucaro had been one of five arrested after a botched attempt to knock off the payroll at a Brooklyn construction site on Bay Ridge Avenue. Bucaro had been arrested while in a sedan mid-getaway by cops from the Fort Hamilton station.

The 1925 bust went down at the corner of Bay Ridge and Fifth Avenues, when police spotted five men parked for a long time and decided to question them. As cops approached the car, the driver started the motor. One cop got up to the driver's side window and ordered the driver to shut the motor off. Instead, the men piled out of the passenger side of the car and right into a pair of policemen with guns leveled at their bellies. Bucaro on that occasion was found to be in possession of an incriminating map that showed where the money was supposed to be. He was charged with attempted robbery and possession of dangerous weapons.

Bucaro went away for a while and got out during the autumn of

1927, at which time he immediately resumed his career as a guy who often unsuccessfully tried to steal things. He became notorious around the Bridge Plaza Court when he was arraigned before Magistrate Healy twice in the same week for separate robberies.

On November 18, Curly Bucaro was one of eight men arraigned for a holdup of a candy store on Metropolitan Avenue in Williamsburg. And then again six days later as one of five men who attempted to hold up a craps game at the corner of Scholes Street and Gardner Avenue, an incident in which one man was shot in the spine and paralyzed. In both cases, witnesses to Bucaro's crimes had memory issues once in court and claimed they'd never seen Bucaro before.

So, there was a disconnect between the Bucaro who appeared in court after trying and failing to steal something and the Bucaro on the streets, a respected soldier of the Natale "Joe Diamond" Evola crew, who later worked the same bootlegging and narcotics operations as Galante and mysteriously traveled to Sicily a few times to do a thing for a guy. These old-time mobsters, we get a skewed vision of them because we learn far more about their failures than their successes.

Evola was born in Bay Ridge, Brooklyn, in 1907. Like Galante, Evola's parents came from Castellammare. He was a lifelong bachelor and even when he was a top hood, running the Bonannos for a while, he lived with his mother in Bay Ridge.

For a time after Meenahan put out the Bucaro APB, Curly remained at large. It wasn't until a month and a day after Galante pleaded guilty and headed up the river, February 9, 1931, that Detective Meenahan, his leg feeling much better, got word that Curly Bucaro had been spotted.

"He was at Diana Dance Hall and he's coming back tonight because there's a girl he's sweet on."

Meenahan knew the joint. It was at 14th Street and Third Avenue in Manhattan. In fact, the Diana was well known to the New York police. The women who worked there were known as "dime-a-dance girls." Of course, if you paid more than a dime there was a chance she would do more than dance.

The dim light hid the grubbiness, and when the mood was right dime-a-dance joints had a glaze of class. Ella Fitzgerald used to sing the dance tunes on 14th Street before she got big.

Not long before Meenahan went there in pursuit of Bucaro, an undercover investigator suspecting prostitution visited the Diana and gave a detailed report. He talked to one young lady who told him she was from the Bronx. He asked her "if she would step out for a wild time." She said she couldn't talk about it right then, but . . . as she had never been to one, if we would take her to a particular cabaret in Harlem she would discuss it there. The joint had a grip on plausible deniability and went un-raided.

Meenahan and Detective Charles Hemendinger put on their Sunday best, like they were out for some old-fashioned courtin', and entered the Diana Dance Hall undercover. They struck up a conversation with Bucaro.

Afterward, Meenahan told Hemendinger there was no doubt. "That's the guy," Meenahan said.

Bucaro was arrested and arraigned before Magistrate Frederick Hughes, who held Andy Curly without bail.

CHAPTER SIX
While Galante Was Away . . .

THE CASTELLAMMARESE WAR raged for two years, lots of guys juked on both sides. The young rebels of those early days thought that the early bosses were stuffed shirts—Mustache Petes, they called them—and looked at them with disdain. The new generation thought the old bosses were exchanging raw earning potential for dignity and respect.

The first guy to get hit in the war was Gaetano Reina, shotgunned to death by a young Vito Genovese on behalf of the Castellammarese. Next to go was Vito Bonventre, a Castellammarese, taken out that summer outside his garage. Galante had been off the streets for eight months when a group of Castellammarese hit men whacked Giuseppe Morello at his East Harlem office. An innocent bystander saw too much and was also taken off the board. The war was not limited to New York City. On October 23, 1930, Joe Aiello, a friend of the Castellammarese, was hit in Chicago. Joe the Boss lost a man on November 5, 1930, when Castellammarese whacked Steve Ferrigno. Masseria lost a capo on February 3, 1931, when Joseph Catania was gunned down.

Surely, had he been on the streets, Galante would have been in on some of this action and would have been a target.

Galante was still away when Luciano put an end to the Castellammarese War by taking out Joe the Boss Masseria and proclaiming himself the ruler of all rackets.

That happened on April 15, 1931, at Gerardo Scarpato's Nuova Villa Tammaro in Coney Island, on West 15th Street, the current site of the Banner Smoked Fish seafood market. Luciano asked Joe the Boss to join him for lunch on Coney Island. As the notoriously gluttonous Joe arrived smacking his lips, a car sat around the corner packed with some heavy-duty company: Albert Anastasia, Bugsy Siegel, Vito Genovese, and Joe Adonis. Siegel had been donated to the effort by Meyer Lansky who was only too eager to rid the New York mob of a Sicilian pureblood.

It was a little after noon. The owner of the joint, Gerardo Scarpato, greeted the men personally. Scarpato was one of the kings of Coney Island. In addition to the Villa Tammaro, he owned the Sea Side Inn on Surf Avenue.

The men ate and ate. And ate. Masseria initiated the seemingly endless meal by ordering the squid and Luciano the pork chops *al finocchio*. Both men ate spaghetti and drank Italian red wine. The feast lasted for three hours.

By the time the men were logy and ordering espresso, at that moment a blue sedan pulled up out front. Seeing that, Luciano patted himself on his belly, belched, and left the table to go to the can.

As soon as Masseria was alone at the table, four gunmen burst into the restaurant and opened up on Joe the Boss. Sluggish from the food and wine, Joe danced, but not well enough. He couldn't avoid the path of six bullets, at least one of which hit him in the back of the head and killed him instantly.

Fourteen more slugs tore up the restaurant wall behind Masseria. Luciano came out of the restroom and took a seat, the scent of gunpowder still heavy in the air and getting into his suit. When police arrived, they found in Joe the Boss's hand an ace of spades, a mob symbol for "ran out of luck." Sitting alone was Lucky Luciano.

"I was in the bathroom when it happened," he told the police. "By the time I came out, still wiping my hands, the gunmen were gone and Joe was dead."

A few days later, Masseria was laid out in a $15,000 casket with silk cushions. Engraved on the lid were the words "Giuseppe Masseria." At the funeral parlor you could hear crickets but no sobbing. His widow didn't even show up.

As the Castellammarese War raged, Galante sat shivering in a place that made the Middle of Nowhere look like Grand Central Station. When people think of New York, their first thought is of the city, with its lively bustle and cloud-fucking skyline. Those who've driven from New York City to Chicago know a New York of wide rivers, rounded and wooded hills, while bus travelers see the state's crystal lakes, and cozy villages of white houses with kelly green shutters. Those who have coursed the state's Southern Tier may recall Canisteo's living sign. The cliffs and falls of Letchworth State Park are awesome. In the west, the piston-power of Niagara Falls is still a favorite for honeymooners. But comparatively few know that New York also includes a vast area of wilderness commonly referred to by its scattered residents as "Up North." The Adirondack Mountain area, where bears outnumber people, includes everything from Albany to the Canadian border, a practically untouched forest, wilderness larger in acreage than any in the United States.

The area has remained wild largely due to governmental action. In 1885, the state legislature passed the Forest Preserve Act, assuring that the huge Adirondack Preserve area "shall be forever kept as wild forest lands."

And so, a long time ago, because of that massive expanse of rough terrain, the Adirondack area was thought to be an excellent place to build a maximum-security prison, a prison surrounded by so much treacherous wilderness that most prisoners didn't think of escape. Get past the big wall and you might fall off a cliff or a bear might eat you. Best to stay in.

Transferred from Sing Sing, Galante began his sentence in Dannemora on October 3, 1932, which up there was the first week of winter. While in Little Siberia, Galante was passed from shrink to shrink. They couldn't figure him out. He got a kick out of hurting people, so it was no surprise when a psychiatrist officially diagnosed Galante as possessing a major personality disorder. He had no conscience, no emotions. Hell, he didn't even have much measurable intellect.

The shrink's report said that Galante was neat in appearance but dull emotionally. He had a mental age of fourteen and a half and an IQ of 90. He was shy with strangers and had zero knowledge of current events. He couldn't name the holidays or say which months they came in, and other items of common knowledge were confusing to him.

We do not know how much of this was an act. Galante was a tunnel-visioned crook and might have malingered to improve quality of life by pretending to be mentally handicapped.

The doctor's diagnosis after examining Galante was that he was a neuropathic with a psychopathic personality. Ya think?

CHAPTER SEVEN
Prison Riot

IN 1932, GALANTE WAS TRANSFERRED from Dannemora to Great Meadow Correctional Facility in Comstock, New York, about a half hour's drive north of Saratoga Springs, where the horses run in the summer and the mineral waters run all year long.

The landscape outside Galante's new digs wasn't as formidable as that in Dannemora, but life inside the walls was every bit as harsh. The name, of course, implies a peaceful and beautiful space, but all of that was destroyed when construction on the prison began in 1909.

At the time Galante entered Great Meadow, there were 1,103 inmates, about three-quarters of them under the age of thirty. The prison was designed to give strict discipline to young offenders.

For the first decade and a half of Great Meadow's existence there was no wall surrounding the grounds. Most inmates were first-time offenders. It was only after prisoners began to be transferred to Great Meadow from other hellish New York State prisons that a wall was constructed. That was in 1924. The prisoners themselves built the wall, three thousand feet of it, enclosing a twenty-one-acre space.

As far as Galante was concerned, the transfer to Great Meadow was a positive one because it meant he was reunited with Cousin Moey, his best friend and constant companion when on the outside.

Now Moey became his best friend on the inside, so it was only a matter of time before the pair got in trouble together.

Galante took his prison affiliations with him from prison to prison, certainly his gang mentality—and of course he was a psychopath no matter where he went. So, when he got to Great Meadow trouble was expected, and trouble came.

At 7:30 a.m., January 26, 1933, Galante, Moey, and their prison friend Salvatore Agro, described at the time as a "professional desperado," were in the prison yard prepping to go to the shops to put in a day's work.

Agro, aka Salvatore Truppiano, was in his mid-thirties and grew up on Varet Street in Williamsburg. He was in prison for the 1928 Sunday shooting of his twenty-four-year-old neighbor Leonard Kletz. What the beef was, no one recalls. Kletz was severely wounded in the shooting, and Patrolman Samuel McCarter shot Agro through both hands before finally capturing the fleeing Agro in his own backyard.

On their way to the prison shops, Galante, Moey, and Agro were jumped by three men, one of whom was twenty-eight-year-old Joseph del Gais, serving ten-to-twenty for first-degree manslaughter out on Long Island. Another was Vincent Bifulco, who had been sentenced in 1926 to twenty years for first-degree manslaughter in Brooklyn.

Afterward, some of the participants tried to pass off the altercation as spontaneous, just somebody bumped into somebody and there was a fight—but there was evidence that the attack was deliberate and planned. For one thing, there was the timing: the fight occurred as prison guards were otherwise occupied, preparing to study the latest methods of using tear gas and gas masks to maintain prison discipline.

By all accounts it was three on three. Shivs came out. The men danced. When prison guards finally arrived, summoned by the whoops of men who enjoyed watching fights, they concentrated on keeping bystanders from joining in. The six dancers were allowed to go, like in hockey, until someone was down.

* * *

Both Galante and Agro were cut superficially, but del Gais was *cut*, a jagged wound along the side of his neck that sprung a gusher. He also had wounds in his abdomen, both arms, and his chest. Del Gais was stretchered, still squirting hot crimson with every beat of his icy heart, to the prison hospital and administered a blood transfusion. The blood was given by another convict, not involved in the fight. But it was too late, and del Gais breathed his last.

In some places down south, I've been told, if a prisoner dies within the prison walls the official cause of death is always a heart attack, no matter how the con actually bought it. Everyone is OK with that. No one asks questions. Southern justice, always brutal, always quick.

But in New York State, the Department of Corrections is more forthcoming with the facts, the details, even the gory ones such as in this case, where you could easily course the trail from the spot where del Gais was cut to the spot where he died by following the splashes of blood.

With a competitive tabloid press in New York, prison officials couldn't get away with shit without an investigation.

The last thing Great Meadow warden Joseph H. Wilson wanted was to be in the news again—but there he was. He'd just survived a rough patch of unwanted publicity. That came after Wilson had a meeting in his inner sanctum with mobster (and childhood friend) Vannie Higgins.

Higgins was born in Bay Ridge, Brooklyn, and developed into one of the top bootleggers in the country. He was known as "Last of the Irish Bosses" and for his ability to escape the grips of the Law. Higgins was OK as long as he limited his operation to Brooklyn, but the second he tried to expand his turf into Manhattan—turf serviced by established bootleggers like Dutch Schultz, Legs Diamond, Mad Dog Coll, and Little Augie Pisano—there was trouble. Higgins and Schultz shot it out in 1928 but didn't hit each other. Higgins was seen fleeing the scene of a shootout at the Owl Head Café at 69th Street and Third Avenue in Bay Ridge in March 1929, a shootout in which Patrolman Daniel J. Maloney was killed in the cross fire. Higgins once stole a shipload of hand grenades and used them on the competition's stills. Higgins was not a nice guy.

Right around the time he was dining with Warden Wilson, Higgins heard a rumor that the mayor of Boston was having an illicit affair with a minor named Starr Faithful. He had Faithful kidnapped and driven to Island Park, New York, on Long Island, where there was an attempt to get her to confess to being the mayor's diddle buddy. The interrogation went bad, and her unconscious body was dumped on the beach at nearby Long Beach. When the high tide came in, she drowned.

So, Warden Wilson was heavily criticized for letting Higgins land his plane on the prison grounds so he and his old buddy could dine together. FDR himself criticized the warden, but Wilson snapped back that it was a free country and he would eat with whomever he pleased.

As for Higgins, after the meal he got in his plane, flew back to New York City, and soon thereafter was shot and fatally wounded in Prospect Park, Brooklyn, while attending his seven-year-old daughter's tap-dance recital.

Now Wilson had some more explaining to do and was in Albany to discuss the fatal knife fight in his prison. After that, it would be up to Commissioner of Correction Walter N. Thayer to tell the public what had happened out on the prison yard.

These explanations, more like press releases, didn't usually need to be terribly detailed. Two desperadoes rubbed out another desperado. People were going to read that and think, good. One less desperado. One less desperate mouth for our tax money to feed.

Those intrepid reporters, sour with sweat, even managed to chase down the warden in Albany, who promised he was leaving immediately to go to Great Meadow to start his investigation.

Galante told authorities that he was not personally involved in the knife fight, although he admitted that he'd been cut during the fracas. He said that he and the dead man were both victims of the same cons.

"And they were?"

"I don't know."

"Their names?"

"Don't know their names."

"What'd they look like?"

"Didn't see their faces."

The authorities told Galante they didn't give a shit if he was directly involved or not. He had been cut in the fight, solid evidence of direct involvement, and all persons involved were subject to the loss of good time—which in effect meant that three years had been added to Galante's sentence.

In the long run, Warden Wilson told the public that the fight was caused by "factional quarrels," acting out upon "enmities aroused by gang warfare outside the prison walls."

He said that the weapons used in the fight were "crude implements" made inside the prison, nothing that needed to be smuggled in.

One of Galante's early jobs was bootlegging liquor, a practice that persisted long after Prohibition was repealed because people didn't want to pay the tax. On July 30, 1934, Galante's still at 71 Wanser Avenue, Inwood, Long Island, operating in his absence, was raided by agents of the Alcohol Tax Unit.

The still was busted up, but cops didn't have enough to bust Galante, who of course was already upstate. A new still was rapidly built and business continued with only a minor interruption. (The same still at the same address continued operation until as late as July 1941. We know because it exploded and the fire department was called. As a result of the fire, which scorched the house's basement pretty good, the still was again busted up by agents of the Treasury Department, and 116 gallons of hooch were seized.)

The New York State Department of Corrections kept a list of people who came to their prisons to visit inmates, so we know everyone who visited Galante. His first visitor was his cousin Charles Bruno, who lived across the street from Galante.

"How come you told them you was me?"

"I didn't."

"Cop says you told them you was me."

"I didn't tell them I was you; I told them I was me," Galante lied.

Later his cousin Joseph Russo came to visit; several siblings and his parents came—plus attorney Nicholas P. Iannuzzi. That was it.

Iannuzzi oversaw Galante's appeals, none of which were successful. The mouthpiece passed the bar in 1930 and entered the workforce as a criminal trial attorney. He would be Galante's lawyer, or one of them, off and on, for decades.

He was a mob lawyer from the start and two of his first clients were Johnny Torrio and Lucky Luciano. During World War II, Iannuzzi temporarily gave up defense work and took a job as the Assistant U.S. Attorney in the Southern District of New York.

Iannuzzi had offices at 2 Lafayette Street in Lower Manhattan, which was also the building that housed Municipal Court. Iannuzzi's big move on Galante's behalf was to serve a writ in Superior Court claiming Galante was being required to serve a longer stretch than that owed to the state.

The building that held Iannuzzi's office had a history. Since the end of Prohibition, it was also the home of the brand-new Alcoholic Beverage Control Board, where New Yorkers could apply for licenses to sell legal booze, ironic in that Galante continued to operate stills for years after government-skimmed liquor was once again legal.

In 1938, Galante was represented by a Mr. Rosenberg, no first name, of the law firm Slade and Ohringer, offices at 299 Broadway in New York, which is downtown. Rosenberg was retained to contest the right of the parole board to withhold the granting of commutation and compensation time on the subject's sentence.

Galante was transferred from Great Meadow back to Sing Sing, closer to home, to finish his sentence. Galante appeared before the parole board on April 12, 1939, and was released on parole on May 1, 1939, after serving eight years of his twelve-and-a-half-year sentence.

The law at that time said that parole was automatic when there was time off for good behavior. The law was repealed soon after Galante was loosed back into the world. Ever since, in New York State, all parolees must be okayed by the parole board. There is no more automatic anything. We've got Galante to thank for that.

The year 1939 was a year of transition for Galante. Not only did he return to the free world, a world on the brink of world war, but his dad died, as well. If possible, Galante came out of prison even harder than when he'd gone in.

He was now a stone pro killer, a hit man, and he went to work whacking guys at the orders of Vito Genovese, then the acting boss of the Luciano crime family. His hits were uncountable. At one point, the NYPD suspected him of upward of eighty murders.

CHAPTER EIGHT

Hit Man

WHILE GALANTE WAS WHACKING guys left and right in what was left of 1939, according to Galante's cover story, he was again employed at the Lubin Artificial Flower Company, located at 270 West Broadway in Lower Manhattan.

Like most criminals, Galante liked his money in cash and within quick reach, but FBI records show that in 1939 Galante had a savings account at the Bowery Savings Bank, a different bank from the one that held his house mortgage. Galante's flirtation with institutionalized finance must've been short-lived, however. A check during later years would reveal that he had "no credit record."

According to the New York State parole board, on July 12, 1940, Galante registered for the draft, as per the 1940 Selective Training and Service Act. He registered in the 22nd Assembly District. He was classified as 4-F, which meant when war came the following year he didn't have to worry about being sent off to tour Europe or the South Pacific the hard way.

In 1877, an Irish tugboat worker from Chicago, Dan Keefe, formed the first local of the Association of Lumber Handlers. The union would survive the 1886 Haymarket riot, in which a bomb blew up seven Chicago policemen, and evolved over the years into the International Longshoremen's Association (ILA).

On February 3, 1941, according to Galante's parole records, he joined ILA Local 856, which represented the boys who worked on the piers of New York City. He was sponsored by his brother Sam Galante and received a Coast Guard pass. For a short time, he "worked" as a stevedore on Piers 14 and 21 for the New York and Cuba Mail Steamship Company and the New York and Puerto Rico Steamship Company.

Less than two months before Pearl Harbor, on September 15, 1941, parole records say that Galante worked as a handyman for the General Electro Plating Company, located at 176-180 Grand Street, NYC.

It is, of course, perfectly feasible that Galante did not show up for these jobs. But they existed on paper and he probably did get paid, but it is likely this is a paper trail designed to keep his parole officer happy while he went about the business of liquid affairs and boot-legged booze.

On August 17, 1942, Galante was allegedly employed by the Knickerbocker Trucking Company at 520 Broadway, at the corner of Spring Street in Soho. The records specified that he was a "helper" on trucking company vehicles. And that was a provable lie, as the "company" only had one truck.

There were also records around this time that Galante was em-ployed in a pastry shop at 13 Prince Street, on the corner of Prince and Elizabeth, and this was backed up to some extent by physical surveillance at that time. We know that, at the very least, Galante en-tered and exited that building on a regular basis. No one knew what he did once he was inside.

Galante told the parole board a lot of stuff, almost all of it fiction. He also told them that he had become a deeply religious man while up north, praise the Lord, that he belonged to the Church of All Na-tions at Second Avenue and 1st Street. He'd been a good Catholic as a kid, too, he insisted, a former card-carrying member of the Cath-olic youth group.

During this time, the savage Galante, now thirty years old, still lived with his recently widowed mom—or next door to Mom, depending on how you want to interpret the records. (Galante listed his residence as at 592 Shepherd Avenue in easternmost Brooklyn, New Lots/Brownsville. Records also showed that Galante's mother lived at 594 Shepherd Avenue, although it is unclear if this was a typo and the same house or correct and the house next door. In different paperwork, Galante's residence was listed as 876 New Lots Avenue, which wasn't far from Shepherd Avenue.)

Whatever his address, Galante wasn't home much. He had four places where he liked to hang out.

First and foremost, he hung out at the Spring Valley Pleasure Club at 238 Elizabeth Street in Little Italy—now the downtown Little Italy that we're familiar with today—apparently where he received his instructions.

He also killed time and played cards at the Musical Club at 18 Prince Street, an address that was raided during the spring of 1940 for bootlegging activities. The hoods there produced grain alcohol, 190 proof, which they used to make liquor and sold to doctors, druggists, and chemical companies.

According to the papers, the head of the illegal booze operation was Mauro Manna of Jersey City. Manna liked to eat at Jean's Clam Bar, a 186-seat restaurant across the street from the docks at 2123 Emmons Avenue in Sheepshead Bay, Brooklyn. The joint remained in operation until the 1980s, when the character of the strip changed, old-time hangouts replaced by high-price condos.

And, finally, according to the surveillance of the day, Galante was known to frequent a candy store on Mott Street in Little Italy, address unknown but near the corner of Houston Street.

The killing and booze business was good, and Galante purchased a piece of a few night spots, including the Bonfire Restaurant in Montreal. His partners in that operation were Harry Ship and Luigi "Louis" Greco. The joint was at the corner of Rue Décarie and Jean-Talon, just outside the Blue Bonnets Raceway.

According to the Museum of Jewish Montreal, Harry Ship was known as the "King of Montreal Gamblers," who controlled the city's top gambling rackets during the 1940s. Ship was a whiz with numbers. He'd had a good education, attending Queen's University but not graduating, and was smarter than your average wiseguy. Ship was just one of a handful of Jewish gangsters in Montreal who rose in power during the 1940s. Guys like Max Shapiro, Harry Davis, and Barney Shulkin also became part of Montreal's criminal underground.

Greco was more of a typical hood. He was a mob boss in Montreal from the mid-1940s until the early 1970s, taking power after his boss, Harry Davis, was whacked on Stanley Street. Greco didn't go to college, like Ship. In fact, he dropped out of school when he was ten (1923) and went to work after his dad died while working for the Canadian Pacific Railway.

Ship was far smarter but always subservient to Galante. In that world it was fear rather than brains that ruled the roost. That didn't mean that Ship wasn't rich as sin. He was, and he lived in a mansion on a hill to prove it.

As a kid, Ship was known as The Boy Wonder, and he was the inspiration for the book *The Apprenticeship of Duddy Kravitz* by Mordecai Richler. Richard Dreyfuss played him in the movie.

Ship's gambling casinos were far more like the luxurious casinos along the Vegas strip than like the smoky back rooms we usually associate with illegal gambling. Ship even arranged a system so that gamblers could be served food at the tables so that the customers wouldn't have to stop gambling.

Ship also believed in giving the customers all the action they wanted or could handle. If a guy came in and wanted to bet on a sporting event in Australia, he'd get unfavorable odds, but he could place the bet.

Ship's number-one joint would be the Chez Parée, a nightclub where you could go to see top Vegas acts, like Dean Martin and Frank Sinatra. Ship enjoyed being a celebrity. When he sponsored a little league baseball team, the name on their shirts was Shipmates.

Ship was busted a couple of times during the 1940s and early 1950s. He slowly but surely frittered away his fortune because, sadly, he was a degenerate gambler himself. His gambling addiction made him vulnerable to the Sicilians of New York City, which probably explains why he found himself partners with the animalistic Galante, a guy Ship probably couldn't stand to be in the same room with.

Galante's other partner in the Bonfire, Louis Greco, was a key figure in the French Connection, a narcotics importation system unlike any the world had previously seen. By 1930, Greco was in jail for sixty-eight days for assault. A 1932 newspaper article called the eighteen-year-old Greco a "dangerous criminal." He worked on the streets as a pimp and once was nabbed by cops for hitting a woman who refused to be turned out.

Of course, you know the deal, some of the Bonfire Restaurant was legit, enough to pass muster should anyone unexpectedly observe, but these businesses served as a front for an eclectic menu of racketeering. Down the line, the Montreal restaurant would serve as a staging platform for massive heroin distribution.

But Galante remained busy killing for profit. His stock rose until 1943, when he was assigned one of the biggest hits in history—a full-fledged political assassination.

CHAPTER NINE
Mussolini's Boy

I have sought with all my strength to elevate the moral and material conditions of the Italian workers here, and I have sought to instill in their souls the same faith in their emancipation that is alive in me. I am a soldier of the ideal.
—Carlo Tresca

As 1943 BEGAN, MOST AMERICANS were focused on World War II, raging in North Africa and in the Pacific. It raged in Eastern Europe, too, where Russia and Germany were fighting a war of attrition on the Eastern Front. On the Western Front, Europe was under Nazi control. There was nothing but the English Channel between Hitler and Churchill. There was a hellish war in the Pacific, too. But our focus is on Italy, where Fascists were in control, led by a guy named Benito Mussolini, who was in Hitler's hip pocket.

In Africa, a combination of American and British troops had landed on the beaches of Algeria and Morocco, where they faced "Vichy French" troops, in theory on Hitler's side. The French troops didn't fight very hard, though, and allowed the Allies to roll over them, which pissed off Hitler so much that he invaded the south of France in spite.

Domestically, on the home front, as they called it back then, the American public was being limited in their activities by rationing. No one was allowed to have more gas or food than they absolutely needed, as most motor vehicle fuel was destined to go overseas. That fuel would power the armored tanks that would eventually roll over the German and Japanese armies.

In New York, of course, there were those who scoffed at the rationing. The city, to stop the abusers, proclaimed that anyone caught "wasting" gas would lose their "food cards."

If rationing had not been as strict as it was, the events of January 12, 1943, might have gone very differently. Galante got to do the things he did that day because concerned officials lacked the gas to follow him.

Here's how it went.

That winter, in New York City, Carmine Galante was fighting a war that only tangentially involved the big battle between Axis and Allied powers. On January 12 Galante was given his latest assignment. For reasons of personal safety and freedom, Vito Genovese had relocated to Italy, where he and Mussolini got along great, but Genovese still had ways of getting a message to Galante if he needed someone liquidated.

Instructions were to whack sixty-three-year-old Carlo Tresca, a New York publisher of an anti-fascist newspaper and the former leader of the Industrial Workers of the World (IWW, aka the Wobblies). Tresca was larger than life, a life composed of kidnapping, murder, large gatherings, revolution—and, finally, violent and sudden death.

Tresca was born in Italy, fled that country as a young man in 1904, a political refugee, and became a vocal progressive when he got to the United States. He moved from picket line to picket line trying to push the power balance away from management and in favor of labor.

Management hates that.

One of Tresca's most famous moves, one that was covered heavily by the news media, was his participation with strikes among Pennsylvania coal miners and silk workers in New Jersey. He worked side by side with Wobbly officials.

Tresca's left-wing policies made him a hero to laborers in America. He was tall, good-looking, and gave emotionally laden speeches that could rivet a crowd, maybe hypnotize it one second and whip it into a frenzy the next.

He and his publications attacked the status quo at every turn. He verbally attacked bankers, bosses, and priests. When Italian American anarchists Sacco and Vanzetti were slated by the U.S. justice system for execution, Tresca tried (unsuccessfully) to save them.

You might be quick to call him a communist, but truth was he was a strong critic of Joseph Stalin, then in charge in Russia, for his "repressive tactics." Tresca was particularly critical of Stalin's actions during the Spanish Civil War, during which Stalin had an uncountable number of anarchists and non-communist loyalists whacked.

But fighting the fascisti was Tresca's true cause, and it was the Fascists who hated him enough to hurt him.

Tresca knew he'd never grow old. Attacking the status quo the way he did, attacking those who tended to have most of the money, would eventually be fatal. He would fight until they had no choice but to kill him.

Tresca's life was considered in danger on January 12 for the simple reason that his life was always in danger. He had been beaten and shot and kidnapped, but he always came back for more, fist raised high—power to the people! He drove Mussolini crazy.

Like any chronic protester who likes to handcuff himself to barricades, Tresca had been arrested many times—three dozen, according to the New York *Daily News*. He'd spent time in jail.

According to the *New Yorker* magazine, Tresca spent his time "fanning volcanoes." Those who knew him said he was proud of the massive number of enemies he had made in his life.

Experts said that he might've revolutionized the labor movement in the United States if it weren't for one factor—he never learned to speak English very well, and xenophobic Americans never quite trusted anyone who spoke "American" with an accent.

Tresca looked like he'd just come from central casting. He had fanaticism written all over him; with his crazy eyes and calamitous beard, he was prone to shaking his fist when he spoke. Beginning in 1920, when a bomb went off on Wall Street, the police always visited Tresca every time there was a bomb in Manhattan.

"They are nice boys," Tresca said about the officers who visited him anytime something exploded. "They come to me, they ask me what I know, I never know anything, and so we have wine."

Tresca had lunched for most of that afternoon with novelist John Dos Passos. During the early evening, Tresca was on his way with his friend Giuseppe Callabi to visit the offices of the paper Tresca edited, *Il Martello*, where they planned to meet four other men to discuss the anti-Fascist Mazzini Society.

When the four men did not show up, Tresca decided to stop waiting. He and Callabi left the office building and headed for a restaurant. Tresca was not particularly worried. He had been on Mussolini's hit list for twelve years at least, and he was still breathing. But on this evening, his luck ran out.

The roots of the conspiracy that eventually did in Tresca began in 1937 when Vito Genovese, whose hits were often carried out by Carmine Galante, was wanted for murder and skipped to Italy, with $750,000 in cash on his person.

Genovese used the money to get in nice with Mussolini's upper-echelon Fascists. Mussolini sided up with Hitler and Japan. Back in America, Tresca was making a stink and getting under Mussolini's skin, so through Genovese it became the job of the American Mafia to take care of it.

Another contributing factor to the timing of the hit on Tresca was a specific incident in which he angered an enemy. But make no mistake: from the second Genovese cozied up with the Italian Fascists, Tresca was dead man walking.

Galante was almost off the hook. Tresca had survived one attack in which his throat was slashed. Two days before Galante went to work there was an apparent attempt on Tresca's life when a car tried to run him over as he crossed a Manhattan street. The car was a Ford sedan, perhaps the same car that was involved two days later.

Today it is difficult to imagine just how dark it was on a Manhattan street during any evening during World War II. There were blackout rules, lights-out, across the United States, but particularly in big cities, to make it harder for potential German or Japanese bombers—which as we now know never came.

It was about 9:40 p.m. and Tresca and Callabi had gotten as far as the corner of 15th Street and Fifth Avenue. Carmine Galante had already been noticed by eyewitnesses, a short guy with tiny feet, pacing nervously. Someone must've given Galante the heads-up—"the guy with the beard, Lilo"—because Galante approached Tresca from behind with long, confident steps, gun out. He opened fire and the instant his gun was empty he fled, leaping into a waiting dark sedan, which peeled rubber as it left the scene. One eyewitness thought there were two people in the front seat of the car when the shooter dove into the back.

Callabi was not hit, but Tresca took a bullet to the back of the head and crumbled to the sidewalk, mortally wounded. Because of the lights-out conditions, no one, it seemed, got a good look at Galante's face—and if they did, they were smart enough to keep their mouths shut.

Police canvassed the block thoroughly asking if anyone saw or heard something that might be helpful. All bystanders claimed to be blind and deaf. Searching up and down the block, a cop recovered a loaded revolver from behind a cluster of dented ash cans (necessary back then because everyone burned coal in their furnaces). Police theorized that there might have been one gunman posted at either end of the block, so that they would have had Tresca covered no matter which way he turned after leaving the newspaper office building.

Tresca's body was picked up by the usual meat wagon—that is, the New York Medical Examiner hearse. The body was moved to the Manhattan morgue, where an autopsy was performed by assistant medical examiner Dr. Milton Helpern.

If that name sounds familiar, it is because Dr. Helpern would go on to have a legendary career. From 1954 until his retirement in 1973, he was the chief medical examiner for all of New York City, and his forensic work in crime cases earned him the tag "Sherlock Holmes with a microscope." He went on to become a key witness in several sensational murder cases. In 1967, Dr. Carl A. Coppolino might've gotten away with murdering his wife if Dr. Helpern hadn't used state-of-the-art techniques to find trace amounts of an injectable muscle relaxant in her system. The doctor also had a way with juries. When Helpern testified in a court of law, everyone believed him, and many defense attorneys didn't bother to cross-examine him. The Perry Mason mystery novel *The Case of the Hesitant Hostess* by Erle Stanley Gardner was dedicated to Dr. Helpern.

Dr. Helpern determined that Tresca had been felled by two bullets, one striking him in the back and the other in the back of the head.

Soon after the shooting, an abandoned Ford thought to be the getaway car was found at the 18th Street entrance to the Seventh Avenue Subway, a few hundred yards from the scene of the murder. Police impounded the car, and the squints went over it with a fine-tooth comb. No prints. It was almost physically impossible for an automobile to have no fingerprints anywhere, inside or out. Very suspicious.

Galante first became a suspect in the Tresca assassination because of a report from his parole officer. We know about it because of a declassified FBI report regarding the hit on Tresca. During the late afternoon of January 12, not long before Tresca's murder, Carmine Galante reported to his parole officer, offices at the corner of Lafayette and Worth Streets in Manhattan, maybe a mile south of the shooting site. He had with him papers designed to prove to his PO that he was gainfully employed as a trucker, making a cool twenty-five dollars a week. (That was the trucking company with only one truck.) His entire parole office had been alerted to keep an eye on Galante, as they'd received reports that he consorted with felons.

Earlier that day, Galante's parole officer had spoken to the beat cop and asked that he follow Galante a bit after he left the building to see what the little guy was up to. So, after Galante delivered his papers establishing his employment as a truck driver, he left and was followed on foot by Patrolman Fred Berson of the NYPD.

As the officer shadowed him, Galante hurried up Worth Street to Lafayette. Parked ahead at the curb was a car, the driver waiting with the motor running. As Galante approached the car, the rear passenger-side door opened, as if by magic.

Galante, who had already been walking very fast, now broke into a run for the last few strides to the car. Galante disappeared inside with a small duck of his head. The door slammed behind him and the car pulled away all in one fluid motion, reportedly driven by Galante's close friend Joey Beck.

Berson wrote down the license number: 1C 9272. He would have loved to follow further because he thought Galante was behaving oddly. Antsy. He seemed impatient while at his parole office, like he was itching to leave, to get on with some unspoken business. Galante had someplace to be.

Berson would have loved to have continued tailing Galante in a car, but there was no gas.

When the men from the parole office noted the similarity immediately between the car found abandoned three blocks from the kill site and the car Galante had been seen leaping into, they called New York police. The plate numbers matched.

"I know some of his favorite haunts. I could help you look for him," the parole officer said.

On January 13, police took the guy up on it and it worked like a charm. They'd checked a couple of joints to no avail and were on their way to a third when they saw Galante walking down Elizabeth Street in Little Italy.

"Galante, get in the car."

"What for?"

"Material witness to the Tresca murder."

"You got the wrong guy, fellows."

"Just get in the car."

Galante got in. They took him to the precinct house and booked him as a material witness. The district attorney's office was all over Galante. D.A. Frank Hogan personally handled the questioning. They were in a small room without windows; the light was in Galante's eyes. It was going to be the third degree.

"Settle in, Lilo. You're going to be here for a while. You need anything?"

"Coffee black. Ashtray."

"Sure."

Coffee and an ashtray were hurriedly brought. As Galante took a sip and lit up a stogie, the detective was already starting his first question.

"Just want to ask you a few questions about your movements yesterday," Hogan said.

"Sure, what do you want to know?"

"You visited your parole officer yesterday."

"That's right."

"What time was that?"

"I never know what time it is."

"OK, what did you do after you left there?"

"I, uh, ducked into the subway."

"Where'd you go?"

"Uptown."

"Where?"

"Went to a movie."

"What movie?"

"*Casablanca*." (It was true that the Bogart movie was at that time running in first-run theaters.)

"What was the movie about?"

"I don't remember."

"After that?"

"Went to see a broad."

"What's her name?"

"I don't remember."

"Uh-uh." The D.A. shook his head from side to side. He had caught Galante in a lie right off the bat.

"Parole office was keeping tabs on you; saw you get into a car at Worth and Lafayette."

"What of it? I didn't shoot nobody. I was never anywhere near where it happened."

Hogan was scratching his head. The Tresca hit was a big deal, hyper-political, of global importance, and their primary suspect was a dim-witted hood who didn't know the difference between fascism and *pasta fagioli*.

A lineup was scheduled so Tresca's friend Giuseppe Callabi who was standing next to Tresca when he was killed, could have an opportunity to positively identify Galante as the assassin.

It all could have been different. The world would've been rid of Galante. But no. Callabi weaseled.

"Could be," Callabi said. "It was dark. I had my back turned at first. I don't know."

Galante again got his picture in the papers. The headline screamed that the assassin had been arrested! And he was a local hood, from East New York, a neighborhood the *Daily News* described as "spawning ground of the Abe Reles murder syndicate."

The problem with the evidence against Galante was it was missing a key piece. Authorities knew that the car Galante got into after seeing his parole officer was one and the same as the car found abandoned after the shooting—but they couldn't definitively say that this car was identical to the one used in the shooting, only that it was similar. Which only goes to show, no one ever writes down a license-plate number when there are bullets flying around.

District Attorney Hogan was further discouraged when he learned that the car that possibly linked Galante to the crime could not be connected to Galante in any way. It had been bought by someone else, not even a known crook, for $300 from a place called Cornfield Motors. I don't know where that is, but I don't think it's Brooklyn.

Hogan saw his hold on Galante crumbling and decided to drop the "material witness" gambit. It allowed police to hold a man, but only for so long. All his mouthpiece had to do was file a writ of habeas corpus and they'd have to spring him—which is what happened.

February 5, 1943, Galante's lawyer filed with Judge Philip J. Mc-Cook, seeking Galante's release. Six days later a judge named Peter Schmuck (again, seriously, that was the man's name) denied the writ.

D.A. Hogan thought of a better way to keep Galante off the street. He called the parole board and asked them to help develop a case against Galante for parole violation. Galante was re-questioned, and this time the grilling went on all night, until the D.A. was the one sweating. Galante gave up nothing.

Later the district attorney described Galante as a "tough nut to crack. This fellow has been in prison for years. He is prison-wise," Hogan said.

When the questioning ended, Galante was taken to City Prison on Centre Street, the hellhole known for thirty years as The Tombs. The charge: suspicion of parole violation.

As all of this was going on, the Italian-American Labor Council and the Il Martello Group, composed of employees of Tresca's newspaper, arranged for the removal of the slain man's body from Bellevue Morgue to the Frank E. Campbell Funeral Chapel at 81st Street and Madison Avenue.

The body lay in state until the evening of January 15, when it was transported to the Manhattan Center Auditorium at West 34th Street and Eighth Avenue for an elaborate Saturday morning ceremony called a "commemorative international mass meeting."

New York's Italian American population, at least those who hated Mussolini and fascism, arrived en masse to say farewell to Tresca, the man they called The Fire Eater. The Manhattan Center to-do was part funeral and part anti-totalitarian demonstration. Most of the speakers were labor leaders. The crowd was heavily peppered with detectives who were there to make sure there was no trouble and to seek clues as to the identity of Tresca's assassin. After the ceremony, Tresca's body was transported in a long funeral procession to Fresh Pond Crematory and Columbarium in Maspeth, Queens. The procession went out of its way to pass the spot where Tresca was killed.

Although no one particularly suspected them—why would a commie kill a commie?—Robert Minor, assistant general secretary of the Communist Party of the United States, made a big stink about how they didn't do it and to do it would have been alien to everything they stood for.

"Any person holding views even remotely tolerant of individual acts of terror would be expelled from the party forthwith," Minor said, "as is made mandatory by the constitution of the party."

The Tombs was an eight-story brick structure with cone-shaped towers, built in 1902. Back then, the construction project came with a decent budget, but after the politicians all took their skim there wasn't anything left for the niceties, like functioning plumbing. The jail looked like the sort of place that would have a dungeon, but in reality it *was* a dungeon. "Squalid" was the word most people used. It was a place where a guy could meditate on his sins while rodents ran over his face and water dripped down the walls of his cell.

As Galante rotted in the Tombs, the city was in the process of moving prisoners into the shiny new "Manhattan House of Detention," which had just been built adjacent to the Criminal Courts Building. Now crooks didn't have to go outside to attend their court hearings.

But Galante was in the old jail, the hole, just him and the vermin, stewing in their own juices. Twenty-four hours in the Tombs was cruel and unusual. Galante had to stay there for eight months in hopes that he would talk, but he never did. For that matter, he never would.

Galante's attorney following his 1943 arrest was Frank Delli Paoli, who served a writ on Galante's behalf to release Galante because he was being held without charge. The district attorney would later decide not to waste too many of his resources on trying to solve the Tresca case. They knew who pulled the trigger but couldn't prosecute. The similarity between the car Galante got into and the one used in Tresca's murder moved Galante to the head of the suspect class. But that was where the case against Galante remained. Police and prosecutors were "reasonably certain," to use the FBI's phrase, that Galante was Tresca's killer. But that wasn't good enough. Galante would never go to trial. So, they were stuck with trying to figure out who ordered the hit—and the list of suspects was long. Tresca had too many enemies. The chances of figuring out which was behind the shooting seemed remote.

The investigation into Tresca's murder did not result in a prosecution of the killer, but it did bear unexpected fruit. D.A. Hogan had ordered hundreds of phone taps after the murder, with an emphasis on Italian American leaders, in hopes that he'd record someone giving up Galante for the Tresca hit. No one did, but the D.A.'s office did listen in on one conversation that was downright enlightening and resulted in a major political scandal. The phone call in question was to City Judge Thomas Aurelio, who had just been nominated to the State Supreme Court, and from mob boss Frank Costello.

"Thanks for everything," Aurelio said.

"It went over perfect," Costello said. "When I tell you something is in the bag, you can rest assured."

"I want to assure you of my loyalty for all you have done. It's undying."

"I know," Costello said.

Costello became a primary suspect in the Tresca hit, as the man who put out the contract, "probably" as a direct favor to Mussolini. It was a theory. Later, authorities came to believe that the order to hit Tresca was based on more personal reasons.

With Galante in the Tombs, the parole board was placed in charge of keeping him behind bars. Their investigation examined Galante's behavior since his release from Sing Sing on May 1, 1939. He'd had steady employment, for Lubin Artificial Flower Company, as a longshoreman, and with the General Electro Plating Company. For a short stint he received unemployment insurance (August 1942) but soon got a new job with the one-truck Knickerbocker Trucking Company.

Years later, the FBI would theorize that though Tresca's career as a spokesman for labor was quite large, the offense that put him on a hit list might have been very small. It was rumored that Tresca's fatal mistake had been an insult of a man named Frank Garofalo, a man the FBI called one of the leaders of the Castellammarese gang.

The actual insult remained private, but investigators put two and two together and came up with a theory as to the subject matter. Garofalo and Assistant U.S. Attorney Dolores Paconti of the Southern District of New York had, as the FBI put it, "gone out" with each other. Tresca had apparently uttered a comment aloud about Garofalo and Paconti that got under Garofalo's skin.

Garofalo became a suspect in the actual assassination. At the time of the shooting, he lived on East 58th Street. As a legit business, Garofalo operated the Colorado Cheese Company at 176 Avenue A on the Lower East Side. Garofalo was not a guy you insulted. His old pal Lucky Luciano had his back, among others.

Who was the third man in the Ford sedan? One theory was that it was a notorious Mexican communist who'd been used in the past as a mob trigger and was also mentioned in a plot to assassinate Leon Trotsky.

Not everyone thought Tresca was bumped off by Galante because Tresca insulted Garofalo and his fed gal pal. Newspaper columnist Walter Winchell was out there pitching international conspiracy theories, saying Tresca had been iced by his own bodyguard under the orders of a publisher in competition with Tresca. The bodyguard, like Garofalo, had been insulted by Tresca, but the bodyguard's diss happened back in 1934. Winchell didn't seem to care that nine years is a long time to hold a murderous grudge.

Was this a new theory, or was it the same theory seen sideways? Frank Garofalo had once worked as bodyguard for a man named

Generoso Pope, who happened to be the publisher of a foreign-language newspaper.

We do know that a friend of Tresca's told the FBI that Generoso Pope was on his short list of people who had the means and motive to whack Tresca. The info specifically was that Pope ordered the hit and "his bodyguard" pulled it off.

The FBI assumed that the bodyguard being placed under suspicion was Frank Garofalo. The feds noted that "Pope and his gang" were once attacked in the offices of *Il Martello* and this might have been retaliation. Tresca had long been anti-Pope. In 1934, he had written an exposé recounting how Pope intimidated his fellow newspaper editors and how Garofalo handled gangster-type activities on Pope's behalf. As we know, at the time of the Tresca hit, Galante claimed to work for the Knickerbocker Trucking Company. Well, it was Galante's supposed employer at that firm who retained Samuel DiFalco, city councilman and chairman of the Democratic Club (itself a cover for gang activities), as its legal counsel. DiFalco was Generoso Pope's nephew and godson.

The FBI's informant said that there had been rising tensions between Tresca and Pope. Tresca had been invited to a dinner on September 10, 1942, and said that he would only show up if assured that Pope was not going to be there. Then, when Tresca arrived at the dinner and found that Frank Garofalo was in attendance, Tresca commented that "Garofalo is not just a fascist; he is a gangster." Interestingly, Garofalo was at the dinner with Dolores Paconti, the Assistant U.S. Attorney, and it was Tresca's snarky comment about Garofalo and Paconti that some think sealed Tresca's fate.

Garofalo was an interesting guy. He was born in Italy on September 10, 1891. He became a U.S. citizen on September 8, 1931, but for his entire life spoke English only with a thick Italian accent. His FBI shadow once described him as a "rather distinguished"–looking man, five seven, 170, brown eyes, gray hair, needed glasses to drive.

He lived in a fancy doorman apartment house where he occupied a four-room apartment with his brother Vincent. They didn't have a phone and frequently used the pay phone in the building's lobby.

There was a doing-business-as (DBA) license attached to the Garofalo apartment: High Grade Packing Company. Uh-huh. Police could find no vehicle listed to either Garofalo or his "company."

The feds looked at this picture and decided the whole packing-company bit was a subterfuge to "give an aura of respectability" to Garofalo and offer him a seemingly endless number of plausible excuses for his frequent trips to Florida and Southern California.

There were other companies he was linked to also: M&G Coat Company, R&R Cloak Company. He had ties with Joseph Barbara—who will become very important to our story—and Barbara's soft drink bottling company in Endicott, New York. The FBI called Barbara a "known hoodlum." Barbara had a substantial record, including an arrest for murder.

An FBI memo assigned Barbara great power: "Barbara is known to control all of the area racketeers in this vicinity and to have widespread gangland connections." The words would become prophetic, as Barbara's rural home would one day be the site of the most famous mob meeting of all time.

Barbara, investigators determined, was born on August 9, 1905, in Italy, entered the United States on May 28, 1921, and was naturalized on May 22, 1927. His FBI files reflected that he was convicted for violation of the OPA laws in 1946 in Utica, New York. The OPA laws were price-control, anti-inflation measures put in place by executive order of President Franklin Roosevelt. The laws placed ceilings on all prices except for those of farming commodities. Barbara's crime today would be called gouging.

The fed surveillance picked up bits and pieces here and there through careful observation. They knew that Galante and Garofalo were both into the illegal booze racket, bootleggers years after Prohibition. The fact that these men were guests now and again with the owner of a bottling plant was interesting. It made the FBI suspect that Barbara was doing more at his Endicott bottling plant than making ginger ale. Also, a fed analyst opined, there were ingredients that could be legitimately ordered for a soft drink manufacturer, sugar for example, and then diverted into the illegal booze business.

The FBI speculated that narcotics and gambling might also have been among the topics of conversation when Galante, Garofalo, and Barbara got together. Who knew what else these men talked about when they socialized? Just having them all in the same room was scary enough. Maybe, the FBI theorized, they talked about "administration policies" or "arbitration of the Italian element of the American syndicate."

Garofalo packed a .32 Smith & Wesson. For years he carried it legit, licensed to protect the payroll of his many companies, but the license was yanked in 1943 when the state determined that he was "no longer in business."

Everyone agreed that Garofalo had powerful friends, friendships that went straight to the top, to the upper echelons of what the FBI was calling that year the "Union Siciliano of the United States." The largest gang in the NYC union, they boldly stated, was the Castellammarese Gang, which happened to be the gang of Galante and Garofalo.

Garofalo was technically clean. Zero criminal record. Still, Tresca had reportedly insulted Garofalo and now Tresca was dead. Galante was said to be Garofalo's friend and Galante was behind bars, his name in all the papers as the alleged political assassin.

The New York District Attorney's Office tried for years to tie Galante in with Garofalo, but they couldn't do it. One cutout between master cylinder and torpedo was all it would take the feds to hit a brick wall, like a pack of hounds suddenly losing the foxy scent. And before the RICO (Racketeer Influenced and Corrupt Organizations) bullshit plausible deniability on the part of organized crime amounted to a license to kill.

So, instead of Galante being nailed for the Tresca assassination, he was found guilty of parole violation and up the lazy river he returned on November 23, 1943, to serve the remaining portion of his armed robbery sentence.

CHAPTER TEN
Back to Prison

ON JANUARY 22, 1944, GALANTE was transferred back up north, for the second time in his life to the Clinton Correctional Facility in Dannemora, so he could spend the rest of winter freezing his Sicilian nuts off in Little Siberia. In February, the CCF warden wrote a letter to the Commissioner of Correction in Albany to ascertain the date on which Galante could be released.

The warden said he'd done some calculation and concluded that Galante had been sentenced to serve too much delinquent time and that the stint should actually be only one year, ten months, and ten days.

The point of contention, apparently, was whether Galante should be credited for time served for parole time. There was confusion at the time of the sentencing, the warden maintained.

Even up there within spitting distance of Canada it can't be winter all the time, and spring finally came. One pleasant morning, May 25, 1944, Galante had company.

Two attorneys made the trek through the wilderness to Dannemora.

I've been to Dannemora, went to visit my uncle Bobby Darrow, and it scares the shit out of you. Yeah, the prison itself, but the surroundings, too. There was nothing but woods for miles and miles. You could drive for an hour and see nothing but trees and a bear—

which is outside of a Brooklyn boy's comfort zone. In 1944, Dannemora must've been even scarier.

The men entering CCF's mighty gates that beautiful spring morning were Thomas Dougherty of Dougherty & Madden and Marcus L. Filley of Decatur & Filley, both of Troy, New York. The former visited Galante; the latter met with another top hood incarcerated there.

The outcome of this was a letter, reportedly from Carmine Galante. He complained that he was one of two Carmine Galantes in trouble and some of the things he was attributed to were the work of the other Carmine Galante.

The letter had a shot-in-the-dark feel.

That summer, on July 31, 1944, the lawyer Dougherty applied for a writ of habeas corpus to the Special Term of the County Court, in nearby Plattsburgh, where it was received by F. Claude O'Connell, a Clinton County judge. The writ was quickly dismissed in Clinton County Court.

But Galante's lawyers weren't through. A notice of appeal from the order of Judge O'Connell was filed in Clinton County late that summer, and that autumn the appeal was denied by the New York State Supreme Court in Albany.

Still, Galante's legal team worked tirelessly and eventually found a judge who saw things Galante's way. On December 21, 1944, Galante was discharged from Dannemora on a court order signed by the Hon. Andrew W. Ryan. Judge Ryan said that it appeared to him as if Galante had already served his entire maximum sentence and ordered Galante's immediate release.

The Department of Corrections had been planning to release Galante at the Ides of March 1945, but this court order moved that date up—and Galante was home for Christmas 1944. He had served two years, three months, and twenty-two days in delinquent time.

This was yet another indication that there were people in powerful positions, in law enforcement, the justice system, and the world of politics, who were inexplicably interested in keeping Carmine Galante on the streets.

Galante's stock had only gone up while he did his time. The whacking of Tresca was very high-profile, a tough hit. Galante got the job done without emotion and kept his mouth shut afterward, even if it meant more jail time for parole violation. His spot in the Bonanno Family rose to "trusted lieutenant."

A free man, Galante moved into a leadership role for the first time in his life, running a crew out of the Lower East Side in the city, making policy and fixing rates.

Galante's personal life was changing fast as well. He'd only been home for a few weeks when he fell in love with a woman who must have had a lovely voice, as she worked in radio. She was Elena Ninfa "Helen" Marulli, twenty-eight years old, a resident at 247 South 3rd Street in Williamsburg, Brooklyn. Helen's parents were born in Italy. Dad's name was Joseph. Mom's maiden name was Bullara.

Lilo and Helen were wed on February 10, 1945. Standing up for Galante was Anthony Marulli, the bride's brother who would become a member of Galante's crew, and of course Cousin Moey.

The wedding ceremony was performed by Father Celsus Repole, and witnessed by Michael Consolo and Mary Caso, at Our Lady of Sorrows, a huge church built in 1868 that sits on Pitt Street between Rivington and Stanton Streets, a few blocks east of Little Italy. The church is a mishmash of three architectural styles: Romanesque, Byzantine, and Victorian, and known for its massive tubular-pneumatic organ. When the bride came down the aisle, everyone on the Lower East Side knew it.

On the marriage certificate, the groom was listed as Camillo Galante, which tended to support his birth certificate as real, and his occupation as longshoreman.

Galante and Helen had three children, a boy, James, born January 27, 1946, and two girls, Camille born January 24, 1951, and Angela, born November 14, 1952.

Either Helen had a cover story or Galante was a modern fellow who had no trouble with his wife working out of the home. Whichever, on July 3, 1948, records showed that Helen, no longer reading copy into a microphone for a living, was employed as a saleslady at a store at 104 First Avenue in Manhattan.

As we'll see, Galante lost his Helen mojo and spent the last twenty years of his life with his goomara, with whom he had two additional children.

CHAPTER ELEVEN
Bootlegger

GALANTE, NOW THIRTY-SEVEN YEARS OLD, was next arrested on September 4, 1947, caught red-handed while dismantling a still in Park Slope, Brooklyn. While agents of the Alcohol Tax Unit (ATU) looked on, Galante was among those taking the still apart and placing the pieces inside a 1938 Cadillac. Also on the scene, and already loaded, was a 1937 International truck, to the brim with copper sheeting, tubing, and other parts necessary for the construction of a still.

The owner of the Cadillac later had his lawyers petition the Secretary of the Treasury to have his luxury automobile returned, and this was done. The fate of the International truck is unknown.

The still, according to police, could produce nine hundred gallons of alcohol a day. It had been built in the cellar of the tenement, near the corner of Berkeley Place and Fifth Avenue. Also arrested in that bust were John Longo, Nicholas Palmiotto, and Galante's good friend Joey Beck. Longo lived in the building in which the still was found and ran a tinsmith business out of the first floor.

The bust made headlines in the *Brooklyn Eagle*, largely because Galante was assumed to be Carlo Tresca's killer, so the fact that he was in trouble again was news.

The quartet of bootleggers were taken to Manhattan Police Headquarters and questioned all night. All equipment and both vehicles were seized by the ATU. The bust itself was handled by the NYPD, which promptly turned Galante over to the ATU guys for questioning. Trying to get information out of Galante was as frustrating as ever for authorities.

"Where do you live?"

"Two-Seventy-Four Marcy Avenue."

"What do you do for a living, Galante?"

"I work for my brother."

"Where?"

"Grocery store. In the neighborhood I live."

"That's it?"

"I'm a longshoreman."

"What are you doing around here?"

"Shopping. Shopping for olive oil."

"How do you know these other guys?"

"Don't. Never met 'em."

Galante tried to tell the authorities that he had nothing to do with the still, that he was an innocent bystander, just passing by when the bust took place. Galante was informed that he'd been under surveillance for the previous six months, so he should cut the bullshit. After that, Galante clammed up.

Galante was taken to federal jail and charged as the owner/operator of an illegal still and for possession of the equipment for the manufacture of alcohol. This alcohol violation kicked around for a few years, not causing the out-on-bail Galante too much grief, until it was finally dismissed by a judge on July 6, 1950.

That winter, December 15, 1950, Galante was in trouble again, this time operating a large floating craps game, again with Joey Beck at his side. It didn't have a regular home base—that's why it was floating—but at the time of the bust it resided at 235 West 18th Street in Manhattan. The raid snagged fifty-one hoods.

Joey Beck at that time lived on Elizabeth Street in Little Italy. Along with being a close friend of Carmine Galante, Beck was also a good friend of Harry "Nig" Rosen, aka Harry Stromberg, as well as Natale "Joe Diamond" Evola.

Rosen started out as leader of a juvenile delinquent gang called the 69th Street Gang and developed into a southwest Philadelphia hood whose influence included much of the Eastern Seaboard. During the 1930s, Rosen worked side by side with Meyer Lansky and had a piece of a drug-importing business that brought babonia into the United States from Mexico. In later years he became a legit shipper, working for Tommy "Three-Finger" Lucchese, transporting dresses from the Garment District to wherever they needed to go.

Evola was from Castellammare and worked the Garment District. He was another rising star in the Bonanno Family and would one day briefly be family boss.

Galante was still working as a hit man, settling Bonanno beefs, in 1950, at age thirty-nine. Just after the New Year, a small-time numbers collector named Dominick Idone, twenty-four years old and destined to get no older, was pocketing cash that he was supposed to be passing up to his superiors.

Galante got the job of whacking him. His pleasure. And so, at 3:00 a.m. on January 1, 1950, just back from a New Year's Eve party, Idone received a phone call at his home on Mulberry Street in Little Italy. On the other end of the line was a stranger using some rap to lure Idone out to a meeting just down the block.

"Who was that?" Idone's wife asked.

"Some guy, wants to meet me at Pete Rao's apartment." Pete Rao was Idone's brother-in-law, who lived just down the block. "I'll be back in a few minutes."

Idone left and that was the last time his wife and two-year-old son, Dominic, saw him alive. When he got to the front of his brother-in-law's building, Galante met him with a gun in his hand, walked him into the building across the street, and emptied his six-shooter, striking his target in the upper body five times and, as Idone collapsed to the floor, firing his last shot over Idone, leaving the last slug embedded in the dingy hallway's grease-stained wall.

Neighbors heard the shots but didn't call the police, all thinking that the sounds were just part of a New Year's celebration. Idone's body was found the next day, January 2, in the dark hallway where Galante left him.

Police didn't realize that it was current policy-bank mischief that got Idone whacked and instead looked at his past. Idone had been arrested for running numbers as recently as November 10, 1949, a crime for which he was fined twenty-five dollars. He had also been questioned recently about a holdup but was released.

Idone, police suspected, had been part of a crew that, in December 1948 dug a tunnel from the basement next door and broke into the Rocco Carecchia Travel Agency on 86th Street in Bensonhurst, Brooklyn. There they stole $50,000 in traveler's checks. With Idone during the Bensonhurst heist were Charles DiPalermo, twenty-five, Louis "Gigi" Arminante, twenty-one, Salvatore Megrino, twenty-nine, and Joseph Mistretta, twenty, all of the Lower East Side.

Of these men, Charles DiPalermo is of the most interest to our story, as he was the brother of Galante's close friend Joseph "Joey Beck" DiPalermo, he of the long neck and humongous Adam's apple who was also suspected of taking part in the traveler's check heist.

Joey was eventually found, arrested for counterfeiting $1 million in traveler's checks, and sent to a fed pen in Atlanta.

In December 1950, there was a major sweep by NYPD of Little Italy gangsters believed to be involved in counterfeiting, bootleg booze, payroll holdups, and floating craps games. The sweep netted Galante along with dozens of others. All were subpoenaed to appear before a grand jury investigating gambling.

Again, Galante was given extra inches of print in the tabloids upon his arrest because he was the assumed Carlo Tresca assassin. Galante was arrested at five in the morning on December 15, 1950, by police who had been staking out his house on Marcy Avenue in Brooklyn waiting for him to come home.

Galante was hustled over to the D.A.'s office and questioned for hours. Galante might've thought this was about Tresca again or maybe about Idone or another murder we don't know about. He must have breathed a big sigh of relief when the questioning was focused only on floating craps games.

The assistant D.A. who'd handled the Tresca case, Louis Pagnucco, attended the interrogation, so Galante couldn't completely relax. But the questions always focused on gambling. Galante freely admitted that he was friends with the DiPalermo brothers, especially his pal Joe, and they grew up together in East Harlem, but as for craps, his mind was blank. As usual, Galante said he didn't know dick about dick. Galante was in custody for eight hours and was released during the early afternoon of December 16.

As Galante spent the early fifties in and out of trouble, there was some in and out going on at home as well. On January 24, 1951, Helen Galante gave birth to a girl, Camilla. Son James was three days shy of his fifth birthday. On November 14, 1952, the Galantes completed their family with the birth of a second daughter, Angela.

CHAPTER TWELVE
Big-Time Babonia

In 1953, GALANTE'S BOSS, his "father," Giuseppe "Joe Bananas" Bonanno, sent him to Montreal to keep an eye on the huge heroin machine there. He worked there alongside Vincenzo Cotroni, a Canadian crime boss. Galante owned part of a restaurant up there and knew his way around.

During that stint, he lived on Dorchester Road in Montreal, sharing the house with Louis Greco, his Bonfire Restaurant partner. (Because it was considered less than honorable to sell heroin, Bonanno erased this racket from his résumé. In fact, Joe wrote a four-hundred-page autobiography and never mentioned Carmine Galante, a man who had once been his protégé, his driver, and eventually his underboss. Many used the other end of the pencil to write books. Bonanno used the eraser.)

According to the Royal Canadian Mounted Police (RCMP), Carmine Galante entered Canada on February 26, 1954. On that date, Galante walked into the Montreal Immigration Office and announced he wanted to officially enter the country as a permanent resident for the purpose of operating a restaurant full-time. He had five grand in cash on him.

Officials told Galante that he couldn't be officially a businessman in Canada until he got the stamp of approval from a physician. Galante agreed to see a doctor and return with a note. Galante passed his physical and returned to the immigration office on March 1. He was handed "Form 1000" and told to fill it out.

Question number seventeen asked if he had ever been arrested in the United States. He wrote yes. Was he convicted? Again, he wrote yes. After he handed in his completed form, immigration official J. M. Langois asked him about the crime he'd been convicted of.

"I was just a kid. Sixteen. Assault. I got a suspended sentence."

"That's it?"

"Yeah."

"All right, Mr. Galante. We are going to check on this and get back to you."

Galante grunted and left. He told his lawyer Paul E. Fontaine what had happened. The mouthpiece knew the immigration office was going to learn of Galante's extensive criminal record soon enough and, on behalf of his client, contacted the immigration office and said Galante was withdrawing his application for permanent residence.

In the meantime, the Bonfire, already set up for a gambling operation worth an estimated $50 million annually, was prepared and adapted to be a hub in a massive narcotics-smuggling operation.

Why Montreal? We get a clue from a two-and-a-half-year study conducted by Judge François Caron that discovered the Montreal police force to be one of the most corrupt in North America. As was true in many places all around the world, hoods could operate with impunity if they knew which palms to grease.

By December 1954, however, Montreal police were investigating the Bonfire Restaurant. They contacted the immigration office and asked for any records they might have on Carmine Galante. That office dished the request off to the head immigration office in Ottawa. The request for info specified that they were requesting all records going back to 1948 regarding either a Carmine or a Camillo Galante. The immigration head office reported that they had no record of Galante being in Canada until 1954.

On February 22, 1955, Montreal newspapers printed a story about the large number of American hoods who'd moved north of the border to avoid being subpoenaed by the Kefauver Committee, a U.S. Senate panel taking on the rackets and racketeers. The official name of the committee was the Special Committee on Organized Crime in Interstate Commerce.

Two days later, the immigration office contacted the RCMP asking for a copy of Galante's U.S. rap sheet. But this was not done. Laval Fortier, the Deputy Minister of Immigration, explained that he did not want to disrupt any RCMP investigations that were ongoing. Huh?

By the spring of 1955, the RCMP was fairly certain that the American hoods living in Montreal were doing more than operating a restaurant, that they were using the Bonfire Restaurant to traffic narcotics. The RCMP gave immigration a list of goodfellas who were not to be allowed into Canada, and Galante's name was on the list.

Now during all of this, Galante was back and forth unnoticed between Montreal and New York all the time. Galante generally crossed the border at the port of Lacolle, sometimes known on the American side as Blackpool. To put an end to this, immigration in Canada issued a be-on-the-lookout (BOLO) for Galante. If he was located, either in Canada or at the border, an Order of Deportation was to be issued.

In the meantime, there was an uptick in mob violence in Montreal, a city that was not used to seeing hoods getting whacked on its streets. Somebody shot at (and missed) Kenneth "China Boy" Winfred. Benjamin "Baby Yak" Yubacovitz was shot in the leg. For a brief time, these targets were kept in protective custody. In late May two hoods got into a fight. Natale Brigante stabbed Paolo Violi, who in response pulled a gun and shot Brigante to death. Violi was later tried for manslaughter and acquitted.

That summer, there was evidence that efforts were being made by American gangsters to engage all Montreal nightclubs in a protection racket. Sure enough, those establishments that didn't pay up had bad things happen, usually in the form of a gang of hoods breaking in and smashing up the place. This happened to the El Morocco, the Down Beat Club, the Savoy Club, and others.

Even as the uncooperative nightclubs were being wrecked, a Canadian judge issued a warrant for the arrest of Louis Greco, Galante's Bonfire partner.

The next day, RCMP raided Greco's Montreal home on Dorchester Street West, where Galante also stayed when he was in town, and confiscated weapons and $4,000. Greco was arrested on weapons charges, denied bail, and pleaded not guilty. Greco ended up getting off with just a fine, plus a $950 "peace bond," which would be returned to him if he stayed out of trouble for a year.

On October 10, 1955, RCMP arrested Galante and charged him with being involved in an illegal card game, a very small crime for a big hood. But it didn't matter. They wanted him out of the country, and any reason would do when it came to deportation.

On April 30, 1956, Canadian officials decided to deport Galante. Galante, in essence, said, "You can't kick me out. I'm leaving." Also asked to leave at the same time was Galante's most loyal crewmember, his wife's brother Anthony Marulli.

So, technically, Galante was never deported—a fact that Galante's legal team planned to exploit. During the autumn of 1956, Galante mouthpiece Paul E. Fontaine wrote to the Canadian immigration office and asked for permission for Galante to visit Montreal for the purpose of "dealing with business problems" at the Bonfire Restaurant. A permit allowing Galante to visit was issued in November, and during the two weeks that Galante was back in Canada he was placed under constant surveillance.

Galante returned stateside before Christmas and apparently remained in the United States until the spring of 1957, when his lawyer again asked for permission for his client to come to Canada and take care of more "business matters." Canada wanted more info on the intent of the visit and the lawyer explained that Galante needed to have a sit-down with Greco and Ship, his partners. This time, Canada refused the request.

This didn't stop Galante from returning to Canada. He simply stopped asking for permission.

* * *

In the days before RICO, indicting a mobster was a chore. The template for success, set in the Al Capone case, was to go after big-time gangsters' taxes.

The wiseguys at the upper echelon tended to consume conspicuously but come tax time always presented a picture of a man on an austerity budget. Maybe the Treasury Department could have its way with Galante.

Treasury agents investigated and put together a file dedicated to Galante's engagement in lucrative operations, verifying whenever possible Galante's fat-ass wallet.

Another tact, one that went back to Luciano, was to micro-analyze the subject's citizenship status. Sometimes they could send mobsters back to Italy where they came from. That meant a team of investigators from the Immigration and Naturalization Service. The feds liked a story they'd heard that Ellis Island documents seemed to indicate that Galante was four years old when his parents came over on the boat from Italy. The argument that Galante was not a U.S. citizen had to deal with that birth certificate, the one that said his real name was Camillo and that he'd been born in a Manhattan tenement, City of New York Birth Certificate #10302, which looked even to experts like the real deal.

The Immigration and Naturalization investigation raised a few questions but zero answers. Those people coming over on the boat from Italy in 1914, they must've been somebody else. That was Galante's argument. And it was a good one. Everyone knew that immigration documentation back then was done on a strictly close-enough basis. Papers weren't worth shit. You got off the boat as Fiaccabrino and came ashore as Fabri. The immigration investigation stalled like an attack on Mount Cassino. They couldn't kick him out based on what they had. Galante was as American as a square slice.

What about alcohol? The Alcohol Tax Unit was contacted and said that, as far as they knew, Galante gave up running stills in 1947.

CHAPTER THIRTEEN
Consigliere

IN ORDER TO UNDERSTAND the Carmine Galante story, you got to understand the mob's hypocritical, phony, and two-faced policy when it comes to drugs, specifically the dreaded babonia—heroin.

Luciano liked to say, "We don't do that"—that is, push junk. Gambino said no, never, but that was largely public relations, one step toward plausible deniability should some hood be caught trying to get through Idlewild with a kilo in his luggage. There was too much money in opiates to ignore.

Money outweighs morality.

Every time.

Upon his return to the United States in 1956, Galante was made consigliere by Joseph Bonanno. The pair traveled in 1957 to Sicily to recruit an army of men to operate the U.S. heroin business. In his parents' hometown, Galante's recruiting efforts were wildly successful. The recruits, all youthful men, were called by Galante the Zips. Among them were bodyguards, hit men, and drug pushers. I don't know why they were called Zips. Some say they were called Zips because they spoke rapidly. Maybe. The Zip I met didn't talk that fast.

The Zips and a humongous Sicilian heroin cartel came into Galante's life more or less at the same time. In 1957, he was called to a tense meeting in Palermo, Italy, at the Grand Hotel et Des Palmes.

Top Sicilian hoods were there: guys like Don Giuseppe Genco Russo and Gaetano Badalamenti, who controlled large chunks of the Sicilian Mafia pie.

Lucky Luciano was there. You know him. He controlled a large chunk of everything. Up until this moment, the mob's participation in heroin trafficking had largely gone unspoken. Silent. At the Grand Hotel et Des Palmes meeting, that silence ended. Luciano made it clear: the subject was babonia, lots of babonia, smuggled into the United States through Canada. In order to pull it off, though, the Sicilian and America mobs were going to have to make nice and work together. Historically, that was not always the case. But the plan was to turn every African American into a setting-sun junkie.

Galante usually took upon himself—or was assigned—someone to do the thinking for him. In the heroin cartel, that guy was Salvatore "Toto" Catalano, a Sicilian who supervised the drug distribution from a Manhattan home base. Catalano wanted to look like a typical immigrant from Sicily to Brooklyn, looking for a better life in the New World. He got off the boat and took a job working in a relative's Knickerbocker Avenue gift shop. But that was just the cover. Catalano was there to supervise the Zips, known in Bushwick anyway as the Knickerbocker Zips. When it came time to have someone looking over Galante's rugged shoulder all the time, Catalano was perfect for the job. If Galante did something wrong, the boys in Sicily would know within hours.

The massive cartel worked a couple of heroin pipelines. Anyone caught importing heroin into the United States outside the cartel would be immediately removed from the earth.

One of the pipelines already existed but would now be enlarged. This operation had initially been run by Corsican hoods Paul Carbone and François Spirito. The start-up money for the business came from a cache of funds stolen in German-occupied France during the chaos of World War II. This pipeline originated in Indochina, where the poppies were grown, and from Turkey, where there were legal opium producers that supplied pharmaceutical companies with the base materials for codeine and morphine. The poppies were processed into "morphine paste" in a French lab and put on a ship in Marseille for transport to New York Harbor. We know that this pipeline existed before Luciano and the Bonannos got involved because there were busts, twenty-eight pounds of heroin seized aboard the French ocean liner *St. Tropez* in 1947 and fifty pounds seized in 1949 aboard another French ship called the *Batista*. Carbone died, leaving a power vacuum, and Luciano filled it.

For the second pipeline, Sicilians would get the poppy-based opiate from the Middle East to Sicily, where mob-controlled laboratories would convert it to heroin. Then it would be shipped to Canada, and then the United States, where Galante's Zips would oversee distribution. There wasn't much for the American gangsters to do but count their money and kill any fuck who tried to sell dope on his own. The system had glitches at first, but by 1960 or so American inner cities had a serious heroin problem, the birth of which took place in that hotel room in Palermo.

The most trouble Galante got into in 1956 was getting caught speeding—again. For the fourth time. Galante had demonstrated throughout his life that he liked to drive, he liked to drive wild, and he didn't give a fuck about traffic rules. (Or any rules.)

Rules didn't apply to him because he was the boss. He was driving through the town of Windsor, in Broome County. Frank Garofalo and Giovanni "John" Bonventre were with him in the car when a state trooper from the Five-Mile Point substation pulled him over.

Garofalo we've met. Bonventre was the fifty-six-year-old Castellammare-born uncle of Joe Bonanno who didn't come to the United States until he was a young adult. Now he was *caporegime* and close to Bonanno. In fact, Bonventre and Bonanno had once owned a dairy farm together near Middletown, New York, in the Catskill Mountains. According to the FBI, Bonventre had returned to Castellammare in 1950 and had just returned to the United States at the time of Galante's traffic stop, an early harbinger that a massive mob conclave was in the works. Bonventre didn't speak much English, like next to none, so he kept his mouth shut as the cop walked up to the driver's side window, which Galante reluctantly rolled down a couple of inches.

"Driver's license," Trooper F. W. Leibe said.

Galante handed him Joey Beck's driver's license. These were the days before you had your photo on your license.

Trooper Leibe decided that there was something about the cut of Galante's jib. Something he didn't like. Galante was a living mug shot. No matter how wide he opened his eyes, you couldn't see the whites. It was just dark in there. And then there was the way he clamped his jaw on his cigar. It said, *I'm a gangster.* The trooper felt like he'd pulled over a speeder and George Raft, Humphrey Bogart, and Edward G. Robinson were in the car. The trooper couldn't remember ever seeing a trio of men who looked quite so swarthy and mean.

"Joseph DiPalermo, Two-Forty-Six Elizabeth Street, New York City?" (The address was directly across the street from the L&T Cleaners, 245 Elizabeth, a place where Galante was known to spend a great deal of time.)

"That's me."

"What's your birthday, Mr. DiPalermo?"

Galante remained mute. *What the fuck was Joey Beck's birthday?*

"I'm going to have to ask you gentlemen to step out of the car, sir," the trooper said. Galante and his passengers complied.

"Why are you gentlemen in this area?"

Galante and Bonventre had their lips pressed together. Garofalo answered. He said they were upstate to see "the great IBM factories."

"Who are you?" Leibe asked.

Garofalo then presented a card that said he owned and operated the High Grade Packing Company. He had a second card that offered his address as a post office box in Merced, California.

Galante was only in the Binghamton substation of the state police for a few minutes when someone recognized him and his cover was blown. They emptied his pockets and he was found to have $1,800 in cash on him, a fantastic amount in 1956. There were twelve one-hundred-dollar bills and twelve fifties. Police also found on Galante a business card with the name Joseph Falcone on it, with an address, 519 Bleecker Street in Utica, N.Y.

Cops questioned Galante.

"You got any interests outside the country?"

"Yeah, I own a piece of the Bonfire Restaurant."

"Where's that?"

"Montreal."

"Who are your partners?"

"No secret. Harry Ship and Louis Greco."

Police checked the registration on the car and found that it belonged to one Anthony Calendrillo, who subsequently admitted to lending his car to Galante but insisted that he knew him only by his first name, just a casual acquaintance, and had no idea what the guy did for a living.

"I know several of the boys around Abco Vending Machine in West New York, N.J., and don't know the last names of any of them. They're just Charlie, Mike, Joe, Johnny, and Doc," Calendrillo said.

The state police quickly learned that Galante was an executive officer of Abco and that he had a phone that was a direct line to the West New York police, supposedly in case of robbery or fire.

Galante was taken to the Justice of the Peace, Richard B. Klausner, in Windsor. He pleaded not guilty to speeding and operating a motor vehicle without a license. He was released on $600 bail. Galante was given a court date to return.

Then a strange thing happened. A disturbing number of politicians and members of out-of-town law enforcement seemed downright anxious, fretful, about the possibility that Galante would do jail time. When asked about the reasons for their concern, they shrugged.

In mid-October, Galante was spotted by federal surveillance attending a meeting at the Arlington Motel in Binghamton, New York, sponsored by ginger-ale king Joseph Barbara, who would also play host to the Apalachin meeting the following year. Records show that Barbara made reservations at the Arlington for five men. Four of them were Joe Bonanno, Frank Garofalo, John Bonventre, and Carmine Galante.

In the meantime, upstate, Justice Klausner was inundated by men trying to get Galante off the hook for his traffic bust. They tried to convince Klausner to fine Galante $500 for his traffic offenses rather than putting him in jail. The town could use the money, they argued. Galante, they said, had offered to donate the money directly to some boys' group, if necessary, in exchange for his freedom. He had a very poor boyhood and would like the money to do something for boys, they said.

Judge Klausner was not swayed. He couldn't help but feel there was something disproportionate about the fuss Galante's traffic stop was causing, but he stuck to his guns. He responded to the requests for leniency with a harsh synopsis of Galante's criminal career.

A man contacted Galante and volunteered to be his lawyer. Galante took him up on it. That's because the guy was Donald W. Kramer, the mayor of Binghamton, New York. Kramer, a Democrat, was first elected the mayor of Binghamton in 1949 and was re-elected in 1953. His platform had been to modernize Binghamton, a city that had been built before there were quite so many automobiles. Streets needed to be widened, parking made available, and expressways built. Like just about all politicians at the time, Kramer was vocally anti-communist. Not long after he was elected, he created a city sales tax to help pay for those widened streets. At the time that he volunteered to stand at the side of alleged pro killer Carmine Galante, Kramer was still proposing expensive programs to improve his city: a new public swimming pool, a new clubhouse for the public golf course, new sewers, refurbishing of the public library, a new fire station, et cetera. The local newspaper, which put Kramer regularly into its headlines for this or that, ignored the fact that he had a mobster as a client. Traffic court wasn't a beat the paper normally covered, but Galante's case should've been considered news and wasn't. Out-of-town papers, on the other hand, had a field day.

While speaking on a phone he didn't know was tapped, Galante discussed the speeding ticket.

"That state trooper that gave me the ticket shined his spotlight over my car. Lucky he didn't ask me to open the trunk, or the cigar box," Galante said with a low, phlegmy laugh.

On November 9, 1956, Mayor Kramer at his side, Galante again stood before Justice of the Peace Richard B. Klausner for sentencing. Klausner said thirty days in the Broome County Jail for unlicensed driving and fined him $100 for speeding and another $50 for unauthorized use of another's license. All efforts to keep Galante out of jail were in vain. Galante did his time. After the Tombs, and Sing Sing, and Dannemora, a town jail was like taking a vacation.

Galante entered jail on November 9, 1956, and was released on December 3. During that time, he was visited by his brother Sam who was living at the time on the Grand Concourse in the Bronx, and his wife, Helen. A third visitor was a friend named Nicholas Marangello, aka Nicky Glasses, aka Little Nicky, aka Nicky Cigars, aka Nicky the Butler. Marangello, as his nicknames imply, wasn't a big guy and he wore eyeglasses with lenses about as thick as the bottom of a Coke bottle. His rise to the top came when he was Joe Bonanno's designated driver. For years, when Galante was behind bars he would use Nicky as a courier to receive and deliver messages to the boys outside.

Even while Galante was chilling in the Broome County cooler, the efforts to spring him continued. A pair of high-ranking New Jersey police visited with pockets full of bribe money and tried to get Galante released. It didn't work. Turned out, Broome County law enforcement wasn't corrupt. Imagine that.

* * *

Galante had been going seventy in a fifty zone. Such a fuss. Much ado. And more to come. As we'll see, there would be ado about the ado.

On October 25, 1957, boss Albert "The Mad Hatter" Anastasia entered Grasso's Barber Shop, took a chair, reclined, and was toweled up for a shave. At that point, four assassins arrived, two standing guard, two shooters entering the shop. They blew Anastasia away and disappeared into the teeming Manhattan streets.

The hit, along with becoming sensational news around the world, left a major power vacuum in the Five Family system. Who was going to take over the stuff that Anastasia used to be in charge of? To decide, there was to be a meeting, with all of the bosses, or representatives thereof, in attendance. As Bonanno consigliere, Carmine Galante was invited. The meeting was in a place that Galante had been before, Barbara's place up in Apalachin, New York.

CHAPTER FOURTEEN
Apalachin

APALACHIN, NEW YORK, WAS TOO SMALL to be called a village. Two hundred and seventy-seven people lived there, but it was hard to tell where "there" was. There was no downtown. If you were on the road, you could blink and miss it.

It was technically a "census-designated place" on Route 17, about fifteen miles east of Binghamton. It lies within the Town of Owego in Tioga County. The area was named after the Apalachin Creek. The word "Apalachin" is Native American for "from where the messenger returned." The area is best known, of course, because of the thing that happened there in 1957.

Twenty days after Albert Anastasia had his last shave, on November 14, 1957, came the big sit-down. All-Star cast. Top mobsters arrived in large cars wearing silk suits and smoking cigars. The cover story was that there was going to be a barbeque in "Mr. Canada Dry" Joseph Barbara's landscaped backyard.

The real purpose was to evaluate the state of the five-family system as set up by the great Luciano. With Anastasia's elimination, there was fear that chaos would reign—very bad for business. There was also the matter of Anastasia's power and turf, which would need to be divvied.

In sparsely populated areas, cops know every car. They might even know every car just by listening to the engine. The Barbara estate had a reputation as a busy place, with a lot of comings and go-ings, but the parade of luxury cars containing Italian gangsters caught the attention of a local cop named Sergeant Edgar Croswell.

Black Cadillacs and Lincolns. A few limos chartered from the city. Those hoods looked about as out of place as a bow tie at a biker rally. Croswell, no dummy, immediately thought mob powwow and called for backup. In minutes, cops had the place surrounded. They watched through binoculars and jotted down license-plate numbers.

The ever-observant Sergeant Croswell had been aware of possi-ble criminal activities at the Barbara estate since the previous year. So, the choice to use the location for a huge mob convention was a mistake—to say the least.

When enough cops had gathered on Route 17, the road blocked to prevent getaways, they raided the joint. It'd be great to have fucking surveillance footage of that raid. It must've been a comic master-piece. All of these tough guys, powerful men, all puffing out their chests, then suddenly dropping their drinks on the lawn, chucking their ID, and hightailing it into the nearby woods. They ran like es-caped prisoners popping out of a tunnel, like degenerates fleeing the busted craps game. The moment has been called the American Mafia's single greatest humiliation.

When you're a kid and you flee from the scene of whatever be-cause of a siren, you can run forever, from Red Hook to Canarsie if you must. But these guys were middle-aged and older a lot of them. They couldn't run very far at all, and the police had no trouble net-ting most of them and hauling them into their suddenly overcrowded police station. Fifty arrests were made. Among those arrested were Joseph Bonanno, Joseph Profaci, Jerry Catena, Vincent Rao, Carlo Gambino, Paul Castellano, and Vito Genovese. What a haul.

Bonanno was found hiding in a cornfield. The onetime kid sent to America to run things there for his old man, to be paterfamilias of a crime organization that would one day bear his name, was deeply embarrassed by the arrest. His ruddy complexion was downright puce, and he was panting like a hound in the heat.

*　*　*

The stories the hoods told the cops were all over the place, but most of them agreed on one thing. Their decision to drop in on Joseph Barbara was spontaneous, and they were surprised and delighted to see that there were other guests on hand as well. A few admitted that there was a planned event, a cookout, some drinks, but denied that it had anything to do with business, legitimate or otherwise.

Meeting for a barbeque was not illegal, so cops didn't hold any of the mobsters for very long. What was accomplished, however, was that a roster of the mob's upper echelon was now written down, a list of names that future U.S. Attorney General Bobby Kennedy would use as a guideline to fight the mob. (Plus, when the RICO laws were put in place years later, the knowledge that the gangs worked together and that there was a so-called Commission enabled the Department of Justice to broaden the scope of their conspiracy prosecutions.)

Vito Genovese was hurt the most by the Apalachin raid. In his mind, the presumed purpose of the meeting was to abolish the five-family system and to proclaim himself king of the underworld. And the whole thing had been horribly botched. His stock plummeted. Luciano took care of it. He didn't whack Genovese—as Anastasia would have. Instead, he set Genovese up, got him busted on a bull-shit dope charge. While Luciano was at it, he set up Vincent "The Chin" Gigante as well, and both Genovese and Gigante did long stretches.

The damage done to the mob in Apalachin couldn't be measured in jail time. One of the things the mob had going for it was that it really was organized, yet law enforcement didn't know how it worked. Now they had a roster, and that would go a long way toward figuring out the infrastructure.

All invitees to the party were Sicilian. Eleven of those picked up in the raid ended up appearing before grand juries. I don't know who did the counting, but it is said that, combined, the hoods testifying for the grand jury took the Fifth 870 times. There would be no self-incrimination.

Galante was one of the few who attended the Apalachin meeting and got away, disappearing into a nearby woods.

Carmine Galante—though never caught, and who knows how he got home—was identified in the November 15 edition of the *New York Mirror* as one of the sixty hoodlums to "attend the conclave." The paper noted that Galante wasn't at the Barbara home in Apalachin for the first time either. And, because of his need for speed, Galante even knew what the inside of the local jail looked like.

In addition to eyewitness reports, the best evidence that Galante was at Apalachin came from the search and interrogation of a hood named Salvatore Tornabe, who lived in Albany, New York. He kept his lip zipped, but police found in his pocket a written note reminding himself to "get together with Lillo [*sic*]" at the Airmart Motel on November 14 before calling Joseph Barbara in Apalachin.

On a separate note, also found on Tornabe, there was written the word "Acqua-Velva." Police would later learn that this word, which could have referred to aftershave, was also phonetically similar to an alias that Galante was using with increasing frequency, and we'll find out why.

The boys from the press speculated about the reason for the Apalachin powwow. None of them knew a damn thing. Howard Wantuch and Sidney Kline of the *Daily News* speculated that the purpose was to put someone in charge of dope peddling. The news reported that the job of drug czar was given to Galante's best friend, Joey Beck, not that anyone knew where Beck was. They couldn't find him and speculated that he'd fled the country and was in Italy somewhere in the company of another man's wife. Joey Beck the ladies' man—hard to picture.

At the *New York Mirror*, they thought "it would be logical to assume that the manufacture and distribution of untaxed liquor would be the principal matter discussed."

On the other hand, the District Supervisor of the Federal Bureau of Narcotics, John T. Cusack, seemed to know what he was talking about when he testified that the meeting was held to re-distribute power to fill the giant void left by the Anastasia hit. He also testified that Galante was the man who had murdered Carlo Tresca in 1943 and was now working to gain complete control over drugs, gambling, and other rackets in Brooklyn.

Cusack added, "Frank Garofalo is mentioned in the Bureau of Narcotics files in association with the late Willy Moretti and the late Abraham Davidian, a California mobster believed to have been assassinated in 1949 [actually 1950] by elements of the Mafia in California. Garofalo is a close associate of Joseph Profaci, Brooklyn's 'olive oil king' who was at Apalachin."

In 1959, twenty hoods were convicted of conspiracy to obstruct justice by lying about the nature of the Apalachin meeting to FBI agents. The twenty included John C. Montana, a former Buffalo, New York, "Man of the Year" who claimed that he was only at the Barbara estate because the brakes on his car had failed nearby; Natale "Joe Diamond" Evola, whom the press referred to as a "garment district" racketeer; Carmine Lombardozzi, who according to rumor had been on someone's hit list but had his sentence commuted at Apalachin; Joseph "Joe Evil Eye" Magliocco, who was Joe Profaci's brother-in-law; Profaci himself, whose biggest worry at that moment was deportation; and Frank T. Majuri from Jersey.

CHAPTER FIFTEEN
Feds on the Case

THE TAXMAN COMETH. Before the RICO laws, the best weapons the feds had against organized crime were tax evasion charges—so it was important for crooks to keep a legit portfolio in case the government wanted to know where their money came from.

Galante's problems with having too much money were more complicated than most because he had a G-man watching him every time he went outside. There was no losing those government fucks. Shake one tail and another showed up as if by magic. So Galante had to make his criminal enterprises look legit.

During the summer of 1957, Galante officially became the owner of the Rosina Costume Company in Brooklyn, located on 70th Street in Bensonhurst. Galante had filled out the necessary papers to operate a business under that name, DBA papers that said he was president, secretary, and treasurer for the company and his wife, Helen, was vice-president.

As expected, IRS agents checked out Rosina Costume and found it legit: it manufactured women's dresses on a contract basis and had twenty-five employees and thirty-six sewing machines. Local banks and clients had no complaints. The government suspected that dresses might be coming out the front door and heroin out the back. But they had no proof.

The feds watched the place like a hawk. What they saw looked annoyingly legit, with Galante showing up for work, the man in charge. The employees were checked out and found to be card-carrying members of the International Ladies Garment Workers Union, the ol' ILGWU. They were AFL-CIO, Italian Local Number 69.

There was also paperwork stating that Rosina "belonged to" the United Popular Dress Manufacturers Association Incorporated, the ol' UPDMA, Inc. Clearly, Galante had a lawyer set it up. It was cozy.

Rosina both made and sold dresses, their major clients being two Broadway shops, Crystal Juniors and Nina Andrews, Inc. There was a lot of importing and exporting going on at Rosina.

The feds learned Rosina was getting packages in and out of the country via the Latamer Shipping Company. Latamer was owned and operated by Nick Duganis, Nick the Greek, who lived in Astoria, Queens, and was, according to the FBI, Galante's "right-hand man." If you wanted to move a lot of contraband, having an import-export company was the way to go, so the feds were intrigued by the connection. Latamer Shipping had its headquarters on East 49th Street in the city. Duganis and Galante, the investigation revealed, were "in together" in the shipping business, as well as a loan-shark operation preying on racetrack degenerates.

On December 19, 1957, the *Newark Star-Ledger* published an article that stated as true many of the things Galante had denied when interrogated by the Law. The gist of the article was that Galante was a big, big, big-time gangster in Brooklyn, New York, that he was doing monkey business out of a coin-operated machine company in New Jersey, the Abco Vending Company, and that he had a "direct line" from that manufacturing facility to the West New York Police Department, the same police force that seemed so concerned when Galante was pulled over for imitating a rocket on an Upstate New York highway.

Abco had a death grip on the coin-operated machine market that covered a large swath of turf. They sold cigarette machines, bowling machines for bars, jukeboxes, gumball machines, even those scales that said: "Guess Your Weight."

For the record, the *Star-Ledger* said the West New York police chief, Fred Roos, was in way over his head. The chief was asked about the "direct line" to Abco: "I know it doesn't exist now and I do not know of it ever existing. When I was captain, there was a burglar alarm system that went directly from Abco to our station. That alarm now has been discontinued, largely because Abco closed up shop and moved about six months ago."

It was true. Sometime in 1957 the Abco Vending Company fled West New York in the middle of the night and re-surfaced in Union City, New Jersey, re-named the Star Novelty Company.

As for that alarm system, New Jersey Bell Telephone Company mouthpiece Charles Dowd said under oath that the burglar alarm at Abco was a "non-talking hookup" but admitted that a signaling device could be placed at the other end.

In other words, all Galante needed to do to have the local cops come running was press a button.

Although there is plenty of indication that the feds were watching Galante earlier, FBI records say that these efforts were considered "less than urgent" until the first week of 1958 when the "Get Galante" program was amped up based on information that Galante was involved in a "major U.S. narcotics ring." Galante's name had come up as a major player during a January hearing before the New Jersey Law Enforcement Council, a public hearing that elevated Galante on the FBI's to-do list.

J. Edgar Hoover's instructions included this: "In the investigation of Galante, be especially alert to political tie-ins, connections to superiors in the underworld, if any, his underlings, and his means of deriving income, both legitimate and illegitimate and where it might be located."

The amped-up investigation got off to a shaky start. They couldn't follow Galante twenty-four seven anymore for the simple reason that they'd lost him and didn't know where he was. A few informants, not very good ones, were being developed re Galante, and efforts to further develop those sources would be continued as part of the FBI's Top Hoodlum Program.

The active informants were insistent: "Do not burn me. I am dead if you burn me."

On January 9, 1958, a special federal grand jury in the Southern District of New York courthouse in Brooklyn, New York, went through the motions and issued a subpoena for Carmine Galante, along with a shopping list of other hoodlums, to appear and testify. Even as they issued it, they knew the subpoena could never be served because Galante was missing and presumed in hiding.

Subpoena in hand, the U.S. Marshal had to go through some motions himself. He went to Galante's home on Marcy Avenue. The house at that address was a three-family, above average in upkeep in what would otherwise be an average low-income neighborhood. It stood directly across the street from the rectory of the Church of the Transfiguration.

The marshal knocked on the door.

A lady answered.

"Carmine Galante live here?"

"Nope."

"Who does?"

"I'm Mae Leggio. I live here with my husband Joseph."

"You know the Galantes?"

"Yeah, Helen is my sister."

"You know where they are?"

"Nope."

So, the marshal went up and down that block of Marcy Avenue asking about the Galantes but, not surprisingly, could find no one who knew the family's present whereabouts. He found a few who would admit to knowing the Galantes, but none who would admit to knowing where they'd gone.

The marshal spent some time looking just for Helen Galante, thinking that if he could locate the family he could stake the place out and eventually find Carmine. But no one knew where Galante's wife and kids were either. The marshal sent the grand jury notification that after several attempts to locate the subject the subpoena went unserved.

By the end of the month, the feds had put together a bio of Galante. Galante was assigned FBI Number 119495. Their best info they had was that Galante and his family "might have" moved to Italy.

On January 24, 1958, an FBI agent again parked outside the Galante home and kept an eye on the place. The surveillance was disappointing, however, as "no activity was observed."

Four days later, the same agent entered the Brooklyn County Clerk's Office and asked to see the records regarding the home on Marcy. Tax records indicated that the house was in block number 2206, lot number 32, and that the tax records were in the name of Marulli, Helen's maiden name, with a land valuation of $2,550 and improvements valued at $14,000.

The records indicated that on January 16, 1956, the house had been sold by Salvatore and Antonia Maneri to Angelina Marulli and Mae Leggio. The deed on file read that Marulli had a two-thirds undivided interest and Leggio owned the rest. The East New York Savings Bank held a $6,600 mortgage dated October 1, 1955. The attorney for that transaction was Edward Z. Jacobson of Court Street in Brooklyn Heights.

The FBI contacted the Department of Motor Vehicles and learned that Galante's last three automobiles had been a two-tone white-and-green 1955 Olds sedan, a black-and-gray 1951 Buick, and a white '56 Olds coupe. Big, American, and they could haul ass. Galante would never drive a car that couldn't outrun a copper.

The same special agent who had investigated Latamer Shipping was now told by an informant that Galante was hiding out in Havana, Cuba, not in Italy with Luciano as others had said.

An investigator for a Joint Legislature Committee on Organized Crime came looking for Frank Garofalo. (Committees grilling hoods was all the rage in the 1950s. When the fad waned, the committees switched to commies and the TV hearings continued.) In 1958, this committee wanted Frank Garofalo to testify and served a subpoena to someone living on East 58th Street in the city claiming to be Frank Garofalo but who was in actuality his brother Vincent.

With Galante missing, the FBI staked out his favorite haunts, such as Villa Penza on Grand Street in Downtown Manhattan. It was an old-fashioned Italian joint and had been for generations. There was a tiny stage in the back for entertainment on weekend nights. On the wall was a photo of the temporary altar built there in 1926 and some of the kneeling worshipers following the death of silent-film star Rudolph Valentino. Old-timers said Villa Penza had been mobbed up for generations. Even back when Valentino was still alive, you could see hoods in fedoras passing thick envelopes under the tables.

No one at Villa Penza had seen Galante in a while. Neighbors all knew who he was, recognizable by the swagger in his walk, and the cigar that seemed permanently clamped between his teeth.

"That is Lilo," those in the know would whisper.

Hearing the name, old women crossed themselves.

CHAPTER SIXTEEN
Much Ado about Much Ado

JUST WHEN YOU THOUGHT the weird mania over Galante's upstate speeding ticket had finally died down, it flared back up bigger than ever. It would be hard, if not impossible, to come up with a speeding ticket that ever caused more fuss.

During that same first week of 1958, simultaneous to the start of the FBI's "Get Galante" program, the New Jersey Law Enforcement Council (NJLEC) took a closer look at the circumstances around Galante's October 1956 speeding ticket.

The NJLEC opened their January 7 hearing in Newark, New Jersey, with an appearance by two West New York police officers—Captain Chris Gleitsmann and Detective Sergeant Peter J. Policastro—who had allegedly made efforts to intercede with the New York State Police regarding the ticket. Captain Gleitsmann allegedly offered a $1,000 bribe to Sergeant Edgar Croswell to keep Galante from serving jail time on his traffic charges.

By the next day, District Attorney Louis Greenblott, at the behest of Acting New York State Investigation Commissioner Arthur L. Reuter, had sent the bribery matter to a Broome County grand jury, as the bribery attempt had reportedly been made near Binghamton.

After the hearing, Captain Gleitsmann and Sergeant Policastro were suspended from their posts by West New York Police Chief Fred Roos. In addition, Commissioner Ernest J. Modarelli, also named in the bribery attempt, was suspended from his extra $5,000-a-year job as grand poohbah of pistol permits in Hudson County.

Modarelli made himself invisible for two weeks, then re-appeared to meet privately with his fellow commissioners before addressing two hundred West New Yorkers, blasting the NJLEC's attempt to take his testimony at their hearing, a move he called politically motivated and an act of bad faith.

After the hearing, NJLEC chairman Joseph Harrison told New York City reporters that he would submit the contradictions in the testimony between the Jersey cops and the Broome County officers who refused to take the money.

"It is troubling that such efforts and risks would be taken just to get a career criminal out of county lockup," Harrison said.

Also testifying at the NJLEC hearing was John T. Cusack, the District Supervisor of the Federal Bureau of Narcotics, who said the Tresca murder was committed by Carmine Galante, a ruthless man who was now engaged in a campaign to control narcotics, gambling, and other rackets in Brooklyn. Galante was a force of nature out of town, too, Cusack said. Lilo, or The Cigar, as they called him, had an interest in a bookie joint in Pittsburgh, Pennsylvania, that had a race wire, enabling gamblers to post bets nanoseconds before the starting gate opened and the horses were off.

Also in trouble over the speeding ticket from hell was Assemblyman William F. Passannante, a Democrat representing a portion of Manhattan. Passannante reportedly called Assemblyman Daniel S. Dickinson, Jr., a Republican representing Binghamton, and asked him to defend Galante regarding his traffic violations.

Dickinson claimed he agreed to cooperate initially but changed his mind when he learned that Galante was reputed to be a "Mafia thug." He did advise Galante, however. He advised him to plead guilty and take his medicine, which is what happened.

Passannante told the *New York Journal American*, "I know my name has been connected with the Galante case, but I don't know the man. As I recall it, a lawyer—I can't think of his name right now—said Galante had been arrested on traffic charges and he asked

me, I think, if I would take the case. I told him I didn't practice outside of the city, but I would see if I could get him a lawyer. I know
Assemblyman Dickinson, so I called him and asked him to recom-
mend a lawyer to defend Galante. Hundreds of cases like this come
up all the time, one assemblyman calling another and asking for
help. When I learned who Galante was I washed my hands of the
case. I later learned that Binghamton Mayor Donald Kramer acted
as Galante's attorney in court."

Attorney General Grover C. Richman, Jr., of New Jersey appointed
Deputy Attorney General Charles Joelson to investigate the West
New York Police Department. Richman said that he would use state
troopers who'd worked for the NJLEC as investigators.

Joelson prepared a case against West New York Police Commissioner Ernest Modarelli, a case that would be presented to grand juries in Upstate New York. On January 15, 1958, the Broome County
grand jury (Binghamton) opened an inquiry into political influence
acting on Galante's behalf.

The *New York World-Telegram* said, on January 28, 1958, that
among the first to bring Galante's upstate difficulties to the attention
of the government was a "mystery man" from Washington, D.C.,
who first got the government—State Division of Veterans Affairs—
to investigate the Galante case, which at that time featured Galante
in a county jail with no bail. The paper said the mystery man was
well known around Capitol Hill. The man he spoke to at the V.A. assumed Galante was a veteran and agreed to help. The caller reportedly later referred to it as an "innocent call."

Yeah, yeah, yeah.

Another man interested in keeping Galante out of jail for his traffic
offenses was Irving Ellis, who allegedly ran a far-flung gambling
operation that stretched from Maine to California. Ellis's headquarters
were in Montreal, where Galante had interests. An informant named
Donald J. Ferraro of Lake Mahopac, New York, revealed that Ellis
brought up Galante's legal troubles during a business meeting involving scrap metal, and in response Ferraro said that he went to the

Republican leader in his district, a Mr. D. Mallory Stephens, who said he was willing to help.

Stephens referred Galante's case to Assemblyman George L. Ingalls of Binghamton, who apparently did some research on Galante and subsequently distanced himself.

Still, pressure to help Galante kept coming and coming, and eventually politicians were found who did not research Galante's background. A couple of politicians said they were willing to go to bat for Galante.

Galante, the feds falsely believed, was subservient to Irving Ellis, that Galante was Ellis's lieutenant. So, it wasn't just politicians and cops who were working to free Galante but actual mobsters as well.

It is a testament to the incorruptibility of Broome County officials who, despite the persistent pressure, turned a deaf ear to Galante's "friends" in high places. Galante was sentenced to thirty days in jail and served every day of it.

Point is, Galante had a large and powerful machine attempting to help him when he was in trouble. During the late 1950s, the feds referred to Galante as one of the most important hoodlums they had under investigation. Yet there were elected officials on his side. Corruption had clearly wormed its way deep into law enforcement and the American political and justice systems. Money versus morality again. No contest.

The case reached a resolution of sorts during the spring of 1959 when Captain Gleitsmann was tried for misconduct in office. The prosecution claimed that when Gleitsmann drove his West New York cop car to Binghamton to help spring Galante he was using it "for other than official business."

Gleitsmann argued that it was true that he drove to Binghamton, but he didn't do it to bribe anyone.

"I only went there to investigate Galante's activities," the police captain claimed.

A jury didn't buy it. He was convicted and that summer sentenced in Hudson County Court to a year in jail and fined $500. The prison sentence was suspended.

*   *   *

In 1957, when "Mad Hatter" Albert Anastasia was whacked in his Manhattan barber chair, authorities had no clue who the gunmen were. (Although you'll learn the answer to that mystery in my book *Lord High Executioner*, about Anastasia's life and death.) On President Street, we knew the identity of the Barbershop Quartet, but the rest of the world had to speculate, and one of the "usual suspects" was Carmine Galante, referred to in a 1958 FBI memo as "the type who would be given such an assignment as the murder of Albert Anastasia."

By this time, the authorities had Galante figured out. He was no rat and never would be. In 1958, an informant said, "No matter what illegal activities Galante might be caught in or charged with, he has a reputation of not talking."

CHAPTER SEVENTEEN
Wanted

UNABLE TO FIND GALANTE, the fed investigation continued. They had info that he was in Italy, info that he was in Miami and then Cuba. But who knew? So, they made up a wanted poster, something to hang up on the post office for folks to look at while they waited in line for stamps. The poster said that Galante stood five five, weighed 160, and was bald, with a crown of graying hair. His arrest record went back to 1926, with arrests for assault, robbery, larceny, and alcohol violation. He was the prime suspect in the Tresca murder, and he always carried a firearm. He was suspected of killing a cop (De Castillia) and was known to have shot another (Meenahan) who was trying to apprehend him. He'd done a long stint in state prisons. Galante had reportedly been at Apalachin but miraculously escaped on foot. He was known to be active in still operations and narcotics. He was said to be involved in a million-dollar scheme to forge American Express traveler's checks. New info led the feds to believe that Galante had a slice of the Canadian gambling pie as well.

The poster announced in all caps:

HE SHOULD BE CONSIDERED ARMED
AND EXTREMELY DANGEROUS.

The poster contained a list of Galante's known aliases: Joe Dello, Charles Bruno, Joe Gagliano, Joe Galicano, Joe Lelo, Joe Lilo, Joe

Leio, Joe Nelo, Bruno Russo, Charles Russo, Joe Russo, Louis Volpe, and Carl Acquevella.

That last alias would turn out to be the most interesting—by far. (We'll get to that.) His most common nickname was Lilo, the Castellammarese stogie.

In hopes it would offer a clue as to his whereabouts, the FBI constructed a timeline of Galante's travel. At one time, Galante had gone back and forth between Brooklyn and Montreal. Then there was a period when he didn't travel at all. That ended with a January 7, 1958, report that Galante had been spotted that day, hiding right out in the open in Havana, Cuba. A few days earlier Galante was seen in Miami Beach with three other well-known gangsters.

Informants told the feds that Galante was moving his gambling operations to Cuba for good, safe from the FBI, thumbing his nose at the Law, worming his operations into those already in existence at Cuba's hottest nightclub, the Sans Souci, which was owned by Miami/Cuba boss Santo Trafficante, Jr., and run by William Buschoff, aka Lefty Clark.

The Sans Souci was a joint seven miles outside of Havana where America's rich and playful could go and get their ya-yas out. You walked through an arch to get in, a large stone arch, much like the famous entrance to Paramount Studios in L.A. The place was huge, could accommodate three thousand guests, looked architecturally like a Spanish villa, had rows and rows of one-armed bandits (called the amusement arcade), and shows that made a point of being just a little bit wilder than anything you could get in the United States in the late 1950s. An international cast of curvaceous exotic dancers didn't just peel and strut the runway to a brassy band; they re-enacted head-swimming voodoo rituals as they did so, treating the audience to a little Afro-Cuban culture to go with their pasties and G-strings. One of the stages—and its dance floor and tables—was outdoors, "under the moonlight." *San souci* means "without a care," and the casino lived up to its name. It was a place where misbehaving was OK. Leave the wife home and have a ball.

According to a New York Legislature watchdog committee, their info was that Galante had fled the country immediately following Apalachin and was in Italy, a rumor that the sluggish Interior Ministry in Rome was unable to verify.

Fed investigators put together a theory that assumed all of the sightings were correct, that Galante had been staying at Barbara's estate for a couple of days before the big meeting, that after the raid at Apalachin he had fled to Cuba and from there flown to Italy, where he had a meeting with mob boss Joe Adonis, who was in exile.

According to the *New York Herald Tribune* (January 8, 1958), Galante was in Italy, probably going to Lucky Luciano for help.

The *New York Times* reported three days later that Galante's presence could not be verified, that Interior Ministry sources in Rome had conducted an "extended check" and found no evidence that Galante was in their country.

Then in February, there was a new set of sightings: Galante flying from New York to Ciudad Trujillo, with a stopover in Miami. It was possible back then for an American citizen, who merely had to proclaim himself an American citizen, to enter the Dominican Republic without a passport, and no record would be kept of entrance into the country, perfect for a guy laying low. Coming back, the citizen would be required to fill out a form, but the D.R. could be entered incognito.

Those were the days: use a fake name, pay in cash, and you could *disappear*.

In March, there were more sightings of Galante, this time much closer to home, in Manhattan. He wasn't apprehended, however. In fact, he wasn't even approached by law enforcement. Instead, FBI shadows latched on and reported a complete itinerary of Galante's activities. Galante began the day by traveling across the Hudson to Newark and then returning. He and two other men went into the Sheraton East Hotel on 51st Street and Park Avenue but left without taking a room. They drove from there to the Hotel Alrae on East

64th Street. There they took a room under phony names—two of them claiming to be from Miami Beach, Florida.

Galante signed in as Carl Acquevella of Coytesville, New Jersey. There was discussion among the men about where to go eat. One unidentified hood suggested they get Spanish food at Forno's on West 52nd Street. But he was outvoted. Galante drove them across the East River, where they went to Bamonte's Restaurant on Withers Street in central Williamsburg. Upon returning, conversation was looser.

The FBI clearly had both the phone and the room bugged. At one point, a hood called and Galante told him to come on over to the Alrae. When the guy walked into the hotel room he said, "Your sister is a busy girl." This could have been referring to someone posing as Galante's sister, about his actual sister, a code for something else completely, or the visitor wasn't talking to Galante when he said it.

There was an interesting conversation in which the voice presumed to be Galante's spoke about his relationship with Luciano himself. He said he met Luciano, but they were never really friends. When he saw Luciano, it was as a guest.

"But I have had coffee with the man," Galante said. It was like saying he got drunk with God.

"You talk business?" someone asked.

"Naw. Just family and friends talk."

The FBI looked into the possibility that the reference to Galante's sister was to his actual sister, Josephine Meglino, but they didn't come up with much. In 1952, Galante drove a car that was registered to his sister. In 1958, the FBI talked to Josephine and she said, "I don't know," to every question asked, including her age. Frustrated, the feds left her alone.

A second theory, based on nothing I can think of, was that the reference might have been to Galante's cousin Jenny Russo, last known to live in Berkeley, California, but it turned out she'd been dead for seven years.

Every time the feds would haul in a shady street crook, they began their interviews by asking if the poor slob had ever heard of Carmine Galante, Joseph Bonanno, or Frank Garofalo. By the summer of 1958, thousands, perhaps millions, of total strangers were familiar with the names Galante/Bonanno/Garofalo because they had come up repeatedly during televised congressional hearings.

CHAPTER EIGHTEEN
There's Something about an Acquevella Man

THE FEDS RAN A CHECK ON Carl Acquevella and found that it was a real guy who had lived in Fort Lee since 1953. Although it took a while, the investigators eventually determined that he was one and the same as Carmine Galante, that Galante was living a double life, shacked with a girlfriend in an apartment on Linwood Avenue in Fort Lee, New Jersey. The girlfriend was more like a second wife. Her name was Antoinette.

But it took a while to get to that conclusion. First off, an informant trying to put the FBI on a false trail said that Carl Acquevella was not Galante at all, but rather a six-foot two-hundred pounder, middle-aged, with "some hair." He had an old lady named Ann and one child. The report was true, except for the description. In reality, Carl was the same age and weight as Carmine Galante. They had the same fingerprints, too.

The next time the feds listened in on one of Galante's conversations, he was on a hotel phone, having a long conversation with a woman presumed by those monitoring to be his wife. (But they didn't know which wife.)

There was some discussion about how the kids were, how the kids were to be moved "out of the hotel" to "another location." Mention was made of a brother-in-law who had recently passed away.

In the marginalia of the FBI memo reporting this conversation, someone wrote that this woman was Ann rather than Helen, adding the comment: "She lives with the subject as his wife."

OK, so Carl Acquevella was Carmine when he was living with his other wife, but the question remained, why had Galante used this name when registering at a Manhattan hotel?

According to paperwork, Acquevella had worked for the past five years as a road dispatcher for the Calandrillo Trucking Company, of Lodi, New Jersey. He gave the name of his supervisor and said that his weekly salary was $125.

A few hapless witnesses looked at a photo of Galante and said nope, that's not Acquevella, So, for a time the feds were thinking Galante and Acquevella were two people, until they located and interviewed Carl's alleged wife, Antoinette Caputo, a good-looking woman in her early twenties. She stood five three, and was known as Ann.

They showed her a photo of Carmine Galante.

"Yup, that's my husband," Ann said.

The special agent found Antoinette to be unexpectedly chatty.

"How old is your husband?" he asked.

"Thirty-six."

"You?"

"Twenty-three."

"When does he work?"

"My husband's hours are irregular," she said.

"How so?"

"He's out all night, comes home about five in the morning," Ann said. "He spends the day with me and then leaves again in the early evening. Except . . ."

"Except what?"

"Except some nights he doesn't come home. Days at a time."

I'll bet, the special agent thought.

At one point, Ann Acquevella let slip and referred to her husband as "Carmine." At another point she said it was OK that he gambled because he was a "professional gambler."

"What kind of cars do you drive?"

"He drives a black Cadillac and I drive a light blue Cadillac," she replied.

"You have one child?"

"Two. Our oldest girl, Mary, has a broken leg and hasn't been able to go to school since around Christmas, 1957."

(An FBI memo reported that the Acquevellas did indeed have two children, Mary Lou, born in 1951, who attended a Catholic school, and Nina, born in 1955.)

The investigator wrote down Ann Acquevella's stats: five three, 115 pounds, dark hair, dark eyes, and "very attractive."

(The FBI subsequently asked informants if they knew an Ann in Galante's life, and several identified her as Galante's "girlfriend.")

After the interview, the FBI received a phone call from a lawyer claiming to be the mouthpiece for Ann Acquevella, advising the government that they should not question her further about anything without him being present.

When the feds canvassed the Acquevellas' neighborhood, their innocent neighbors learned a great deal about the situation just by the questions the government was asking. For example: "Did you ever hear Carl Acquevella refer to himself as Carmine Galante?"

The neighbors would shake their heads wide-eyed, because now they knew a little something and it was frightening.

The FBI did interview Ann a second time with her lawyer beside her, and her tune was dramatically changed.

She said, "I don't know my husband very well." And, "I have never heard him referred to as Galante. . . . I have never heard him refer to himself as Galante."

That was the last shot the feds had at the "other wife." After that, "Ann and Carl Acquevella" left Coytesville. The feds checked with the post office, but they'd left no forwarding address.

The feds entered the house and found it completely empty. Bizarrely, they couldn't find a single neighbor who'd seen a van, or any indication that the Acquevellas were moving. The couple and their kids had disappeared into the night.

To further establish Galante's double life, agents got into the Hotel Alrae room before the cleaning staff and took fingerprints from personal objects in the room, which were then submitted to the FBI lab, which on May 1, 1958, reported that six of the prints were identical to those of Carmine Galante.

There was no record of Carl and Antoinette Acquevella being legally married, so Galante wasn't guilty of bigamy.

Over the next weeks, the FBI agents made no attempt to pick up Galante or interfere with his activities. They simply followed and observed. So, we see Galante in flashes now, when something happened worthy of a written report.

By mid-March, the FBI had picked up Galante's trail once again. One evening they watched as Galante exited a Manhattan restaurant alone, got into a cream-colored Pontiac parked just outside, and drove off into the night.

An hour later, he was zooming south on the Jersey Turnpike. Like a rocket. He passed a parked New Jersey state trooper and was pulled over for speeding.

"Where you going?" the cop asked.

"I got to get to Bowie Race Track."

"Now?"

"Yeah."

"In Maryland?"

"Yeah. Pronto."

The policeman looked at his watch.

"I think you might have missed the last race."

The cop gave Galante a ticket and sent him on his way. Imagine that. Galante got a speeding ticket and the whole world didn't stop.

Near the end of March, an FBI special agent from the Albany office talked to an informant who positively identified Galante as one of the men at the Barbara home in Apalachin on the morning of November 16, 1957.

It wasn't like this was a big shock. Others had said he was there. The *New York Mirror* and other newspapers had printed that Galante was one of sixty hoods at Apalachin, printed it as fact.

Still, the FBI was concerned about the lack of hard evidence establishing Galante's presence at the conclave, so it appreciated the corroboration.

During the early evening of April 2, Galante was spotted out in front of L'Amorique Restaurant at 54th Street and Second Avenue, in the company of two middle-aged men and a couple of babes, a redhead and a brunette causing a traffic jam with their tits and ass. The men continued to converse on the sidewalk as a 1955 Olds convertible with Jersey plates pulled to the curb, and the women got in.

During the middle of that afternoon, Galante was spotted walking on Park Avenue near East 60th Street, where he climbed into a 1957 Plymouth with Jersey plates that was waiting for him at the curb.

The Plymouth was being followed and so took a circuitous route through Manhattan, meandering until eventually making it to the Hudson River Drive and the Brooklyn-Battery Tunnel.

The car drove the Belt Parkway toward Coney Island and at 5:10 p.m. stopped at the Esso Gas Station on Cropsey Avenue in Bath Beach, where Galante got out, went into a phone booth, shut the door, and made a call.

Galante was sick of wandering in hopes of losing his tail. The shadows, on the other hand, made notes of the streets the car traveled on but made no attempt to stop the men. Sooner or later, they would have to reach a destination, right?

Not before putting a few more miles on the odometer.

From the phone booth, the car drove to Shore Parkway and Ocean Parkway, a ten-lane thoroughfare with a thick mall in the center that traveled through the heart of Brooklyn from the sea to Prospect Park.

They U-turned and headed south on Ocean Parkway, all the way back to the sea. This time, the car stopped in front of an apartment building on Shore Parkway. Galante got out and went into the building, which sat at the southeast corner of the intersection there. Cousin Moey lived there.

Galante went to see his pal. He had the heat following him, couldn't shake it, what to do? Moey gave Carmine counsel, and about twenty minutes later Galante returned to the car.

A woman left the building through the rear exit and entered Galante's vehicle. She was described as a woman with short red hair, about thirty-five years old, and, the surveillance team noted, "very attractive."

With the woman in the car, Galante drove to Manhattan via the Manhattan Bridge and parked in the vicinity of Henry and Clinton Streets on the Lower East Side. The pair went into a building. At that point, the surveillance was discontinued. The assumption was that the pair was in for the night.

Periodic surveillance of Cousin Moey's place was maintained for a week or so, but it was determined that the apartment building there was too large and there were too many exits to keep tabs of, and the effort was discontinued during the first week of April 1958.

The FBI was still fascinated with proving that Galante had been at Apalachin. It made a difference to them, like they thought it would matter in court someday. Which I guess it might've had Galante survived into the RICO era.

Investigators went to every hotel or motel within a fifty-mile radius of the Barbara compound and found that no one checked in during the appropriate time span using either Galante's name or any of his known aliases.

The agents visited each inn in person and showed a photograph of Galante to employees, just in case Galante had used an alias previously unknown to them. These efforts came up empty.

The records of Mohawk Airlines were checked to see if Galante flew into the Binghamton area, again without a hit. All the agents had were multiple witnesses who said he was there, and for some reason that wasn't enough.

*   *   *

Before RICO, the FBI and IRS were close pallies. The taxman put gangsters behind bars. But investigating Galante's finances could be frustrating. Someone who knew their shit was moving Galante's money.

Galante had legitimate investments and had reported legitimate earnings. In 1957, Galante claimed to have made $7,026.17 from the Rosina Costume Company. Out of that, the government withheld $717.92 for tax and Social Security. Although FBI surveillance had indicated that Galante was in charge at Rosina, the paperwork stated that one-third of the business was owned by Galante's brother Sam and the other two-thirds by his wife, Helen. Carmine was the secretary for the company, and the seven grand he'd made there in 1957 was listed as his salary.

While the IRS tried to find evidence of conspicuous consumption out of whack with Galante's reported earnings, the FBI contacted their international counterparts for info on Galante as part of a global narcotics conspiracy.

The feds still had sources who insisted that Galante was an illegal booze guy, had been for years. New evidence indicated those sources were behind the times. Galante, the FBI agents were told, had moved on and was "one of the top narcotics dealers in America."

The story the FBI picked up was that Galante and Luciano were connected with a guy in Rome, Italy, who was caught trying to bring ten kilograms of heroin into the United States. They had one informant who gave a detailed report. Galante was a big-time babonia pusher. Usually, informants didn't drop broad facts like that.

More typical was the info supplied by another "informant" on the fringes of the action, who told the cops that he had no knowledge of any illegal payments being made to Galante, knew no union officials, no racketeers, and that, as far as he knew, there was no racketeering whatsoever in the garment industry. What's more, he knew nothing of Galante's personal life, his associates, or his background. And the anonymous non-source managed to say it with a straight face.

*   *   *

While the feds worked on a case to bring down the dope-peddling ring, the New York police had long been chipping away at the ring's edges, attacking the babonia bums at street level. Sometimes they worked their way up and nailed the pushers' bosses.

Six gangsters were arrested in 1957 and charged with aiding "notorious dope baron" Joseph Basile, who ran a dope distribution racket out of his apartment on St. Mark's Avenue in Crown Heights, Brooklyn.

When the dope squad raided the apartment, they found half a million dollars' worth of heroin and cocaine. This bust included men who had helped Basile hide out while he was on the lam, renting him an apartment in Schenectady, New York, and acting as messengers so he could run his business while in exile.

This is where the bust became close to home for Carmine Galante. The list of Basile's helpers included Joey Beck, who was still on the lam. Beck, officials noted, was expected to be at Apalachin but failed to show up. Beck was in big trouble.

In July 1958 the U.S. Senate Subcommittee on Improper Activities in the Labor or Management Field called undercover U.S. narcotics agent Martin F. Pera to the stand.

Pera told the subcommittee that he had been with the Bureau of Narcotics since November 1948. He testified that Joe Bonanno and Carmine Galante had a meeting with one Santo Sorge, reportedly Luciano's top lieutenant in Sicily, in the days leading up to the Apalachin conclave. The Sorge meeting, it was speculated, "may have prefaced" the ill-fated Apalachin get-together.

Pera testified that Bonanno and Galante left the country together during the autumn of 1957 but were back in the United States in time to be in Apalachin for the barbeque. Pera told the subcommittee that he saw it as significant that Bonanno, Galante, and Sorge were together in Salerno.

*   *   *

The FBI tapped the phone at the Rosina Costume Company. Those monitoring the electronic surveillance learned that Galante and his compatriots often spoke about "the meatballs."

"Are the meatballs ready?"

"The meatballs need to be delivered."

"When will the meatballs arrive?"

The agents checked and found Galante had no legitimate reason to be concerned with the production, preparation, or consummation of meatballs.

An FBI memo commented: "The individuals may have been discussing the distribution of narcotics."

Carmine Galante was a common name, and the FBI did a cursory check of the other men living in the New York area with that name. At one point, they thought they were on to something when they came across a Carmine Galante who worked as a baker at 13 Prince Street and lived on East 3rd Street.

The thing was, he was born on February 21, 1915, same date, different year, as our guy. But this Carmine really was a baker—that he shared a birthday with his underworld namesake was just a wild coincidence.

On April 2, 1958, the FBI listened in on a phone call believed to have been made by Galante from his room phone in the Hotel Alrae. As per mob tradition, no proper nouns were used.

Galante asked, "You take care of that thing?"

"Yeah."

"You got the place?"

"Yeah."

"You see the little guy?"

"No."

"He left for Miami last night. He says he'll see you after the primary. He has a plan."

Later in the conversation, still apparently talking about a politician, the voice on the tape asked, "What do you mean he doesn't want you to go to the whip? Well, this guy better be good if you say he's got the closest thing to the whip?"

"Going to the whip," of course, was a horseracing term, meaning the jockey should smack his mount with a riding crop to make him run faster. In this case, however, investigators suspected "the whip" was an individual.

The voice, presumably Galante, said that he had tried to get reservations on a plane for the next day but was having difficulty.

"If that boy wants any more business, then he better come through. I've seen the wire. Tell him to bring the paper."

There was no mention of meatballs, but the conversation was so vague that nothing could be demonstrated, other than that the conversation was about something that needed to be referred to in a vague manner. "Bring the paper" probably meant "bring the money."

In a later call, a discussion was recorded about the acquisition of "raw materials."

"I'm getting one side of production from a Yankee," Galante said. "Forty-two percent. Milan, thirty percent. I've handled two hundred fifty dresses this week."

The voice on the other end of the phone said he would bill for 30 percent the next time.

"That's right, because you can't hold two permanent registrations as a jobber to a manufacturer," Galante said. "You should call, talk to the floor girl. She could help sort the dresses. For a while anyway, then she's got to close up the bar."

Later Galante said, "The money I gave to get into that place was given to the dead man's people."

On the next phone call, a caller informed Galante that he'd been laid off from his seventy-five-dollar-per-week job, which pissed Galante off.

"I'll find out about it. I will visit him tomorrow about noon," Galante said.

As it turned out, Galante took care of it by phone later that day.

He called a long-distance number and Galante chewed out a man over the previous caller being laid off.

"I will close that place up tight and ruin you guys if you ever decide to fire him again," Galante said.

The man on the other end of the line said the guy could come back to work on Tuesday.

The FBI must have had the room at the Hotel Alrae bugged as well, as they followed Galante's conversations even when he was no longer on the phone. He instructed one of his minions to take an unnamed woman downstairs. And put her in a cab. When the guy got back Galante quizzed him if anyone had been out there watching the place. The guy said no.

Yet another phone call a few minutes later seemed to indicate that something illegal was going on. The caller said that he'd "paid a dollar plus forty big ones"—which the FBI took to mean $41,000— for the lot but expected to get it back. The purchase would be "transferred to the Bonfire" when he was repaid. This was apparently a reference to the Bonfire Restaurant in Montreal, which the FBI theorized to be a point in the heroin pipeline into the United States. The conversation continued regarding the Bonfire. There was gambling there, but it was small-time, for fun. No bet larger than forty-four dollars.

"You guys, when you leave, make sure you're not followed," Galante said.

On the early morning of June 3, 1958, the Federal Bureau of Narcotics arrested "numerous individuals." Early reports by the press stated that Galante had been among those arrested, along with Cousin Moey and Anthony Macaluso.

But the story quickly changed.

Turned out that Galante and another man "escaped a series of raids," although sixteen other hoods were nabbed. Galante's picture was on the front page of every newspaper in the country. Just like at

Apalachin, he proved to be slippery when the boom came down. FBI surveillance continued, so when it came time to nab him they'd know where to find him.

Joey Beck's days on the lam ended on July 3, when Galante's right-hand man was arrested by the FBI and charged in two separate indictments, accusing him of "narcotics conspiracy."

Age had done nothing for Joe Beck's sex appeal. He still looked as much like a bespectacled ostrich as a person. The indictments stated that Giuseppe DiPalermo—that's Beck—was "distribution boss" of a "multi-million-dollar operation."

Beck appeared in Federal Court, Cadman Plaza, Brooklyn, a few weeks later and asked for more time because, as hard as it was to believe, he hadn't been able to come up with a lawyer.

The judge's eyes were following Beck's Adam's apple as it bobbed up and down somewhat violently, but he granted the delay.

When the trial finally happened, the world learned a lot about the narcotics web that Beck ran. He wasn't standing on a corner dealing handshake drugs. He dealt in quantity.

Beck's trial determined that he fully financed a Rome vacation for a New York cabdriver named Vincent Trupia. That seemed like unlikely generosity, and at first agents who tailed Trupia to Rome saw him acting the part of an innocent sightseer.

The agent noticed that, surprise, Joe Beck had made the trip to Italy as well and was also following Trupia, keeping a safe distance. As the agent watched, Beck made a few phone calls from a pay phone and then had a short conversation with Trupia.

The instructions, investigators were to learn, were to go to a specific place in Milan and pick up a package. The U.S. agent instructed Italian police to give Trupia a top-notch search before allowing him to leave the country.

Sure enough, when Trupia tried to fly stateside he was stopped at the airport, and a secret compartment was found in one of his suitcases containing eight kilos of cocaine. Trupia was sweating bullets.

He'd seriously fucked up. He was looking at a long stint on one side and a bullet in the breadbasket from the other.

Cops told him he would make it easier on himself if he cooperated. He reluctantly agreed. He gave info, but it wasn't very good. Police figured he was holding back, trying to get the benefits of his cooperation without ever saying anything that might get him whacked.

While tiptoeing that tightrope, Trupia told police that he couldn't remember exactly where he'd picked up the drugs or who he got it from. All he remembered was a set of three stone steps that were chipped and old and they were "next to a park."

Weirdly, the location rang a bell to one cop, and the spot was put under surveillance, at which time they observed Francesco Pirrico doing business. Pirrico worked for Luciano. Based on that info, Luciano's apartment was searched, and police found a little black book with contact info for the world's top hoods, the uppermost echelon.

Guys started getting nabbed for the crime of being in Luciano's little black book. Another Luciano comrade, Joe Pici, who looked like a movie gangster, with knife wound scars on his forehead and under his chin, was thrown in an Italian jail.

As it turned out, the evidence wasn't solid enough to keep Luciano, so the cat-and-mouse game between Lucky and the Italian police continued. He demanded constant attention. Blink and he was gone.

Elusive when he chose to be, Luciano could, on the other hand, be conspicuous—cruising around the Italian countryside in a gray Alfa Romeo. He couldn't return to the United States. He'd been given a thirty-to-fifty-year sentence after being convicted by prosecutor and future governor Thomas E. Dewey on prostitution charges. For a whorehouse. It was embarrassing. They sent Luciano to Dannemora, where he paid to have a Catholic church built inside the walls. He served ten years and then was let out after promising he would go to Italy and never return.

Luciano was one of an estimated four hundred Italian-born hoods who were deported rather than prosecuted. That was the route they would have gone with Carmine Galante if they had been able to prove that he wasn't Camillo Galante at all, but Carmine, born in Italy four years earlier. But they couldn't prove it, and Galante only went to Italy voluntarily, and always to return.

Luciano lived briefly in Rome but found the Rome police suffocating. He moved to Naples, where the police chief tried to have him banished to Ustica, a small island off the Sicilian coast. Luciano paid off an Italian commission assigned to determine his fate and stayed in Naples.

The Naples cops put him "on admonition," which was a sort of parole. He was allowed to move freely in the daytime, but he had to be off the streets after dark. He was never to be seen in nightclubs or at racetracks—and of course he was never to associate with any known criminals.

Luciano privately said that he didn't blame the Naples police. They were the pawns of U.S. narcotics agents, the real wolverines who were ceaselessly chewing at his ankles. His phone was tapped. They were intercepting his mail.

That was the summer that Bobby Kennedy, as chief counsel of the Select Committee on Improper Activities in the Labor or Management Field (better known as the Senate Rackets Committee), was grilling guys who'd been caught at Apalachin, sometimes on television.

On the first of July, it was John C. Montana's turn to be grilled. Montana was indignant. Montana said he was from Buffalo and it was really just an accident that he'd been at Joseph Barbara's place at the time of the raid.

"I was having car trouble; the rain caused the brakes to malfunction. And I pulled into this place thinking I might find a mechanic," Montana said. He laid it on thick: "I'd just as soon die as take the Fifth. I never did nothing to be ashamed of. What happened to me could've happened to anybody."

Senator Irving M. Ives, a Republican of New York, called Montana a liar: "Your story does not make much sense, I'm sorry to tell you. You may tell some people that story and make them believe it." But not Ives. "Somebody yells, 'Roadblock!' And you run into the woods."

Kennedy got into it, "Didn't you tell Sergeant Croswell that if he let you go you would do something for him?"

Montana replied, "I didn't tell him anything of the kind."

On the same day that Montana testified, James Vincent LaDuca of Lewiston, New York; Russell (Rosario) Mancuso of Utica, New York; and Louis LaRasso of Linden, New Jersey, all at Apalachin, were called to tell their stories.

These three were all union officials. LaDuca told the senators that he was the secretary-treasurer of Local 66, Hotel and Restaurant Employees. Mancuso was the president of Local 186, Hod Carriers and Common Laborers Union, and LaRasso was trustee of Local 394, Hod Carriers and Common Laborers.

Of course, the hoods didn't have much to say, sticking to their cover stories.

That same week, sixty-one-year-old Vito Genovese was called to testify and through thin, dry lips took the Fifth 150 times. I guess somebody must've counted. He did answer a few questions. He told Bobby Kennedy that he was just a "simple man" whose take-home pay was $107.50 a week.

On the Fourth of July, the RCMP received information that Galante was back in Montreal, staying at the Sheraton Hotel. They didn't need a reason to arrest him. Because he was on the prohibited list, his mere presence was a reason to arrest him. An arrest warrant was issued, but when RCMP officers went to the Sheraton, Galante was no longer there.

Galante's real problems were in the United States, however, where the feds had their ducks in order and were finally ready to move on him. Before they could act, however, they had to wait for Galante to return from Canada.

* * *

On Monday evening, July 7, 1958, the feds lowered the boom on the guys bringing the babonia into America. Galante was arrested and charged with conspiracy to distribute narcotics. (In 1959, Galante would be charged with a second set of drug charges, and the two cases would overlap as they worked their way through the courts.) He made bail and was soon back in the sunshine. Authorities wouldn't see him again for another eleven months.

Vincent "The Chin" Gigante was arrested on an indictment that called him Genovese's protégé, a rising star in the American Mafia. Gigante was famously the gunman who put a new part in the hair of Frank Costello in the lobby of an apartment building on May 2, 1957, although acquitted of those charges by a smart jury.

FBI agents arrested Vito Genovese at his home in Atlantic Highlands, New Jersey, and charged him with masterminding a thirty-seven-man ring that smuggled heroin into the United States from Europe. The Senate investigation had concluded that Genovese had personally made an estimated $30 million in dope money.

John Ormento of Lido Beach, New York, on the South Shore of Long Island, was described by the federal indictment as a "top man" in the drug ring. The feds stated that they thought the drugs were coming into the United States through Cuba, Puerto Rico, and Mexico. (It should be noted that Fidel Castro had yet to take over Cuba. Before Castro kicked the hoods out of Cuba they had free reign on that island, with Havana functioning as a sort of Las Vegas, where everything went, where Carmine Galante was trying to worm his way into Santo Trafficante's empire.)

According to U.S. Attorney Paul W. Williams, Genovese was the main figure in the bust. Williams tended to refer to him as the "Italian-born" Genovese, always noting that deportation was an option. If they couldn't get him behind bars—and getting a jury to convict wiseguys was tricky—they could always send him back where he came from. The indictment against Genovese noted that he was referred to within the mob as "the right man," a "mark of distinction."

The federal indictments were based largely on FBI electronic surveillance, with bugs set up in New York City, Las Vegas, Chicago,
Miami, Cleveland, and Philadelphia. The indictment also stated that
the hub of the heroin distribution system was in East Harlem, the
now predominantly Puerto Rican section of Upper Manhattan where
Galante had grown up ages ago.

By July 29, 1958, the feds were spending as much time investigating
Carl Acquevella as they were Carmine Galante. They learned that
Carl had a reputation as a gambler and a bookmaker, that his "wife"
Ann was from Newark, New Jersey, and her father operated a gas
station in that city. "Carl" and Ann spent a lot of time in Montreal,
especially during the summer months. They had two kids.

There must have been a time when Galante truly was living a
double life, traveling from one wife to the other. This is proven by
the fact that his first child with Ann was born before his final child
with Helen.

(Later FBI memos state that Galante's second family "alternated
surnames" between Acquevella and Galante.)

To give you an idea of where the FBI's head was at in 1960, they
divided information regarding Galante's children into "Legitimate"
and "Illegitimate."

After the Apalachin raid, Joe Bonanno went into hiding. He was so
hard to find that the feds speculated that he might have voluntarily
left the country, which would have been ironic, since they tried and
failed to deport him once because they caught him lying about his
criminal record on his application for U.S. citizenship.

At the start of November 1958, federal narcotics agents found
Bonanno living quietly in Tucson, Arizona, where he'd had a home
since the mid-1940s. He was arrested and charged as a material witness in the big heroin conspiracy case. By this time, more than half
of the men known to have attended the Apalachin meeting had been
arrested for something or other and eight of them were already in
jail.

*   *   *

On January 12, 1959, Assistant U.S. Attorney William S. Lynch, of the Southern District of New York, officially declined to prosecute either the Latamer Shipping Company or the Rosina Costume Company, because the fed investigations had found "no violations" of the federal anti-racketeering statutes or the Labor Management Relations Act. With Carmine Galante's brother Sam running Rosina, that Bensonhurst company held tightly to its legitimacy. Whatever was going on in there, the feds couldn't crack it, and they eventually admitted defeat.

In 1959, both of Galante's sisters, Angelina and Josephine, lived on Blake Avenue in East New York, Brooklyn, and both had the married name Volpe. Had they married brothers, brothers who shared a house? Turned out it was just an alias. One of Carmine Galante's aliases was Louis Volpe.

On April 17, 1959, Federal Judge Alexander Bicks sentenced Vito Genovese to fifteen years in prison, calling him the "mastermind" behind the dope-peddling ring that had crippled so many inner cities. Fourteen members of Genovese's crew were also sentenced at the same hearing, before a gallery of sobbing wives and goomara.

In addition to Genovese, the most harshly punished hood was Joey Beck, also sentenced to fifteen years. Beck's major gripe about the sentence was that Judge Bicks had revoked his parole. Beck had been out and about for the duration of his trial.

"I been here every day," Beck said. "I could've laid you ten-to-one that I'd be convicted, but I came in just the same."

Judge Bicks stuck to his ruling, pointing out that Beck had an "impressive" criminal record, no visible means of support, and other indictments pending in Kings County (Brooklyn).

The judge said, "The risk [of flight] is too substantial to warrant bail." And so, Joey Beck went behind bars.

His brother, Charles DiPalermo, Charlie Beck, also a member of Galante's crew since the beginning, was also sentenced in that courtroom that day, although his punishment was not as severe as his brother's: twelve years, and continued bail. The judge noted that Charles had a son who was critically ill.

Also sentenced that day was Vincent "The Chin" Gigante, then a strapping thirty-year-old man working as Genovese's driver/body-guard. He had skated on attempted murder charges in connection with the attempted hit on Frank Costello but got seven years here. Gigante, unlike the other defendants, had an entire cheering section in the courtroom and another rowdy group of supporters outside the courthouse. Among his supporters were his brother the priest and reps from the Children's Aid Society.

The federal government had managed to put some big gangsters behind bars, and they had a few others, like Galante, on the run—but they had not slowed the flow of heroin into the United States. The quantity was tremendous. The only guestimate as to how much came from the Federal Bureau of Narcotics, which said that two and a half tons of babonia were coming into the United States every year.

Galante's days and nights of free movement ended late on the evening of June 1, 1959. To no one's surprise, the capture started as a traffic stop. He was pulled over near Holmdel, New Jersey. Galante was wearing a white cap and working out a shiny new white Chevrolet convertible on the Garden State Parkway between Asbury Park and Keyport.

The cop realized who he had and called for backup. Galante was initially questioned overnight in the Holmdel state police barracks before being transferred to Newark police headquarters. A flock of cops, agents, special agents, and very special agents converged on those barracks. The Federal Bureau of Narcotics was there.

"Where you been, Carmine?" one agent asked.

"I been on Pelican Island." That was an Ocean County community on an island along the Jersey shore, connected by causeway to Bay Shore in the west and Seaside Heights to the east.

Investigators checked into this and found Galante was telling the truth. Galante had gone into hiding in a house on North Sunset Drive on Pelican Island. The house was owned by Gary Muscatello of Union City, New Jersey, who turned out to be a used-car dealer and a Teamster official. That Muscatello stuff was paperwork. The digs really belonged to Cousin Moey.

Neighbors said Galante was living with a "pretty woman" with prematurely gray hair. They had two young children. These, apparently, were the Acquevellas, Carmine's second family.

Neighbors knew something was up and had been keeping an eye on the man and woman because they had behaved peculiarly. Both made frequent trips to a telephone booth two hundred yards from their house.

Observant neighbors also noted that the couple drove a car that had "license plates of a different color." Every time you turned around they were different. The car had Florida plates when the couple first moved onto Pelican Island. After a while, though, that plate was replaced by a Jersey plate, then a few months later by New York State plates, then finally, back to Jersey plates.

With Galante at the time of his apprehension were two of his favorites, Cousin Moey and forty-four-year-old Anthony Macaluso, who lived on Sixth Avenue in the city. Galante's friends were charged with harboring and concealing a fugitive.

Police boasted to the press that, with Galante's capture, they had behind bars "the biggest dope peddler in the country."

Galante was questioned all night and, pretty much as expected, gave authorities nothing of value. He went into his well-rehearsed ignoramus act. His questioners wondered how a man so dim of wit could be in a position of responsibility in organized crime.

It was a question that would always be with Galante as long as he was alive. Was he really the borderline idiot that he appeared to be when interviewed by police? Was it an act? Or, just maybe, were Galante's skills not measurable in intellect?

The following day Galante was arraigned on charges of narcotics conspiracy before Judge Sylvester Ryan of the Southern District of New York courthouse in Brooklyn, New York.

You would think this would be a no-bail sort of case, right? Not only had a ton of taxpayer money been spent to catch this guy, but he'd been on the lam from the law for the previous eleven months.

Galante's attorney, Nicholas P. Iannuzzi, argued briefly that Galante deserved bail, and the judge was like a twig in a hurricane. He was swayed. Galante was granted $100,000 bail and was back on the streets in minutes.

With Galante sprung, Iannuzzi backed off and an attorney named Joseph Brill announced that he was going to manage Galante's defense on the drug charges at the forthcoming trial.

Galante was out of there fast, so a subpoena to appear before the New York State Commission of Investigation was served to Brill. The subpoena compelled Galante to appear before that commission at a date to be determined following his trial on federal charges.

Galante's legal difficulties continued to grow during the spring of 1960. Already under indictment for conspiracy to distribute heroin, Galante was included, along with twenty-nine others in another drug conspiracy indictment.

On May 17, 1960, Galante surrendered in Federal Court to Assistant U.S. Attorney William M. Tendy on the new charges. Tendy was a Fordham Law graduate who was partway through a legendary career as a federal prosecutor. When he died in the 1970s, Rudy Giuliani called him a "giant in law enforcement."

The new charges against Galante had nothing to do with his 1958 indictment, for which he was still out on bail and awaiting trial. This indictment featured twenty-nine co-defendants.

Galante was held in custody from May until September 1960. His arraignment was held before the Honorable John F. X. McGohey, a sixty-six-year-old judge who was part of the fabric of New York City justice. He was born in the city, earned his B.A. in the Bronx at Fordham, his law degree at NYU Law. After a stint in the public sector, as part of publisher William Randolph Hearst's sizable legal team, he received a recess appointment from President Harry S. Truman in 1949, as a U.S. District Court judge, the position he held eleven years later when a scowling Carmine Galante came into his courtroom. Galante pleaded not guilty. Judge McGohey set bail at $100,000—must have been the going figure at that time—which Galante immediately posted, and he was once again set free pending trial.

He gave his address as 40 Park Avenue in the city. FBI surveillance revealed that Galante was no longer living with either of his wives.

So now Galante had been arrested and indicted twice. As it turned out, the second arrest would end up being tried first.

CHAPTER NINETEEN
Trials and Tribulations

IN NOVEMBER 1960, GALANTE WENT TO TRIAL at the federal courthouse of the Southern District of New York on Cadman Plaza in Brooklyn. His co-defendants were down to twenty.

The judge was Richard H. Levet, sixty-six years old, a graduate of Colgate University and NYU Law. He'd fought in World War I and for thirty years maintained a private law practice in White Plains, New York. He was in his fifth year as a federal judge in the Southern District of New York, having been nominated for the seat in 1956 by President Dwight Eisenhower. (Levet would serve on the bench until his death in 1976.)

When Judge Levet learned that a woman scheduled to testify on behalf of the government in this drug conspiracy case had been threatened with bodily harm, his reaction was to revoke Galante's bail, as well as that of his co-defendants, for the duration of the trial. This caused a legal debate.

Galante's legal team appealed the ruling. Did a federal judge have the right to deny a defendant the right to make bond? The case went to the U.S. Supreme Court, where Justice John Marshall Harlan II ruled on February 27, 1961, that the Southern District of New York judge, as intimidation of a witness was alleged, was within his rights to keep Galante locked up during his trial.

On March 20, 1961, four months into the trial, one of the attor-

neys called for a sidebar, a conference between the judge and the attorneys out of earshot of the jury. The defendants were misbehaving
during this trial from the start, but Galante, not a man of many
words, had remained mute. But, for some reason, this sidebar and all
of that whispering at the bench set Galante off.

"Let the jury hear everything!" Galante yelled, among other
things. Although the outburst did not significantly delay the trial, it
earned Galante a sentence of twenty days in jail for contempt, weak
sauce as far as Lilo was concerned, as he was already in jail when he
wasn't in court.

The FBI became concerned with the proceedings when a transcript of audiotapes acquired from the NYPD, based on surveillance
and a confidential source, was made available to Galante's defense
team for "perusal." The problem was, the non-redacted transcript
could be used to determine the identity of the source, which would
put the informant's life in danger. The worries were confirmed when
the snitches who squealed on Galante began to get subpoenas from
Galante's defense attorneys.

The whole trial was shrouded in danger. Anyone who was part of
the process of putting Galante in prison was in danger. And everyone knew it. The proceedings were plagued by defecting jurors.
Whatever was going on behind the scenes, and we can imagine, jurors were terrified of passing judgment on Galante. Many found excuses to be dismissed before the trial was through so they wouldn't
have to face a potentially fatal deliberation.

Those who remained willing to serve had bad things happen to
them.

On the eve of the closing arguments, the jury foreman, sixty-
eight-year-old Harry Appel, "fell" down a flight of stairs in an abandoned building, broke his back, and hit his head, causing a severe
concussion. The belief was that Appel had been attacked.

One judge commented: "Mr. Appel suffered an unexplained fall
into a cellar-way of an abandoned building while walking alone, late
at night, on the Lower East Side, where many of the defendants in
this case have associations."

With Appel's injuries, the alternate jurors had been used up. They were down to eleven.

Five and a half months after the trial began, the judge declared a mistrial—and the whole thing didn't amount to a hill of beans. The enormous waste of courtroom time and assets led some legal experts to wonder if massive multi-defendant conspiracy trials should be held at all.

Was having that many hoods on trial at once a responsibility too large for one judge, any judge, to handle? To keep such a trial orderly demanded an almost superhuman combination of firmness and patience.

On June 2, 1961, a new bail hearing was held for Galante before fifty-six-year-old U.S. Judge Thomas F. Murphy, a lifelong New Yorker who graduated from Georgetown University and Fordham Law. Murphy had earned fame in 1949 and 1950 as prosecutor at the two trials of Alger Hiss. That led to a two-year stint as the New York City Police Commissioner. He was nominated for a seat on the bench by President Truman and served until his death in 1995. (Sidenote: Murphy's brother Johnny was well known in his own right, having pitched for eighteen years for the New York Yankees and Boston Red Sox, and was later a general manager for the New York Mets.)

Judge Murphy set bail at $135,000, a new high for Galante and a far cry from the $600 he'd had to put up six years earlier for his upstate traffic violation. Although both quantities were put up with equal speed. Galante had money. The amount of the bail wasn't really a factor.

The FBI didn't like the feel of any of this, that behind the scenes strong-arming and violence were defeating justice. FBI surveillance began the instant Galante stepped into the daylight. Instructions from J. Edgar Hoover were to give the Galante case, as well as Galante himself, "continuous, vigorous attention."

Galante had this case to worry about; would there be a second trial after the mistrial was declared? But there was more. There was the other case, the Cotroni Conspiracy case, and that trial was slated to start during the summer of 1961. That case was already attracting public attention because of the punching power of the defendants, and by the fact that they didn't all come from the same criminal family. There was Galante, who was a Bonanno, John Ormento and Angelo Loiacano were with Lucchese, and Carlie DiPietro was with Genovese. These were the individuals, according to the lengthy indictment, who distributed heroin obtained from the Cotroni organization into local and interstate traffic. The case began up in Canada with the arrests of Giuseppe "Pepe" Cotroni and Rene Robert, along with the seizure of six kilograms of heroin in 1959.

On September 28, 1961, the U.S. Court of Appeals for the Second Circuit heard arguments regarding Galante and co-defendant Anthony Mirra and the lengthy mistrial they'd endured. Mirra was a lifelong Bonanno. His uncle was Bonanno *caporegime* Alfred Embarrato and four of his cousins were capos. (One of those cousins would eventually be the one to whack him, but that was much later.) Mirra was different from other hoods in that he never touched booze. If it looked like he had a drink in his hand, you could be sure it was just ginger ale.

What do appellate lawyers do after a mistrial? They'll come up with something. Since there had been no conviction, there was nothing to appeal—or was there? Lawyers decided to gripe about the jail time Galante and Mirra had been forced to serve because of contempt of court charges.

In this appeal, Galante was represented by Albert J. Krieger. Co-defendant Mirra was repped by Leo B. Mittelman, and the prosecutors were U.S. Attorneys William M. Tendy and Arthur Rosett.

Five and a half months. It would be hard for any red-blooded American hood to go that long without misbehaving now and again, right? Both Galante and Mirra had accrued some jail time with their impertinence, and each had received sentences of twenty days in jail. As we saw, Galante got his for objecting loudly to a sidebar.

It all seemed silly, because Galante had not been granted bail as he awaited his re-trial, so the twenty extra days didn't appear to matter. Mirra appeared to be the instigator in the courtroom, first to start with the, "Fuck you, Judge." The judge said he'd give him five days in jail for each "Fuck you," so Mirra must have stopped after four. After that, Mirra was quiet. He'd said his piece.

In 1962, Galante was a defendant in two sprawling cases. During the re-take of the mistrial, there were more fireworks. Anthony Mirra, Galante's co-defendant, again managed to cause a major fuss.

On June 4, 1962, Mirra was called to the witness stand to testify on his own behalf and lacked the character to withstand a vigorous cross-examination. At one point, Mirra stood up, picked up his chair, and threw it at the deputy district attorney who was questioning him. The chair missed its target by mere inches and struck the front of the jury box with such force that it broke into pieces. Mirra was arrested, charged with assault, and later tried and sentenced to a year in prison for the outburst.

At Galante's other trial it was the lawyers and jurors who had trouble staying healthy. As the trial started, Nicholas P. Iannuzzi was Galante's lawyer. On April 2, 1962, Iannuzzi made an application to Judge Lloyd F. McMahon to be relieved of his duties as Galante's counsel, and that his job be transferred to a woman lawyer named Frances Kahn, who was confined to a wheelchair because of polio.

Judge McMahon allowed Kahn to join Galante's defense team but refused to allow Iannuzzi to leave and ordered him to remain as co-counsel.

(It's unclear if Iannuzzi was threatened by Galante, but he spent the rest of his life in fear of Lilo. When his son John Nicholas Iannuzzi was admitted to the New York bar in June 1962, the swearing-in ceremony was under the glass-domed courtroom of the appellate division at 25th Street and Madison Avenue. The rest of the family was there to celebrate, but Nick Senior was missing. He had checked himself into Columbus Hospital not because he was sick or injured, but out of fear that he was to be whacked by Galante.)

Kahn, the wheelchair-bound lady mouthpiece, was seldom confused for anyone else. She had gotten a lot of play in the papers in the past year as lawyer for Jack Molinas, the Columbia All-American and former star of the Fort Wayne Pistons of the National Basketball Association (NBA), who was now barred from playing pro ball for betting on his team's games.

Again, the defendants, emboldened by all being in court together, misbehaved in court. Galante earned forty-five more days of jail time for outbursts. The biggest contempt penalty went to co-defendant Salvatore Panico, who was allowed to be in court only if bound and gagged and who was given fifteen months of jail time for repeatedly shouting profanities in court.

Then Frances Kahn accidentally rolled her wheelchair down a flight of stairs and injured herself on June 12, 1962, badly enough that they had to take her to the Doctors Hospital, where she remained for weeks. We're pretty sure this was a genuine accident. Galante by all accounts liked Kahn, and after she recovered from her injuries she continued to represent him, even in appellate court.

When Judge McMahon entered his courtroom the day after Kahn's tumble and there was an empty space where Kahn's wheelchair should have been, there was this exchange:

McMahon: "Nicholas P. Iannuzzi was originally your attorney for this trial, was he not, Mr. Galante?"

Galante glowered at the judge but did not speak.

An attorney for one of Galante's co-defendants, Silvio Cosentino, stood and began to speak: "Your Honor—"

McMahon: "Are you now representing Mr. Galante?"

Cosentino: "No, Your Honor, I—"

McMahon: "Mr. Cosentino, stop winking at me." (Cosentino had a nervous tic in his face that the judge had not previously noticed, apparently.)

Cosentino: "I'm not winking; I—"

McMahon: "I know a wink when I see one. Now stay seated. Mr. Galante, would you mind standing?"

Galante continued to glare but did slowly rise to his feet.

Cosentino: "May I just make a statement for the record, Your Honor?"

The judge angrily slammed his hand on his desk.

McMahon: "Another word out of you, Mr. Cosentino, and I shall hold you in contempt." The judge returned his attention to Galante, "Nicholas P. Iannuzzi was your original lawyer at this trial, isn't that right, Mr. Galante?"

Galante remained mute.

McMahon: "I asked you a question, Mr. Galante."

Galante: "I really don't want to say anything, Your Honor. I'd like Miss Kahn to speak for me."

McMahon: "She isn't here."

Galante: "We should wait, then, so she can speak for me."

McMahon, when he was assigned to preside over the trial, was determined to keep it on schedule. He wasn't going to let Kahn's accident slow things down. This wasn't the first time that someone had tumbled, in a wheelchair or not, down a flight of stairs while Carmine Galante was on trial.

McMahon: "When I agreed to Miss Kahn representing you, Mr. Galante, I did not dismiss Mr. Iannuzzi. I want him back here this afternoon so this trial can proceed."

Another of Galante's lawyers had a heart attack on June 18, only six days after the first incident. Amazingly, Galante had no trouble finding lawyers to replace those on the disabled list—the Bonannos probably had a whole bullpen of them—and the trial went on without interruption, at near light speed in fact.

The government put forth its case in an orderly manner, at a crisp pace, and demonstrated how Galante and his co-defendants had conspired to import copious amounts of heroin and to dilute and distribute the drugs once they arrived.

At the Cotroni Conspiracy trial, being held simultaneously, the principal government witness was Edward Lawton Smith, who described in detail the machinations of the system, how the labor was divided up within the organization, how they worked hand in hand with a crew of Canadians led by Pepe Cotroni, who handled the exportation of the drugs from Canada, across the border, and straight down the Hudson River to New York City. The jury learned about the men who worked in the receiving centers in New York, where the heroin was "cut" and packaged for sale. Distributors would then dispose of the drugs through a wide variety of selling outlets. The man in charge of the whole shebang, the chief executive of the heroin importation business, was Carmine Galante.

Smith testified that in late April 1957 a man named Mancino took Smith to a meeting in a Montreal apartment and Carmine Galante was there, along with two Cotroni brothers and a man identified only as "Angelo"—probably Cousin Moey.

At one point during the meeting, Galante picked up a valise, put it on the coffee table, and opened it. Inside were clear plastic bags filled with a white powder. Smith and Mancino took the valise to New York and Mancino took it into a joint called Frank's Bar & Grill in Brooklyn, where it was reportedly delivered to John Ormento.

Smith testified that he didn't go into Frank's Bar but instead returned immediately to Montreal. Smith told the jury another story from late June 1958 when he, Anthony Mirra, and another man drove to 56th Street and Sutton Place in Manhattan and pulled to the curb. Nearby Carmine Galante was standing at the corner. They got out of the car and approached Galante, who told them "the stuff" was in a nearby car. Smith and Mirra removed a suitcase from the trunk of the nearby car and brought it to their own car. Galante asked Mirra if he knew what he was supposed to do. Mirra said he did and Galante gave him ten hundred-dollar bills. Smith testified that he'd been told to change hotels but hadn't done it, which pissed Mirra off. Mirra told him that Galante gave the order for him to switch hotels and if he didn't do it he would end up being dragged behind a truck.

When Galante needed to meet with some of the men in his charge his preferred meeting place was a joint called Johnny's Keyboard at

687 Lexington Avenue (between 56th and 57th Streets, now the site of the Fitzpatrick Hotel). During the 1950s, the nightclub was a competitor of the Copacabana, where you could go see (and dance to) performers like Jackie Kent and his "cocktail drums" and hear the romantic ballads of Joe King, and Russ Haddock, who happened to be the son of Judge Ambrose Haddock.

Smith's testimony had Galante coming and going. It showed him amid the group that was importing drugs. It showed him in physical possession of the drugs and with knowledge and supervision of the entire operation.

The re-trial and the Cotroni trial both ended in convictions for all defendants. On June 10, 1962, a jury found Galante and twelve co-defendants guilty of conspiracy to violate narcotics laws.

At the sentencing hearing two days later, Judge McMahon said, "The evidence on the trial shows that you were the leader, the chief executive, of this vicious criminal enterprise. You have a criminal record which proclaims your total contempt of the law. You are a threat to the public safety."

Galante was sentenced to twenty years in the fed pen, only half of what Judge McMahon gave to Big John Ormento, who got forty years, starting immediately, no bail during the appeal process. About Ormento, the judge said, "You are a hardened criminal and an incurable cancer on society. You are totally undeserving of any mercy."

Here's a scorecard of the defendants and the sentences imposed that day:

Joseph Fernandez, thirty-five years

Samuel Monastersky, thirty years

Carlie De Pietro, twenty years

Carmine Galante, twenty years

Anthony Mirra, twenty years

Salvatore Panico, twenty years

Angelo Loiacano, twenty years

William Bentvena, fifteen years

Carmine Panico, twelve years
Salvatore Sciremammano, twelve years
William Struzzieri, twelve years

At the same sentencing hearing, the judge said that he would continue to deny the defendants bail pending their inevitable appeal and remand them immediately to federal custody.

"If these men were released on bail there would be danger to the public," Judge McMahon said. "To the jurors and to court personnel."

The judge said he didn't have high hopes for those appeals, saying they were bound to be "frivolous" because "many questions of law have been deliberately created by the defendants in an obvious plot to frustrate justice by terrorism.

"It is too plain for argument that the general pattern shows a deliberate design by all of the defendants to frustrate justice by provoking a mistrial or creating error," Judge McMahon said.

With this conviction, Galante's status apparently in his other trial became moot, and twenty years remained his time to serve despite separate but similar convictions, a matter of Galante being caught twice doing the same thing: being a big-time narcotics dealer, maybe the biggest. Well, they wouldn't have to worry about him for a while. Save the taxpayer a buck.

That summer, the secretary to wheelchair-bound Frances Kahn, an ex-con named Israel Schwartzberg, was arrested and charged with obstruction of justice. Schwartzberg, it turned out, was a Bronx hood known as "Big Mizo" who proclaimed himself a "confidential law clerk" upon being released from prison.

Schwartzberg, the charges said, had gone into hiding with documents that could have aided Galante's defense. Schwartzberg waited until the trial was finished before coming out in public again and was promptly arrested.

The defendants appealed their convictions and on June 13, 1963, four of them were granted new trials by an appeals court, but not Galante. Following Galante's conviction, his appellant counsel,

O. John Rogge of New York City, appealed the conviction to, at the very least, get Galante a new trial. Representing the United States was Jonathan L. Rosner, and Circuit Judge Irving Kaufman presided.

The appeal began with a request that Galante be granted bail pending his appeal. However, precedent indicated that bail should only be granted to convicted criminals who "will respond to the demands of justice." And that the granting of bail must always be at the discretion of a judge, as there were criminals for whom no amount of bail would be an effective deterrent to flight. The appellant court noted the fact that Galante had proven himself in the past to be a flight risk and had hidden from authorities for years as a fugitive from justice when indicted on drug conspiracy charges. Of all the types of felons, the judge said, drug offenders were most apt to skip bail. What's more, Galante was comfortable traveling abroad. He had international friends and frequently left the country.

Galante was heading for the fed pen, and not just any pen: the Rock.

CHAPTER TWENTY
Rock and Rat

GALANTE'S NEXT HOME WAS ALCATRAZ, aka The Rock. It was like Dannemora in one sense: the guards didn't worry much about escape attempts. The prison had the reputation of being the number-one hellhole in American corrections—prisoners called it Hellcatraz—a place so brutal that it made sane hoods go off their rocker.

For many years there was a strict code of silence and anyone making a sound risked a stint in "The Hole," named after the hole in the floor that served as the toilet.

It was also three thousand miles from Williamsburg. The prison perched atop a craggy island in San Francisco Bay only a mile and a quarter offshore. Those who'd tried to escape found that swimming to the mainland was impossible because of the swirling currents in the bay. Thirty-six men tried to escape from Alcatraz. Twenty-three were caught, six were shot and killed, and the others drowned or presumed drowned. The site was originally an army fort built in the middle of the nineteenth century. In 1910 construction began on the prison building, which was used for a generation as a military prison. The U.S. Department of Justice acquired the island in 1933, and by the time Galante arrived there it was well known as the home of the "worst of the worst" where cells were forty-five square feet in size with claustrophobic seven-foot-tall ceilings.

Galante would probably have spent much of his sentence on The Rock, but in 1963 it was closed, necessitating Galante's transfer.

The prison didn't close because of the inhumane conditions. It closed because it was falling down. The constant bombardment on its walls of salt spray from the bay had crumbled the structure. It was either close it or fix it, and fixing it was too expensive.

The year 1963 will be remembered as a time when astronauts were heroes, young and old did The Twist like they did last summer, and a beautiful glowing family lived in the White House—until November 22 anyway. On President Street it was remembered as the First Year of the Rat.

That was the year that Joseph Valachi turned songbird in the vaulted hearing room of the Old Senate Office Building in Washington, D.C., in front of a Senate Select Committee and, because of the heavy TV and radio coverage, the entire world.

As many of you might know, it was through Valachi that America picked up the phrase "La Cosa Nostra"—our thing—as a synonym for the Italian Mafia in the United States. Valachi might have used the phrase generically, but it had a ring and it stuck, so much so that future FBI memos would refer to the Italian mob as LCN.

Valachi, in addition to giving the mob a favorite moniker, also laid out the way it was organized, that there were five families (related by activities rather than common ancestry), led by a godfather and made up of crews, each with their own capo running the show.

While chain-smoking cigarettes, Valachi told the committee about his crime career, which started as a kid in East Harlem, running with a burglary gang of teenagers known as the Minutemen, how he became a made man in 1930, taking the vow of omerta, which meant death if he revealed the secrets of the secret society.

He testified that the syndicate protected its friends—no matter what business, or funny business, those friends were involved in—as long as they did what they were told when the time came. For many businessmen this meant paying a skim. For Valachi personally, it meant doing favors, like following orders to whack guys who'd failed to do the right thing.

There were famous examples of guys who'd needed to be iced

because they were in the mob's way. He recalled for the senators that in pre-WW II Brooklyn a guy named Peter LaPlaca had the misfortune of being a witness to a murder committed by Vito Genovese and his Queens lieutenant Michael Miranda. LaPlaca was a resident of the rathole known as the Raymond Street Jail when someone slipped him poison and forever silenced him.

The other classic example, Valachi said, was the death of turncoat Abe "Kid Twist" Reles, who proved to be a canary that could sing but not fly, shoved out of his sixth-floor room at the Half Moon Hotel on the boardwalk at Coney Island, falling seventy feet to his death below. He was supposedly being protected by five police guards, but his security team did him no good.

Some hits looked like suicides. Valachi's third example was Bronx drug dealer Joe "Pip the Blind" Gagliano, who supposedly hung himself in his Bronx County Jail cell after talking to the district attorney.

Some hits could never be confirmed because the victim disappeared so thoroughly.

Some of the things Valachi said struck close to home. I was just a kid, but on President Street all ears were on the radio as they broadcast Valachi's testimony live. There was a lot of cursing when he started talking about Anthony "Tony Bender" Strollo, who had backed the Gallo brothers over the Profaci Family. Tony Bender and his goomara had disappeared in 1962.

Valachi said that he was spilling what he knew because he was a dead man anyway. He lived in Atlanta Federal Penitentiary, where there was an open contract on his life. He said that his main nemesis was mob boss Vito Genovese, who'd given him the "kiss of death" in his prison cell—an actual kiss on the hand that made Valachi's blood run cold.

"If you went back to jail this afternoon, what would happen, Mr. Valachi?" a senator asked.

"I would be dead in five minutes."

Now Valachi's testimony is famous, and it is pertinent to our story here because among those in his prison whom he suspected of being out to kill him was the terrifying visage of Joseph "Joey Beck" Di-Palermo, Carmine Galante's lifelong friend and right-hand man.

After the kiss of death, Valachi kept his head on a swivel. He was ready to defend his life every time he was approached, every time someone placed their hand on his shoulder. He broke prison rules to purposefully be put into solitary. He knew which guys to keep an eye on. There was "Trigger" Mike Coppola, and John "Dio" Dioguardi—but mostly there was Beck, who Valachi felt was the leader of the prison death squad.

"I knew DiPalermo [Beck] had been assigned to kill me, so I decided to get him before he got me," Valachi testified. One day he walked out onto the prison yard and found things eerily quiet. He was alone. The place was deserted. Then, in a rush, he saw Beck and four or five other men coming at him.

"I had a piece of iron pipe in my hand, and I lashed out," Valachi said.

The guy he hit wasn't Beck, however. It was Joseph Saopp, who suffered multiple skull fractures and died thirty-four hours later. Saopp had the misfortune (in at least two ways) of resembling Beck, although it is hard to imagine anyone looking enough like The Ostrich to cause confusion.

Valachi was tried for the Saopp murder, convicted of murder in the second degree, and his sentence increased to life. None of which served to take him off Vito Genovese's hit list. And so, with nothing to lose, Valachi became the first high-profile rat, a desperate attempt to save his life.

And it worked. Valachi received special protection inside prison and lived another nine years before dying of a heart attack in prison at the age of sixty-six.

Galante was still on The Rock in San Francisco Bay when his name next came up in an FBI investigation. The feds had bugged the home of New Jersey crime boss Sam "The Plumber" DeCavalcante (the real-life inspiration for Tony Soprano).

While under audio surveillance, DeCavalcante said that Carlo Gambino was complaining that Salvatore Vincent "Bill" Bonanno, Joseph's son, grabbed $150,000 from some Bonanno guys in Montreal that was supposed to go to Galante.

When the federal government closed The Rock on March 21, 1963, Carmine Galante was transferred to the fed pen in Lewisburg, Pennsylvania, which was psychologically less unsettling, for the simple reason that it was built on the mainland rather than on a tiny island surrounded by roiling waters.

Nonetheless, what was outside the prison wasn't nearly as important to prisoners as what was inside, and the Gothic architecture made some of the guys in the striped uniforms feel as if they were doing time in a haunted house.

The hellishness of Lewisburg could devastate a man. Al Capone spent three years there for tax bullshit, entering the pen a cocky boss and exiting thirty-six months later a wary jailbird.

Lewisburg had a rep as a wiseguys' prison, and there was even one stretch of cells known as Mafia Row, so Galante had guys to talk to, guys in the same biz. Among his fellow inmates was a powerful union leader named Jimmy Hoffa. Also, there was a young John Gotti, whom Galante took a liking to. Two ruthless fucks will find each other, even in a structured setting such as a penitentiary.

"When you get out you can work for me," Galante said.

Gotti, a Gambino on "Charlie Wagons" Fatico's crew, thanked Galante. "I already got a job," the future Teflon Don said.

Galante admired him for his loyalty.

After time in Lewisburg, Galante was transferred to the Federal Correctional Institute at Milan, Michigan, forty-five miles outside Detroit, which compared to Alcatraz and Lewisburg was like a country club. Milan had once been a women's prison and after that for a time a prison for youthful offenders. There were no cells with a hole in the floor for a toilet.

In Milan, Galante became king of the handball courts, not be-

Carmine Galante's dad grew up in Castellammare del Golfo in Sicily, a hub of organized crime activity. The bosses there were always named Bonanno, so when young Joe Bonanno came to America to run operations for his family, young Carmine knew where his allegiances lay. So many mobsters came from Castellammare that they went to war with the rest of the American mob. Galante's pure bloodline served him well in the Bonanno Family.
(ALAMY Stock Photo)

As far as we know, the first guy Carmine Galante ever killed was thirty-four-year-old Patrolman Walter Orlando de Castillia, born in 1895. On March 14, 1930, de Castilla's job was to guard the delivery of the $7,267 payroll of the Weinstein Martin Shoe Company warehouse. But he was instead gunned down by Galante and others.

(Yearbook photo)

Joseph Bonanno (center) came to America as a young man to "run things" for his dad in Castellammare. He was a tad more gentlemanly than his fellow fathers on the commission, and when it came time for him to go, he was treated in kind. Instead of having his brains blown out in some south Brooklyn gutter, Bonanno was allowed to "retire" to Tuscon, Arizona, spending his days at poolside counting cactuses.
(ALAMY Stock Photo)

At about 1:00 p.m. on Christmas Eve, 1930, Galante, still shy of his twenty-first birthday, participated in a botched holdup in Bushwick, Brooklyn, and had a shootout at a teeming Williamsburg intersection with this man, Detective Joseph Meenahan (shown here on the occasion of his retirement). Galante and Meenahan wounded each other, and one of Galante's errant bullets struck an innocent bystander, six-year-old Shirley Hershowitz of Bedford Avenue, in the thigh.
(Brooklyn Daily Eagle, the Brooklyn Collection, Brooklyn Public Library)

Italian-born revolutionist Carlo Tresca as he appeared in 1910 at the age of thirty.
(Author collection)

On January 11, 1943, Carmine Galante committed his most notorious murder, the whacking of the Italian anarchist publisher of *Il Martello*, Carlo Tresca. Galante shot Tresca twice, once in the head and once in the back, and left the scene in a car. Here, Tresca's stiff lies on the sidewalk at Fifth Avenue and 15th Street in Manhattan.
(New York Daily News Archive/Getty Images)

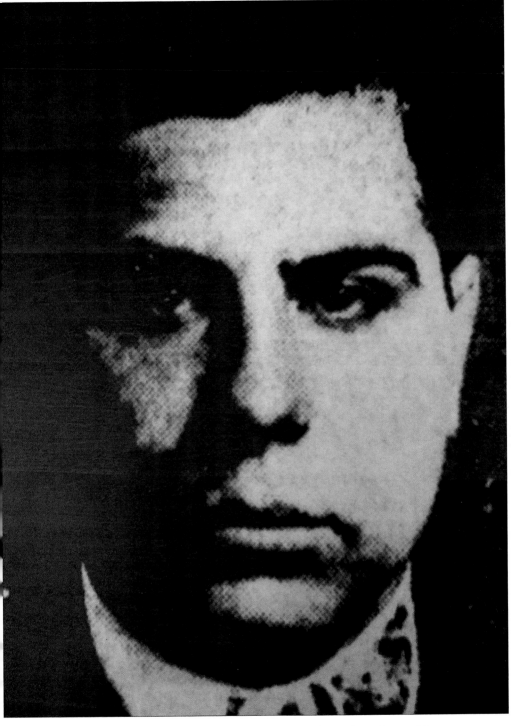

The first time Galante got his picture in the paper in Brooklyn, the caption writer got his name wrong, calling him "Rocco" Galante. The accompanying article, about Galante being the number-one suspect in the assassination of anarchist Carlo Tresca, got his name correct.
(Brooklyn Daily Eagle, the Brooklyn Collection, Brooklyn Public Library)

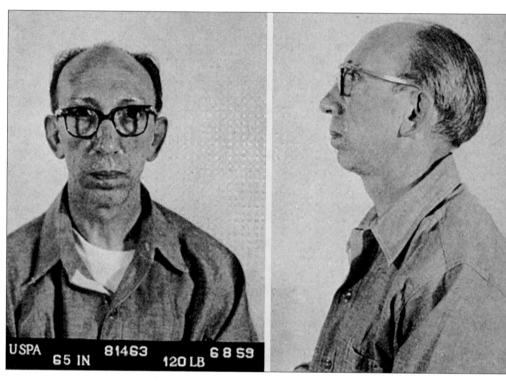

USPA 65 IN 81463 120 LB 6 8 59

Galante's most trusted friend was Giuseppe "Joe Beck" DiPalermo, starting out as a juvenile delinquent and growing up to become the "dean of dope dealers." He was also a stone killer like Lilo. Imagine this mug being the last thing you see. *(Author collection)*

Although Galante had two "wives," and had children with both, he was only legally married once, to Helen at Our Lady of Sorrows Church. The church was built in 1868 and sat on Pitt Street between Rivington and Stanton Streets in Little Italy, a mishmash of three architectural styles: Romanesque, Byzantine, and Victorian. The church was known for its massive tubular-pneumatic organ. When the bride came down the aisle, everyone on the Lower East Side knew it.

(Author photo)

Carmine Galante was arrested in front of this building on September 4, 1947, caught red-handed while dismantling a still at 5 Berkeley Place in the Park Slope section of Brooklyn. While agents of the Alcohol Tax Unit looked on, Galante was among those taking the still apart and placing the pieces inside a 1938 Cadillac. Also on the scene, and already loaded to the brim with copper sheeting, tubing, and other parts necessary for the construction of a still, was a 1937 International truck.

(Author photo)

When Galante was released from the Federal Penitentiary in January 1974, he was pissed off by the fact that he couldn't whack Frank Costello on account of Costello dying of natural causes the previous year. One of Galante's first orders was: "Blow up that fucker Frank Costello's fucking grave. Fuck with that fucker's tomb." So Galante's boys, some of them original Zips, went out to buy the dynamite and headed to St. Michael's Cemetery in the East Elmhurst section of Queens. The subsequent police report read that the doors to the tomb had been blown right off, and that the "remains were disturbed."

(Author photo)

Santos Trafficante sits at the bar of the Sans Souci, seven miles outside Havana, Cuba, where anything went. Trafficante ran the joint. Galante wanted in, but in the long run Castro's revolution came through, the mob fled, and by the 1960s there was goat shit in the Sans Souci's roulette wheels. By then Trafficante's biggest enemy was JFK, and you know how that turned out.
(ALAMY Stock Photo)

My uncle Joe, called "Joe Shep" on the street, was a made man in the Genovese family.
He knew them all. Albert Anastasia, Joe Adonis, Lucky Luciano, Frank Costello, Vito Genovese —
and Carmine Galante. When Galante came to President Street in 1974, Uncle Joe was his liaison.
(Author's collection)

This is about what Galante looked like when I met him a couple of times during the mid-1970s. His last federal mugshot, and if and if you look closely, a rare glimpse at the white of Galante's eyes.
(Federal Bureau of Investigation)

In what might be the most famous mob rubout in history, Carmine Galante, big-time dope dealer and cold-blooded killer, was blown away on the patio behind one of his favorite restaurants on Knickerbocker Avenue in Bushwick, Brooklyn, on a hot summer day. Here's the scene behind Joe and Mary's not long after Galante was rubbed out. Crime scene investigators are working the scene, and someone has been nice enough to throw a blanket over Galante's ghastly remains so the boys can dust for fingerprints without distraction.
(ALAMY Stock Photo)

Carmine Galante was buried in the southeast corner of St. John Cemetery, Section 25.
His common-law wife, Antoinette "Ann" Acquavella, outlived him by twenty years
and was subsequently buried in the same plot.
(Author photo)

cause he was good at the game but because everyone was afraid to beat him.

At one point, he told the other handball players that, from that moment on, anyone playing against him would have to hit the ball high on the wall so that he would be able to return it. Only he would be allowed to come in and kill the ball.

"I am to win all the games," Galante said.

When one opponent disobeyed the rule, Galante walked up to him and slapped him across the face.

"I rule everything," Galante said. "And when I get out of this prison, I will show this to everyone."

Galante finished his sentence at the fed pen in Atlanta, Georgia. Upon his release, an FBI informant told the feds that Galante was what was becoming a rare animal in the underworld. He was a Castellammarese, a Sicilian, who understood the language and the customs of the old country. He was, in essence, one of the last of the Mustache Petes, in style and manner more like the previous generation, his dad's generation, than like the Young Turks, some of them not that young anymore, who broke the rules and made organized crime their own thing, an American thing. Galante, the informant explained, would be assuming a leadership role in the Bonanno Family when he got out. And his ambition would know no bounds as he sought to become boss of everything and to win all games.

On October 21, 1964, Joseph Bonanno, one day before he was scheduled to testify before a grand jury, was kidnapped in New York City by men reportedly loyal to Stefano Magaddino. The story was seen as fishy by many because news of the kidnapping came from Bonanno's lawyers, who said that Bonanno was snatched as he was going into his lawyer's office building on Park Avenue and East 36th Street. Maybe. Electronic surveillance in Jersey revealed that, according to Sam "The Plumber" DeCavalcante, the Commission knew nothing of the kidnapping and presumed that Bonanno had merely gone on the lam. Back in Manhattan, FBI bugs picked up conversations among Bonanno's soldiers, to the effect that Don Peppino had split the scene and left them holding the bag.

According to the official story, Bonanno was held captive in Buffalo, New York, for nineteen months. He was released only after he agreed to retire to Arizona and allow the Commission to pick his successor as the head of the Bonanno Family, which would retain his family's name.

In 1966, Bonanno was picked up by authorities and brought before a grand jury, where he refused to say anything about anything. He was jailed for a time for contempt and, upon his release, fled once again to the great American Southwest, where he kept tabs on the underworld by reading newspapers beside his swimming pool. Eventually, everyone who cared knew he was in Tucson, Arizona, but no one bothered him.

In 1968, Don Peppino had a heart attack. His son Bill Bonanno was a thorn in the family's side while Don Peppino was away. He'd gone to war (the "Banana War") with Gaspar DiGregorio over filling the power vacuum created by Joe's departure. DiGregorio at one point asked Bill to come to a peace meet on Troutman Street in North Brooklyn. Arriving for the meet, Bill and his boys were greeted by gunfire, although no one was wounded. When peace was negotiated, part of the deal was that Bill would join his old man in Arizona. Don Peppino liked retired life, easy on his ailing heart, but the younger Bonanno became antsy and soon enough found himself involved in California rackets. He ended up being convicted on the West Coast of fifty-two counts of mail fraud and sentenced to four years in prison.

CHAPTER TWENTY-ONE

Digging under the Jersey Chicken Coop

FOR YEARS, GALANTE HAD OWNED a piece of land five miles northwest of Lakewood, New Jersey, about sixty miles from New York City, which backed up against a small home and yard that, on March 24, 1967, was dug up by the feds, revealing two bodies.

The site was an old rural chicken farm belonging to a family named Celso. They'd converted a large chicken coop into a modest five-room yellow bungalow on Cook Road in Jackson Township.

The federal diggers began the process by knocking on the Celsos' door and giving Joseph Celso and his wife, Rosa, their search warrant, which specified the names of the two bodies they were looking for. One was Angelo Sonnessa of Nutley, New Jersey, last seen in September 1961. The other was Kenneth Later of New York City, missing since April 1963.

Observers could tell that a stool pigeon who knew the facts was involved here, as the feds went directly to the correct spot and dug up the bodies. To recover one body, before they could get to earth they had to smash through six inches of concrete. Someone who was there when the bodies were buried was talking. For obvious reasons the source of the info was a deeply guarded secret.

Sonnessa's remains were found in a small tunnel that had once been used as a moonshine mash pit. Later's remains were in a rusty fifty-five-gallon oil drum filled with hydrochloric acid. His remains were discovered with a plastic bag over the head and wire binding the ankles together. The two bodies were only feet apart, with a narrow gravel road running between them.

This wasn't the first time the Celsos' property, adjacent to Galante's, was raided. In April 1960, agents from the Alcohol and Tobacco Tax Division raided the joint and busted a still, right in the same spot where the bodies were found years later. Almost as a footnote, there had been a second bust in 1962 at the Celsos' for running numbers.

The feds set up floodlights they borrowed from the Naval Air Station at Lakehurst, eight miles away. Now they could dig night and day. Shovels were too puny, so they brought in a bulldozer.

Sonnessa, who lived in Nutley with a woman described as "not his wife," was a former partner in a Jersey contracting firm and had been a former key informant for the Federal Bureau of Narcotics. He'd testified against Galante's co-defendant Big John Ormento, who was a major cog in the global heroin network until he was sent away, largely because of Sonnessa's testimony—so it was easy to see why Sonnessa was buried where he was. His contracting partner had been Joseph Vecchio, who'd been indicted (along with Galante) in May 1960 for heroin distribution. Vecchio died a month after Sonnessa's disappearance in a Secaucus, New Jersey, car accident.

The other body was that of Kenneth Later, who had no police record. He was a former stockbroker, a nightclub booking agent, a securities dealer, and a "man about Broadway"—so the reasons for his whacking were more mysterious. Speculation was that he was an expert in moving money around, perhaps washing it in the process, a skill that might've helped some gangsters and made him the enemy of others. Later was fifty-five years old when he disappeared on March 29, 1963. He told a friend that he had to see a guy and then he was headed out to Aqueduct to bet the ponies. He never arrived at the Big A. There was doubt about whether he was going to the track to bet or for another reason, like lending or collecting money from the degenerates who practically lived there. We do know that Later had been to the track every day that week, so either he was a degenerate himself or he was exploiting degenerates.

There had been a rash of hoods getting disappeared over the previous seven years, many of whom were suspected of being rogue heroin dealers. Even in prison, Galante didn't like competition.

The 1967 discoveries by the Jersey chicken coop also included a moldy orthopedic shoe that was linked to a missing Bayonne, New Jersey, restaurateur named Barney O'Brien, who was friends with a lot of big-time Jersey politicians and had a clubfoot that necessitated the special shoe.

O'Brien was listed thereafter as "presumed dead," though his body wasn't found. No one had seen O'Brien since the fall of 1962 when he parked his car in front of his house near Newark Bay but never made it inside.

O'Brien had a history as a longshoreman and had been permanently barred from the waterfront at Port Newark in 1955 because he'd been caught in a kickback racket. His sister claimed he'd gone straight after that, but sisters don't always know. She theorized that some hood had tried to get O'Brien to do something he didn't want to do and he got himself whacked when he refused, but it was just a theory.

Police wouldn't say why, but they also believed that a thirty-five-year-old gang playgirl by the name of Barbara Delmar—wife of an ex-con named Teddy Delmar, a journeyman hood without the necessities to make it big—was buried on the farm. Down in Houston, Texas, the FBI questioned a guy named Joe "Joe Rogers" Stassi, a Damon Runyon character type who might have been a Genovese, about Mrs. Delmar, who disappeared from her home in Danbury, Connecticut, after receiving a phone call from Stassi. Stassi was free on $150,000 pending sentencing on a narcotics conviction. He told the FBI that "she was probably with Ken Later," thus the suspicion that she might be under the chicken coop.

And she wasn't the only babe authorities hoped to find the remains of. They were also looking for the va-va-va-voom Nancy Sue Shelton, whose red hair and blue eyes made her a hood favorite. She disappeared on September 24, 1964, after having a "chat" with the wife of a convicted narcotics pusher in her luxury apartment on New York's fashionable East Side. She, apparently, said too much.

The feds had a lengthy list of others they hoped to find, all of them in theory enemies of Carmine Galante, who remained more dangerous than ever despite being behind bars.

These included:

Fiore "Fury" Siano, Joe Valachi's nephew, his sister's son, named by blabbermouth Valachi as one of the hit men in on the 1952 bullet-to-the-head bump-off of narcotics informant Eugene Giannini in 1952 in Harlem and the dumping of Giannini's body in front of an East Harlem building on 107th Street. Siano was busted in 1954 as a member of a "Harlem dope gang," selling cocaine and heroin. Siano was also reportedly the killer of ladies' man Steve Franse, whom Genovese blamed for alienating his wife's affections. Siano was slated by the government to be the number-one witness against Vito Genovese when he vanished during May 1964. When last seen, Siano was with three unknown males entering Patsy's Pizzeria on First Avenue:

Anthony "Bootsy" DiPasquale, who was under indictment for narcotics trafficking when he disappeared.

Nicholas "Bulldog" Martello, born in 1907, originally from Astoria, Queens, and eventual Jersey dope-case stool pigeon. Allegedly with the Lucchese Family, the Bulldog had been in the rackets since the 1920s. His first arrest was for rape in 1926. During the summer of 1931, his car was used (probably with him in it), in the horribly botched hit attempt on shifty-eyed dope peddler Tony Trobino in East Harlem, a fiasco that somehow left one child dead and four other children wounded from shotgun blasts. The target was unscathed. In 1958, Bulldog was arrested on drug charges and soon thereafter fell off the face of the earth.

Joseph "Joey Surprise" Feola of Yonkers, New York, who
controlled a big slice of the garbage waste disposal
business in Westchester County. He tried to move into
Jersey, which was DeCavalcante territory, and vanished in
1965.

Sebastiano "Benny the Sicilian" Bellanca, born 1904 in
Cattolica, Sicily, arrested on dope charges in 1954, then
jumped bail and was never seen again by authorities. Benny
had been a courier moving back and forth between New
York and Montreal, meeting frequently on the Canadian
end with Giuseppe Cotroni, and on the New York end with
someone the FBI only knew as "Mr. Lilo," who of course
turned out to be Carmine Galante.

Morris Taubman, aka Morris Tannenbaum, notorious racketeer who worked out of New York, Chicago, and Detroit.
Served seven years in the federal pen in Milan, Michigan,
for pushing dope and was named in a 1952 fed indictment,
accusing him of conspiracy to violate narcotics laws. While
working in Detroit, he was part of the Waxey Gordon narcotics ring. He handled large amounts of heroin whenever
he was a free man but maybe sometimes went light on the
tribute.

And Bonanno soldier Salvatore "Little Sal" Giglio, aka King,
born 1906 in New York City, friend of both Lilo and Joey
Beck, with an arrest record that dated back to 1937, one fed
conviction for narcotics conspiracy. Little Sal is not to be
confused with the Sal Giglio who had been dead since
October 5, 1963, when he drove his car off the
Metropolitan Avenue Bridge through a fence and plunged
twelve feet to his death into Newtown Creek, the watery
border between westernmost Brooklyn and Queens. Little
Sal was another associate of both Pepe Cotroni and Lilo
who shuttled back and forth across the Canadian border

during the 1950s. He was described by the FBI as a "major underworld narcotics trafficker." Giglio was deported from Canada and subsequently vanished.

None of the suspected victims were found under the chicken coop. As the digging went on, wiseguys muttered to themselves that they were wasting their time. Some bodies were just unfindable.

CHAPTER TWENTY-TWO
Top Echelon

DURING THE EARLY-MORNING hours of January 24, 1974, Galante was released from Atlanta Federal Prison after serving twelve years of his twenty-year sentence. He was scheduled to be under the supervision of the U.S. Board of Parole assigned to the Southern District of New York until about 1982—a moot point as Galante didn't live that long.

Galante entered a world that was different from the one he'd left. For one thing, people looked different, especially the men. The high-and-tight haircuts of the early 1960s were gone, replaced by perms, hair-hidden ears, and sideburns the size of an eight-track tape—men having grown steadily hairier ever since the Beatles appeared on *The Ed Sullivan Show* in 1964. Galante never learned much about culture, but now there was a counterculture, a movement of anti-war, anti-establishment young people. Women were on the Pill and the number of them "saving themselves for marriage" was down to a nunlike few.

Galante, as he walked through the gates of the Atlanta fed pen, didn't look out of place, but he did look out of time. Edward Kirkman of the *Daily News* called Galante "Little Caesar," a reference to a Prohibition-era gangster story.

Galante learned upon his release, if he didn't already know, that the Law had done much to clog up his pipelines of heroin into the United States. The system set up in Palermo, Italy, at the Grand

Hotel et Des Palmes by Lucky Luciano was being piece by piece dismantled by the authorities.

In 1971, the Turkish government banned the growing of poppies and production of opium. In 1972, federal narcotics agents from the United States and France seized 110 pounds of heroin at the Paris airport. Another French seizure nabbed 210 pounds, street value $38 million.

Closer to home, the crew of Lucchese associate Vincent Papa was smashed. This proved to be embarrassing for the Law because several NYPD officers were found to be dirty. Whenever drugs were seized in quantity by police, the bags of white powder would be put in an evidence room where dirty cops would pick it up and return it to its rightful owner.

So that no one would notice the missing evidence, bags of cornstarch were put in the drugs' place. This system was busted when bugs infested the evidence, something that wouldn't have happened had there been heroin in those bags.

Papa was personally responsible for stealing an estimated $70 million worth of heroin from the NYPD evidence room, a theft that formed the basis for the great movie *The French Connection*.

The investigation into the NYPD theft unearthed some embarrassing stuff, such as the fact that the Central Intelligence Agency, the famed CIA, in charge of defending U.S. interests abroad, had known from the start about the heroin pipeline and had done nothing. One imagines they were paid to look the other way—or maybe exchanged immunity for overheard chitchat involving Italian communists.

Point is, Galante was going to have to look for new ways to earn. He would need to fix new games so that he always won. If he couldn't start up a racket, he'd bully his way into a piece of someone else's rackets, a practice that most certainly shortened his life.

The instant Galante left the Atlanta pen, the FBI activated their dormant investigation into all things Galante, once again proclaiming him "armed and dangerous."

Galante went from the prison directly to the Atlanta airport, bought a ticket under the name C. Galante, and—accompanied by son James Galante (from his first family) and daughter Nina Galante (from his second)—boarded a flight for New York, landing at 8:08 a.m.

He emerged both powerful and vengeful. FBI informants laid it out for the feds. Galante controlled the Bonanno Family and "will definitely make a power play with Carlo Gambino in an attempt to become the one-and-only crime lord of New York City." Galante, as they say, had visions of grandeur.

Galante rented two apartments, one on East 38th Street in the Murray Hill section of Manhattan, in a new multi-storied apartment building. There he placed his common-law wife, Ann. She lived on the twentieth floor in apartment 20B.

The other was on Waverly Place in Greenwich Village. Technically, two of Galante's daughters—his children with Ann—lived there, but it was actually his new headquarters. The shadowing agent got as far as the front hallway. Under apartment 8's mailbox was written the name Galante.

Anticipating further difficulties with the law, Galante retained famous attorney Roy Cohn to be his legal counsel. Cohn was the first of Galante's lawyers to be legitimately famous in his own right.

Cohn was a New York City kid, born in the Bronx, schooled at Columbia. He earned his B.A. and his J.D. by the time he was twenty. He had a great-uncle who owned Lionel Trains and an uncle who went up the river for passing bad checks. Cohn first got his name in the papers as the U.S. prosecutor of alleged nuclear-secret spies Julius and Ethel Rosenberg, a case that ended with the Rosenbergs getting the electric chair. In 1954, Cohn represented Senator Joseph McCarthy, the ruthless commie hunter, whose anti-Red campaign had evolved into a reckless and falsified attack on political enemies. Cohn was a confirmed bachelor and lived with his mom until he was forty.

*   *   *

Kirkman also noted that Galante's release spelled trouble among the ranks. Here was a guy whose ambition knew no bounds, and he was walking into an underworld where it had been years since Carlo Gambino had had a suitable rival for the title of Boss of Bosses. The Young Turks of the old days, the ones who'd wiped out the Mustache Petes, were now old themselves. The bosses were ancient, and their top lieutenants, lifelong friends usually, were just as old. It was a time when fresh blood was needed, a world in which a guy like John Gotti could make major progress. But what about an old Little Caesar like Lilo, who could think of nothing—nothing!—but power and vengeance?

When Galante walked out of prison, vowing to take control of everything everywhere, one of the dangerous men he pissed off was Carlo Gambino, who didn't believe in heroin trafficking.

Under twenty-four-seven surveillance, Galante rounded up the troops and told them Gambino could wait. His first job was to gain control of the Bonanno Family, so he ordered a few hits, just to let the official leader of the Bonannos, Philip Rastelli, know that he was back.

CHAPTER TWENTY-THREE
Costello's Tomb

OF THE ZIPS RECRUITED BY GALANTE, the one who stood out most in a crowd was Cesare Bonventre. He was easy to spot because he may have been the tallest mobster in history. In a world where a lot of wiseguys were five five, five six, Bonventre stood six feet, seven inches. He was also a man of style, with thick, black slicked-back hair, Italian-cut suits—which had to be made specifically for him because of his size—and designer shades. In a world of Italian American mobsters, guys who took their fashion sense from Hollywood movies, Bonventre took his fashion cues from Sicily. He even carried a small leather bag over his shoulder for his stuff, a man purse, hip in Sicily but unheard of in the American underworld.

His nickname in the mob world was, naturally, The Tall Guy. He had been easy to recruit because he had family already made and already in America. His uncle was John Bonventre, who was in the Bonanno Family and rose as high as underboss. He was also a cousin of Baldassare "Baldo" Amato, whom I would one day have espresso and cannoli with.

Cesare was born in Castellammare in 1951 and was brought over to America when Galante got out of prison, specifically to be Galante's bodyguard.

* * *

Galante was shadowed everyplace he went. His six-seven body-guard just made the job easier. Galante and Bonventre couldn't even get lost in crowds. The Tall Guy's head poked up.

Galante, with feds in tow, made early visits to the L and T Cleaners on Elizabeth Street. The special agent keeping tabs on Galante remembered Galante's pre-prison habits, as he commented in his written report that Galante did not frequent the cleaners as much as before he went away.

On January 31, 1974, Galante was loving life. Everything had that new freedom smell. Another thing had changed since Galante went away a dozen years earlier: He no longer drove. Now he always had a driver pick him up and drop him off. Sometimes bodyguards would drive. Other times his daughter Nina would play chauffeur. On this day, Galante was driven around town in a white-over-red Caddy by his nephew, who lived out on Long Island in Nassau County.

They rode from Manhattan to Bath Beach in an Oldsmobile bearing Jersey plates. Galante visited the Magic Lantern, a bar owned by his son-in-law, Nina's husband, Louis Volpe, located on Bath Avenue. Volpe lived at Eighteenth Avenue and 79th Street in Bensonhurst, just north of Bath Beach.

As exhibited by his handball games, Galante's days of losing were over. FBI informants—one of whom turned out to be Bill Bonanno, son of Joseph, turned rat—laid it out for the feds: Galante controlled the Bonanno Family and would "definitely make a power play with Carlo Gambino in an attempt to become the one-and-only crime lord of New York City." Inside the Magic Lantern, Galante was observed talking to swarthy men in Sicilian-accented Italian. It looked like Galante was conducting business.

The swarthy men were Knickerbocker Zips, the Sicilian guys who did more than just drive and bodyguard. Galante gave them capo status so they could operate with their own crews, and they had their headquarters in a variety of pizza parlors and pastry shops up and down Knickerbocker Avenue in Bushwick.

With the Bonanno Family in disarray, ranks depleted, the Zips formed the infrastructure for a new family, Lilo's Family. And Galante was conducting business out of the Magic Lantern. He took over a gambling and loans op that was running out of Penn Station. He chipped away at Gambino power by demanding a piece of the action in Manhattan sweatshops.

Galante had grudges. Rastelli, whom the Commission had named top Bonanno, and Gambino underboss Aniello Dellacroce. Galante and Dellacroce, vicious down to their toenails, were two peas in a pod and so naturally hated each other's guts. Besides, Galante still held a grudge against Dellacroce because he'd whacked a couple of Galante's heroin dealers.

But there was nobody Galante hated more in the world than Frank Costello, tops on Galante's list of guys who would die before he did. Problem was, on February 18, 1973, while Galante was still in Atlanta, Frank Costello died of throat cancer in Doctors Hospital in New York City at the age of eighty-two. Costello's body was taken to the Frank E. Campbell Funeral Chapel in Manhattan. Galante heard the news and was beyond pissed. Smoke came out of his ears. Costello had deprived Galante of the pleasure of killing him.

Costello's death was reported heavily in the news. America had an interest in Costello, getting to know him when he testified before the Kefauver Committee on national television. He was memorable as the guy whose face they didn't see. He agreed to be on television only if his face was never shown, so TV cameras focused on Costello's finely manicured hands during his testimony, which he delivered in a raspy voice straight out of Central Casting.

Costello answered more questions than most of the hoods who testified. He didn't take the Fifth at all, which made him different. He also said absolutely nothing of value to the Kefauver Committee. He admitted to being a bootlegger and a bookmaker years before. Who wasn't? But that was a long time ago and these days he knew less than nothing about organized crime.

They asked him what he'd done to his credit as an American citizen.

"I paid my taxes," Costello said. Everyone laughed. Oh yeah, America remembered him.

His obituary was action-packed. Illegal booze, gambling, a famous assassination attempt featuring parted hair and a celebrity gunman known for his chin, the attempt to deport him during the late 1950s, a man who'd aged out of hood activity, who'd been laying low during the last years of his life, seldom leaving the Central Park apartment that he shared with his wife, Loretta.

When Costello died, there was a small fuss about the size of his funeral convoy, about the size of the flower arrangements around his coffin, and, finally, about the size of his tomb, which was larger than many Manhattan apartments. Joking—sort of. A caretaker at St. Michael's Cemetery was a blabbermouth, told a reporter that the plot alone cost Ms. Costello $4,880.

"She paid in cash," the caretaker said.

On that five-grand plot they built an elegant marble mausoleum. The contractor who built the structure later said he had no idea that its occupant was infamous.

"I didn't recognize the name," the guy said, a smart contractor. He said that he'd taken the job from an elderly man named Amilcare Festa, who turned out to be a trusted neighbor of Frank Costello's mother. The contractor was paid in cash, a series of packets, each containing fifty hundred-dollar bills.

This stuff about Costello's legacy being the fanciest tomb in the whole fucking cemetery appeared in the papers and Galante had Nina read it to him while he sat and drank wine and brooded.

That shit stuck in Galante's craw. When Galante got out of prison in January 1974, one of his first orders was: "Blow up that fucker Frank Costello's fucking mausoleum. *Fuck with his body!*"

Costello had been dead for months, but the mission was ordered with urgency. If Galante couldn't blow Costello up when he was alive, he would blow him up while he was dead.

So a few Zips, The Tall Guy and a couple of others, went out to buy the dynamite and headed to St. Michael's Cemetery in the East

Elmhurst section of Queens, where Costello's final resting place was about to lose its doors to an explosion that could be heard all the way to Astoria.

The police report said that the doors to the tomb had been blown right off and that the "remains had been disturbed." Not too many guys have the stomach for that kind of ghoulish work. They grow 'em tough in Castellammare.

CHAPTER TWENTY-FOUR
Rastelli

DURING THE FIRST YEARS OF THE 1970S, with Joe Bonanno still counting cactuses in the great American Southwest, there was a revolving door of sorts as to who was running the fragmented Bonanno Family. Paul Sciacca laid claim to the position in 1971.

He was replaced by Natale "Joe Diamond" Evola, who had an advantage because he was an original Sicilian, from Castellammare. Evola was a key figure in Galante's heroin distribution system and spent ten years behind bars, from 1959 to 1969, for conspiracy to distribute narcotics. He wasn't into broads and lived much of his life with his mother in Bay Ridge. On August 28, 1973, Evola was taken off the board by cancer, dying at age sixty-six in Columbus Hospital in the Bronx.

Other hoods sought the top spot but lacked the juice. Gaspar DiGregorio and Bill Bonanno made unsuccessful moves to run the Bonannos. Aspirations aside, Gaspar never achieved a seat at the Commission table. Gaspar was once sprayed with machine-gun fire and suffered a heart attack, but it was the smokes that killed him. He died of lung cancer in 1970 at the age of sixty-five.

Evola was replaced at the top spot—this time officially—by Philip "Rusty" Rastelli. One of Rastelli's capos was Anthony DiGregorio, Gaspar's son.

* * *

The power vacuum caused by Bonanno's exile in 1968, often referred to euphemistically as his "retirement," was only partially responsible for the revolving door. There was also the government, which seemed to have top Bonannos behind bars at all times, so there always needed to be a distinction between boss and acting boss.

In 1974, right about the time Galante was getting out of prison, the Commission met at New York's Americana Hotel. They named Rusty as acting boss of the Bonannos. Despite the Commission's decision, Galante continued to behave as if he were boss, taking orders from no one.

Rastelli's life and Galante's ran parallel paths in many ways. He was born in New York City on January 31, 1918. On April 29, 1943, he registered for selective service—the draft.

In 1948, Rusty married a gal named Connie Pietrafesa, mean as sin, a Brooklyn gal, no uglier than a bulldog, and dragging along a couple of brats from a previous marriage. Rusty took on a lot.

Connie was just as well known to police as her mobster husband. She'd been arrested numerous times for performing abortions. The Rastellis didn't get along much—and would eventually take turns shooting each other.

If you read my last action-packed book, *Mafia Hit Man*, which among lots of other stuff contains the true facts regarding the whacking of Joey Gallo, you know I got the info from someone who was there. Joey's killer was a guy named Carmine "Sonny Pinto" DiBiase, whose first kill was that of the best man at his wedding, Mikey Errichiello, on Christmas Day years earlier in a Little Italy social club they ran together.

DiBiase stayed in Little Italy for a few days after the whacking of Errichiello but then split and went completely off the grid for seven years. During part of his time on the lam, DiBiase was hidden by Rusty Rastelli, who lived on 58th Drive in Maspeth, Queens.

It wasn't long before DiBiase wished he'd found a cave of his own to hide in.

The Rastelli house was tumultuous, to put it mildly. Connie and Rusty were at war. Rastelli liked to stay out for obvious reasons, he was a busy guy, and it eventually got to the point where the Rastelli house wasn't a good place for Sonny Pinto to hide because Rastelli himself was on the run.

Rastelli was suspected of whacking thirty-six-year-old Michael Russo on December 13, 1954, with a bullet in the back of the head on a Bath Beach sidewalk. Rastelli's beef with Russo had to do with a grandiose heist they had planned for a Queens bank, which didn't come off because Russo backed out at the last minute.

Rastelli needed two tries to dispatch Russo. On December 3, 1953, he allegedly shot Russo four times but didn't kill him at 56th Road near 48th Street near Calvary Cemetery in Queens. During the first shooting, Rastelli drove Russo to the cemetery and told him to run, then fired at his back.

After the first shooting, cops hauled Rastelli in, but he said he didn't know nothing about no Russo. A grand jury subpoenaed Russo. Hearing that, the lovely Connie Rastelli approached Mrs. Russo and told her there was money in it if Russo didn't testify.

Russo went before the grand jury and when they asked him who shot him he said, "Philip Rastelli." Hey, why not? He didn't have long to live anyway. Rastelli wasn't going to give up.

The second try did the trick. It happened on Bay 41st Street in Bath Beach, Brooklyn on December 12, 1954. Rastelli allegedly didn't make the same mistake, none of this "three steps" shit, and shot Russo point-blank, DOA at Coney Island Hospital.

The next day, Rastelli walked free, but cops picked up Connie and charged her with the attempted bribery of the murder victim's wife. It turned out that Connie had made several attempts to buy off the Russos.

Also hanging around the Rastelli abode during that time was Ralph Santora, a friend of Rusty's from East Williamsburg, who was allegedly around for both Russo shootings. Santora was younger but already had a lengthy rap sheet as a bookie. He, too, didn't have long to live.

DiBiase, Rastelli, and Santora were all hiding out from the cops at the same time for a stretch. It is unknown if they did that separately or together. Rastelli played his cards smart. He was under indictment for the first shooting of Russo but only heavily suspected of Russo's killing, with Russo being the sole witness against him for the first incident.

The war between Connie and Philip Rastelli had been bubbling under the surface for years. Things were better for a time when Rastelli was living in Montreal on St. Catherine Street while Connie remained in Maspeth, but late on the evening of December 18, 1961, with Rastelli back in Brooklyn, it boiled over.

Connie shot and wounded her husband outside a home on South 4th Street, across the street from Continental Army Plaza in Williamsburg. Police came, arrested both of them, and charged Connie with felonious assault and Philip with possession of a gun. Both were released on bail and advised to go their separate ways.

After the shooting, Connie moved out of the Maspeth home and got herself a place of her own in Williamsburg. She tried to stay out of her husband's way, as he was pretty angry with her.

On February 9, 1962, a judge dismissed Philip's gun possession charges. Anyone who thought the Rastellis would let bygones be bygones at that point were sadly mistaken.

Connie reportedly tried to get rid of her husband in another way, going to the FBI and suggesting that they investigate her husband's activities as a drug trafficker. The feds thanked her. Rusty had quite an arrest record—murder, extortion, loansharking, gambling—but nothing involving drugs. Connie's tip opened a new vein of research.

On March 4, 1962, the forty-nine-year-old Connie was in the hallway of her home on North 7th Street, Williamsburg, when she was shot five times and killed.

Connie's hydrant-shaped body was discovered at 11:20 p.m. by her son, twenty-nine-year-old James Fernande, one of the brats Connie dragged along when she married Rusty, now all grown-up.

The papers loved the story. The husband was suspected in the Russo murder, the victim had recently shot her husband, and she herself had a record dating back many years, with two busts for abortions and another for attempted bribery (that of Mrs. Russo), but had always beat the rap.

No one was ever charged in Connie Rastelli's murder—but everyone knew.

His domestic woes over, Rastelli could concentrate on organized crime again, and he rose in the ranks. On April 19, 1963, Rastelli attended a Bonanno Family meeting, capos and up, at the Hotel Wentworth in Manhattan just off of Times Square.

Not long after Connie Rastelli's murder, Rusty married a woman named Mildred, about whom not much is known. Although some sources say that in 1964 Rastelli felt Cupid's arrow one more time, and married a Canadian woman named Irene McKee, it is Mildred who is buried beside him. (As of September 1972, Irene was living in Ottawa, Canada, and had no contact with Rastelli or any of his hood friends. By 1975 she was deceased.)

Rastelli, of course, being an Italian man, didn't allow his marriage status to affect his dating life, a fact that became public in the most brutal way when, on May 8, 1965, he was driving a car with a couple of broads along Woodhaven Boulevard in Queens when he hit an abutment. One of the women was thrown from the car and died. She was twenty-nine-year-old Caroline Minkus.

One of the advantages Rastelli had over Galante was not just that he was out during the 1960s while Galante was in but also that he had friends within the Bonanno Family who wanted to see him succeed. On December 1, 1965, the FBI learned that Rastelli was aligned with the Gaspar DiGregorio crew and was also allied with Armand Pollastrino.

* * *

In January 1970, Rastelli was subpoenaed to appear before a grand jury that was investigating loansharking. He refused to answer questions.

On June 30, 1970, flamboyant Nassau County District Attorney William Cahn charged Rastelli with contempt of court for not testifying before the grand jury—a charge that down the line would buy Rusty an extra six months in jail.

Cahn was one of those two-faced guys. He was political and liked to portray himself as a mob buster, but he couldn't keep himself on the straight and narrow. He eventually went down in disgrace, after eleven years as D.A., in 1973 after he was caught double-charging the people of Long Island for his travel expenses.

Twelve months later, on June 20, 1971, a new grand jury indicted Rastelli and four others on loansharking and conspiracy charges. Judge Pierre Lundberg set bail at $50,000. A month later, both Rastelli and Anthony DiGregorio (Gaspar's son) were held on sixteen-count indictments in connection with loansharking. When the tabloids reported this, they quoted a cop as saying Rastelli was a known organized-crime bigwig, but without clear allegiances. He seemed to work for a combo of the Bonannos and the Colombos.

On February 4, 1972, the FBI learned through an anonymous informant that the upper echelon of the Bonanno Family featured Evola as boss, Rastelli as underboss, and Nicholas "Nicky Glasses" Marangello as consigliere.

Upon analysis, this info seems faulty. During the days when Galante considered himself boss, Marangello was his underboss, all unofficial of course because the Commission was on Philip Rastelli's side. Marangello had been a faithful soldier for Galante for years and had been used to relay messages to and from Galante while Lilo was behind bars.

Nicky Glasses was also a superior earner. He ran a large-scale sports book and gambling operation (with a side biz in loans) out of the Toyland Social Club on Hester Street in Chinatown. He was one of the guys who would buy into the Donnie Brasco act and during the 1990s was sent away for RICO bullshit.

In December 1972, Rastelli was tried for loansharking in Suffolk County (eastern Long Island). On December 29, 1972, the jury convicted Rastelli and his four co-defendants. All five defendants were allowed to stay free on bail during the appeals process.

On January 14, 1973, the *Daily News* reported that, according to an anonymous member of the NYPD's morals squad, Rastelli owned a piece of a notorious after-hours joint on East 60th Street in the city called The Zoo. The joint was publicly known as a "juice bar" with no liquor license but in reality was a hangout for jazzed-up speed freaks who would pay the four-dollar cover charge to have a place to dance and do lines of blow or meth out in the open. Not long after they learned that Rastelli owned a piece of the joint, the NYPD raided it and shut it down after finding drugs and guns inside. By 1974, the club was closed and had been replaced by an indoor mini-golf course.

On February 5, 1973, Rastelli was sentenced to four years in the Suffolk County jail for loansharking. The judge again, however, allowed Rastelli to remain free on bail during the appeals process.

Rastelli's legal obstacles wouldn't go away. On March 23, 1973, Rastelli pleaded guilty to his Nassau County contempt charges and on April 12 was sentenced to six months in jail for contempt of the Nassau County grand jury. No bail this time. Rastelli was ordered to begin his sentence immediately.

Piling on, it was only eleven days later that Rastelli was brought up on new charges, involving the systemic extortion of mobile lunch wagons, sellers of New York's infamous "dirty water dogs."

It was around this time, summer of 1973, that Natale "Joe Diamond" Evola died of natural causes. Rastelli was popular among the Bonanno capos and was named boss. Nicky Glasses, a longtime Galante loyalist, was reportedly promoted from consigliere to underboss.

* * *

Which brings us to the time when Galante was released from prison in Atlanta and began his campaign to accrue power and wreak vengeance. During the late winter of 1974, Galante began a campaign to take away from Rastelli, piece by piece, soul by soul, all he found near and dear.

Rusty had a forty-one-year-old stepson named James Fernande— one of Connie's brats, Connie at this point dead almost exactly twelve years—who ran Rusty's gambling operation in Williamsburg. Galante ordered Fernande hit, and on March 6, 1974, it was done. Fernande was shot to death, four bullets to the head in his Williamsburg clothing store, the Northside Clothing Outlet on North 7th Street.

Fernande was last seen alive at 2:45 p.m. on March 6. His wife discovered his body a little more than two hours later. No weapon was recovered. A quick check indicated that Fernande had a record of thirteen arrests dating back to 1954, mostly involving forgery and drug charges.

The timing of Galante's release from prison and the whacking of Rastelli's stepson did not escape the mob reporters at the *Daily News*, who, on March 28, published a story in that paper predicting a war between Galante and Rastelli.

Galante wanted Rastelli to officially step aside. The whacking of his stepson was just a nudge.

Neither the seventy-three-year-old Gambino nor the fifty-six-year-old Rastelli seemed bothered by Galante's re-emergence. Rastelli wasn't that heartbroken when the kid was hit. The threat to his power, of course, was a concern, but Rastelli didn't want guys to think he was afraid of Galante—although he must've been terrified. Galante was nuts and would do anything.

Gambino wasn't hiding either. He had been seen in public several times since Galante left Atlanta, always with his usual two bodyguards, Vincent Failla and Ettore "Tony Russo" Zappi.

There was a major difference in power between Gambino and

Rastelli. Gambino had an army of 6,000. On a good day, the Bonannos would number about 250. Galante would chip away at Rastelli's
power first using his usual method: decreasing the surplus population.

There was also a major difference in health. Whereas Rastelli was
robust, Gambino was fading.

As Galante sat in his Waverly Place apartment, he took a good, hard
look at the Gallos and President Street, where I was a young man,
hanging out, learning the ropes, and doing what I was told. I had
some great teachers.

The Gallos were unpredictable, defiant. We numbered less than
a hundred, but we had avoided being totally dominated by anyone,
including Gambino. Still, we weren't at our strongest. There had
been a lot of defections from the Gallo crew after Joey got
whacked, guys who didn't want to follow Albert "Blast" Gallo and
instead went back to the Colombos, to whom they technically belonged anyway.

Galante may also have felt that the President Street Boys could be
pushed around, now that Blast was the only surviving Gallo brother.
Before Galante could take on Gambino he figured he'd best make a
deal on President Street.

CHAPTER TWENTY-FIVE
Galante Comes to President Street

BEFORE I CAN TELL YOU how I met Carmine Galante, I've got to tell you about the Block. That's the block, technically two blocks, on President Street in Red Hook between the piers at one end and the Brooklyn-Queens Expressway at the other—an enclave that was easy to defend. The western end of President was now geographically isolated, and that was where the Gallo crew hung out, ran business, shot the shit, and planned tactics and strategy.

I was there because my dad was Ricky Dimatteo, a pro boxer and bouncer who started out on President Street as Larry Gallo's bodyguard, but Larry passed away in 1968 of natural causes and in 1972 Joey Gallo was whacked in Little Italy, leaving just Blast Gallo to carry on the family business. By 1974 my dad was a much-respected elder of the Gallo crew. I was a teenager, hanging around with my friend Anthony "Goombadiel" DeLuca, on call in case somebody had something for us to do.

The meeting with Galante was set up through Uncle Joe, whom I called Uncle because he was very close with my father. Uncle Joe was called Joe Shep on the streets, a made man in the Genovese Family. He was born in Manhattan, a juvenile delinquent on the Lower East Side. When he was eighteen he moved to Church Avenue just off Flatbush, and later he lived on Ocean Parkway in Coney Island.

He started out as a petty thief and a stickup man. He was arrested for the first time at the age of twenty (with two other guys) in April 1932 for holding up eleven men and three women in an apartment on South 3rd Street in Williamsburg. They got away with about $160 in cash and were arrested within minutes of leaving. Uncle Joe went away for a while after that, but while he was inside he did some quality networking, and by the time he got out he was on the good side of some big boys.

He knew them all. Albert Anastasia, Joe Adonis, Lucky Luciano, Frank Costello, Vito Genovese. Uncle Joe started out as a driver for those guys, going out on scores, making getaways. He got turned over to Joe Adonis and put in charge of running the gambling and shylocking out of Joe's Italian Kitchen in Brooklyn. After Lucky Luciano got his prostitution sentence commuted and left for Italy, Uncle Joe started running with Frank Costello. Luciano at one point left Italy and went to Cuba, via Argentina, where he worked with, among others, Santo Trafficante, to turn Havana, Cuba, into a gambler's paradise, a project later realized in full in Las Vegas but destined for failure in Cuba on account of Fidel Castro, who didn't want mobsters or reptilian American tourists in his country.

Anyway, Uncle Joe went to Havana with Adonis and met Lucky in person. Uncle Joe went over to the Genovese crime family, where he was bumped up to capo. That was when he started to make his move in the unions. He was Costello's right-hand man for years and dealt with the labor unions.

Ricky and Joe would hang out together at the Gondola Hotel in a restaurant owned by Joe Morola. They played cards once a week, legendary games with some big pots. After cards, they'd go to Sheepshead Bay to the old Randazzo's restaurant. They'd bring the wives, my mom, Dee, and Joe's dear wife, Ann, who looked like Carol Channing and was a very classy woman. We all loved Joe and Ann.

In 1974, looking to consolidate power under his auspices and thinking he saw a potential ally in Blast, Galante came to the block. It was a big deal. Everybody was on their best behavior—except for Galante, of course, who remained his animalistic self. The meeting was in the main club, which was Roy Roy's club, actually Roy Roy's mom's club.

Roy Roy was Rosario Musico, born on President Street in 1942. He was wild from day one, growing up in his mom's club, getting rough and tough. He was an asset to the Gallos when he was still a kid, and he stayed a loyal member of the crew for decades.

Roy Roy's mom was a sassy, loud woman with a husky voice made of whiskey and tobacco. The club was our hangout, but (other than in times of war) it was open for business, too, and a popular spot for Red Hook's thousands of longshoremen. She also ran numbers out of the joint.

I knew Roy Roy well because he oversaw us young guys on our way up. He was assigned to teach us the ropes. By "normal" standards, Roy Roy was not a great role model. He was both a ruthless gangster and a party animal. He could down a bottle of scotch over the course of a night and smoke a couple of joints to take the edge off. He was rebellious and did not like to be told what to do. Back in the old days, the rules on the block were no mustaches or beards, but Roy Roy hated to shave and wouldn't shave until Larry or Blast would yell at him.

So, it was sometime in 1974 when my dad got word that Galante needed something. This is enough to turn your blood to ice water. It turned out that Galante was looking for guys who would have his back if a full-fledged civil war among the Bonannos broke out. The Gallos had been having their own civil war on and off with the Profaci/Colombo Family for decades, so they understood a family that had fallen out of order.

We all went into Roy Roy's club before the meeting. We knew the instant the car pulled up out front with Uncle Joe and Lilo in it. When Blast was ready, he gave a gesture, and someone went to the door to give Uncle Joe the high sign. After that, Uncle Joe and Galante came into the club, walked past me and into a back room where we could look and see what was going on, but we couldn't hear.

What I saw was that Galante never sat down. He talked with Uncle Joe and Blast and my dad for three fucking hours, and he stood the entire time.

Galante seemed to me like danger personified. He was rough around the edges. Now, on President Street we weren't exactly society—except for Joey and Joey was gone. Nobody stuck their fucking pinky out when they jiggled the ice cubes in their Dewar's, so if Galante seemed rough to us, he was rough. Here was a guy who, not only couldn't you imagine him laughing; you couldn't imagine him smiling.

He was like a concentrated freeze-dried wiseguy, with anything resembling civilized behavior boiled away. Me and Goombadiel, seventeen years old at the time, acted as gofers, getting coffee and drinks for the back room.

Apparently Galante said that he needed a "union favor" and would do a favor for a favor, but Blast said that cash would be just fine. How that took three hours I don't know. I might've been on a need-to-know basis and I didn't need to know.

I met Galante later that year. Another sit-down had been scheduled between Galante and a member of the President Street crew, this time on Galante's home turf. The Knickerbocker Avenue meet involved a guy in the Gallo crew we called Louie the Syrian. His real name was Louie Hubella, and he was one of a handful of guys on President Street who not only weren't Sicilian but also weren't even Italian. He really came from Syria.

Louie was a stand-up guy and a charter member of the Gallo crew, tough as nails, a World War II veteran. He ran a sports book and lent money to Brooklyn's Arab population, then clustered along Atlantic Avenue, the major thoroughfare that separated Downtown Brooklyn from South Brooklyn. When Louie wasn't on the block, he was at the Court Terrace Lounge on Atlantic Avenue conducting business.

Back in the day, Louie had been one of Joey Gallo's favorites. Joey appreciated guys who could scare the shit out of people. Joey could do it, and so could Louie the Syrian. When Louie cracked his knuckles, guys shit their pants.

Joey ran a massive protection racket. Half the businesses in Brooklyn paid Joey to leave them alone. Joey knew he could trust Louie. If a guy owed money, Louie came back with it. If a guy didn't want to be "protected," Louie convinced him of the wisdom in paying the money. But that was earlier. By 1975, Louie was the consigliere of the Gallo crew and he had been one of Joey Gallo's pall bearers.

The deal with Galante had nothing to do with gambling or loansharking, however. Appropriately, considering the way Galante made his millions, it involved drugs. But, in this case, it wasn't heroin; it was hashish.

Louie had gotten a load of hashish off a merchant ship floating in the waters somewhere off Red Hook. The men on the boat threw the hash overboard, and Louie retrieved it. But there was too much—so much that Louie couldn't get rid of it all through his own people. He only knew one guy who could snap his fingers and distribute a shitload of hash and that was Galante. Thus, the meeting at Galante HQ in Bushwick.

I drove Louie to the meet. Goombadiel came along, too, and rode in the front with me.

The meet was at Joe and Mary's Italian-American Restaurant on Knickerbocker Avenue, which is famous now because of what happened there later, but at the time it was just another Italian restaurant just like a thousand others I'd been in.

Joe and Mary's looked tiny from the outside because it was narrow, only about twenty feet wide, tucked between a pizza parlor and a lawyer's office. But it was deep, long, and in the back there was a patio where diners could eat in the fresh air and sunshine. It was also a place where the diners did not have to worry about electronic surveillance devises.

When we first got there, I went out on the patio briefly. It didn't mean anything at the time, but later I'd realize the importance of the spot. While the meeting was going on, Goombadiel and I sat inside with Baldo Amato, one of the Knickerbocker Zips, and had espresso and cannoli on the house.

At the meeting, I was later told, Louie the Syrian asked Galante if he could take the ton of hashish we had lying around. Galante said no, but he knew someone who could. After the Knickerbocker Avenue meet, we packed up two cars with the hashish, which came in bricks that weighed three pounds apiece. Galante's cut was 20 percent.

A sidenote: On September 2, 1974, I was out on the sidewalk on President Street when Louie the Syrian Hubella was shot. I had turned my back to him for a second, heard the shot, and turned back to see him on the ground bleeding from the head. He was taken to Long Island College Hospital and reported in poor condition. Nine days later I was standing at the corner of President and Columbia Streets when Punchy Illiano was shot in the neck and shoulder as he was buying lunch from the hot-dog guy on the corner. Louie the Syrian and Punchy were both in the hospital for more than a month. Punchy was never the same, suffered nerve damage that would affect him for the rest of his life.

After that, I spent months with my head on a swivel. The shootings had nothing to do with Galante, though. It was Colombo-Gallo War shit, a sniper friend of Carmine "The Snake" Persico trying to take out the President Street Boys one by one with rifle fire.

During September of 1974, the FBI noted that Underboss Nicky Glasses was getting out of prison just as Rusty Rastelli was scheduled to go in and theorized that Nicky might take over as Bonanno acting boss when that happened.

On September 6, the feds noticed that John Gotti and Carmine Galante were simultaneously physically present in a joint called Humperdinck's Supper Club on Northern Boulevard in Bayside, Queens. Gotti owned the place. Galante was visiting.

The feds knew that Gotti and Galante had met in prison and were confused when Galante's reported archenemy Philip Rastelli also entered the club. The place wasn't big enough for the three to avoid one another, but if there was a meeting no one knows what was discussed.

Interestingly, the club would, in 1976, convert into a disco known as Elephas and become the scene on June 26, 1977, of the penultimate attack by the terror cult known as Son of Sam. (If you thought David Berkowitz was the lone Son of Sam killer, you should read my co-author Michael Benson's book *The Wicked King Wicker*.) The victims were shot with Sam's trademark .44 Bulldog while making out in a car parked outside the club. They were twenty-year-old Sal Lupo and seventeen-year-old Judy Placido. Both recovered from their wounds.

Three days after the Humperdinck's meeting, Galante appeared before a federal grand jury in the Southern District of New York.

"Rat out, Galante; everybody's doing it."

"Fuck you."

Galante refused to answer questions.

By this time, the entire underworld had become convinced that Galante was a force of nature, a guy who was going to push and push until he was stopped. And there was only one way to stop him.

On December 9, 1974, Galante appeared before yet another federal grand jury, Eastern District of New York, where he again refused to answer questions. He invoked the Fifth Amendment to all questions except for his name and address. Why did they bother?

CHAPTER TWENTY-SIX
Power Hungry

GALANTE'S TAILS WERE ALWAYS THERE. Galante ignored them. Initial reports said that Galante's busy daily itinerary was similar to his movements before he went away, so they correctly assumed that not much had changed.

One new stop on his daily routine was in Bath Beach, probably a card game. Galante's favorite hangout spot when he got out was the Bath Beach Civic Association located at Bay 11th Street and Bath Avenue in Bath Beach, Brooklyn.

The club belonged to Bonanno capo Anthony Spero, who, unlike many who kept pigeons, cared for three hundred or so exotic birds up on the roof. The feds kept track of the comings and goings at the club and said that associates of the Gambino, Genovese, and Columbo crime families all hung out there.

Galante's criminal career received another boost on March 5, 1975, when Philip Rastelli, his nephew Louis Rastelli, Anthony DeStefano, and Carl Petrole were all indicted by a federal grand jury regarding their lunch-wagon racket.

The following day, Rusty was arrested and taken before Federal Judge Thomas C. Platt, who released him on a personal bond of $50,000. In court, Rastelli denied having anything to do with organized crime and insisted he was a $200/week employee of CAI Trucking.

Asked his marital status, Rusty left out the messy details. He said that he had been a single man ever since a quickie Mexican divorce in 1965.

On March 16, 1975, Rusty's nephew Louis Rastelli, named in the lunch-wagon indictment, was found dead with a .357 Magnum in his lap. The official manner of death was ruled suicide. Who knows? Maybe it was.

A year earlier, Rusty had lost a stepson to a mob hit; now the nephew was dead from a bullet through the head—and again the finger of suspicion was pointed at Carmine Galante.

Galante stayed out of trouble with the law until March 27, 1975, when he traveled to Florida. He checked into the Diplomat Hotel, with spectacular ocean views, on South Ocean Boulevard in Hollywood, Florida, between Miami Beach and Fort Lauderdale. The Diplomat, at that time, was a popular meeting spot for crooks who needed privacy and anonymity.

As these things go, after a while it stopped being quite so private. It was so popular that various law enforcement agencies had a pretty much permanent stakeout across the street, keeping track of the comings and goings. Many gangsters, but there was special excitement when Galante entered the lobby.

Galante checked in at the Diplomat but failed to register in Florida as an ex-felon. That was a violation of a Florida State statute, and a week after he arrived Galante was arrested by agents of the Broward County Sheriff's Office Organized Crime Task Force, acting on a tip from the FBI shadows. Galante did not resist arrest and, after posting $500 bond, was released. He gave his address as Waverly Place in Greenwich Village.

Around this time, an FBI informant whispered into a special agent's ear that Galante was now boss of the Bonannos.

On April 2, 1975, Galante voluntarily appeared at the sheriff's office and registered as a felon. Later that day, he re-appeared at the Diplomat Hotel, registered as Carmine Galante, and gave as his address the East 38th Street apartment that he shared with Ann. He was assigned room 110.

Authorities in Florida wanted badly to find a reason to put Galante back behind bars but came up only with information that Galante "might" own stocks and bonds under a pseudonym, that being Steven Schwartz.

Rastelli's problems were much worse. He was out on bail, already convicted of loansharking. On June 6, 1975, the last of Rastelli's appeals fell through. He was ordered to begin his four-year incarceration on July 8. He did not flee but rather took his medicine. As had been done before and since, Rastelli ran his rackets from behind bars, using members of his family (brothers Marty and Carmine), and trusted friends such as soldier Joseph Charles Massino to relay messages to the outside.

By this time, Galante no longer spent time with his first wife and family, but he did take care of them financially. On paper anyway, Helen was an officer and received funds from the Alpha Investment Corporation in Dorval, Quebec, Canada. The principal of that corporation was Louis Greco, one of Galante's old partners in Montreal. Helen was also associated in Bonfire Limited, on DeLane Boulevard in Montreal. And back in 1962, Helen told authorities that she owned half interest in the ABC Pretzel Corporation, located on Kosciuszko Street in Brooklyn.

On June 28, 1975, Galante's eldest daughter from his second family, twenty-three-year-old Mary Lou, was married to Craig Trobiano at Our Savior Catholic Church on Park Avenue in Manhattan at 3:00 p.m.

After the ceremony, cocktails were served at 5:30 in the Regency Room, then dinner at the Cotillion Room, both in the luxurious skyscraper Pierre Hotel, sticking forty-one stories up at East 61st Street and Fifth Avenue in Manhattan, across the street from Central Park.

The hotel was so tall that for a few years, before they moved to the Empire State Building, ABC Television had its broadcast tower atop the Pierre. As for the Trobiano wedding, there were "only" 160 guests, an intimate affair as far as mob weddings go.

At the reception, there was a line of men paying their respects to Lilo, who accepted the tributes with a puffed-out chest and billowing cigar. He looked like a mini-Mussolini.

The choice of location was interesting. In 1972, three years earlier, the Pierre was the site of *The Guinness Book of World Records'* largest heist, $27 million, reportedly orchestrated by members of the Lucchese Family.

If you want to check out the ballroom at the Pierre, watch the movie *Scent of a Woman*. That's where Al Pacino does the tango.

In August 1975, Galante flew to Los Angeles, where he met with some of the guys running the lucrative Southern California porn business. At that time, Gambino had porn sewn up on the West Coast, with Gambino's former bodyguard, seventy-one-year-old Ettore "Tony Russo" Zappi, running the show out of North Hollywood in the Valley.

Galante's porn guy was Mickey Zaffarano, who was worming his way in. According to sources inside the Anaheim Police Department, Galante wanted a piece of the action. An informant revealed that, along with cutting himself a slice of the porn pie, Galante had a scheme whereby he would consolidate Lucchese and Colombo guys on the West Coast into their own family, one that he would father.

Those of you who remember the 1970s recall that porn was everywhere. The local neighborhood theaters that used to show second-run features now showed XXX movies. Times Square went all porn. Dirty bookstores spotted strip malls in cities from coast to coast.

And there was a reason for this. During that decade the porn biz became organized like never before, like a mini-Hollywood, with studios and production and distribution all organized in something that mirrored legitimate corporate structure.

Every step of the way the companies had different names, different ownership, so if the authorities took a keen look at it, they'd fail to see that it was all connected. But it was. And it was turning into Big Business.

During his stay in Southern California, Galante visited Disneyland, FBI shadows in tow. According to reports, Galante walked around the amusement park in a white T-shirt, a "Coney Island" baseball cap, and puffing at a cigar.

The visit couldn't have been for pleasure alone, however, as he regularly stopped at pay phones throughout the day to presumably talk business. He also strolled up and down Disney's Main Street and took a crack at driving a go-kart around a track, something he did just as recklessly as when he'd driven actual cars.

Galante's "more for me" tour included stops in Reno and Lake Tahoe, but he returned east in time for his niece's wedding on August 28 in Wethersfield, Connecticut. While the wedding was going on inside the Church of the Incarnation on Prospect Street, the FBI was outside taking down license-plate numbers.

That summer Galante built a summer home on the northeast corner of Tulip Avenue and Wakeman Road in Hampton Bays, New York. The new house was described as "one-family" and was valued at approximately $60,000.

When it was complete, he moved his daughter Mary Lou and her new husband into the house. Galante himself liked to spend weekends there, where he grew a surprisingly lovely garden, exercising a green thumb he'd developed during his twelve years under federal supervision. He also used the Hampton Bays home for at least one summit meeting, when he and Cousin Moey hosted Russell A. Bufalino, the renowned out-of-town boss who ran the Pennsylvania rackets.

When Galante and the feds on his trail bumped into each other, there was a surprisingly friendly chat. Galante wanted them to understand. He'd gone straight. He was a legitimate businessman, owner of the Abco Vending Company of West New York, New Jersey—

coin-operated machines—and a Little Italy dry-cleaning shop. He said he mostly cared for his family and tended to the tomatoes in his daughter's garden in Hampton Bays. He was older and he was enjoying life.

The guys selling drugs for Galante were having a tough time of it in 1975. Naturally, Galante thought it was Rastelli making the trouble—and he was probably correct. On September 7, thirty-eight-year-old Carmine Consalvo, who happened to be Carmine Galante's godson, "committed suicide" by plunging off the balcony of a twenty-fourth-floor luxury apartment in Fort Lee, New Jersey.

Consalvo had gotten himself into a jam. He'd been indicted as part of a heroin-importing conspiracy worth $30 million. They had him by the nut hairs, and he was in a position to improve his lot in life if he sang.

Sometimes when that happens, and it gets out that it's happened, guys are taken off the board simply because they *might* rat. It's a pre-emptive move. So, whether he jumped or was tossed, he wasn't going to flip.

On November 11, a twenty-seven-year-old Galante loyalist named Mario Paniccioli of Staten Island was found murdered in Brooklyn. Paniccioli, an alleged hit man among other things, was at the time of his death on his way to court, where he was on trial for the murder of a twenty-seven-year-old bartender named Eugene Glabick in a shootout linked to cigarette-smuggling operations. Jury selection was to begin that morning.

A truckload of bootleg butts had been hijacked in February 1975, leading to a bloody beef. The hijackers were reportedly John Consola, twenty-seven, and Joseph Doria, thirty-eight. Less than twenty-four hours after the cigarette-napping, Consola was shot five times by Paniccioli while sitting at the bar of Club 24 on 86th Street and Twenty-Fourth Avenue in Bensonhurst. He survived, but Glabick, who tried to come to his aid, was shot dead. Only hours later, the other hijacker, Doria, was found liquidated in a Staten Island woods.

Doria's brother owned Club 24. Paniccioli, who had a record dating back to 1966 when he was caught in an Upstate New York town trying to pass a counterfeit ten-spot in a snack bar, was arrested and charged with the Club 24 shootings, but the justice system never got a crack at him. Street justice was too swift.

Paniccioli was in a car—dressed for court in a black suit and tie, white shirt—driving along tree-lined Bedford Avenue between Glenwood and Farragut Roads near Brooklyn College in the peaceful Midwood neighborhood at nine in the morning when two shots shattered his windshield. Wounded, he jumped out of the car and tried to make a run for it.

The gunman, who witnesses said looked to be no older than a teenager and was wearing a fur cap, dropped to a knee, held his automatic pistol with both hands for better aim, and squeezed off eight shots, which dropped the fleeing Paniccioli. The killer then stood over his fallen victim in front of a home on Bedford Avenue and pumped his final two bullets into Paniccioli's head. The killer took off on foot and presumably escaped in a waiting car. Police reporting to the scene found eight shell casings at the scene.

Thirty-two-year-old Frank Consalvo, Carmine's little brother, also died by falling off a building. What are the chances? Frank plunged to his death in December 1975 when he fell from a fifth-floor window of a Little Italy tenement. Frank C. had once been Gambino underboss Aniello Dellacroce's driver-bodyguard. It was a message from Galante to Dellacroce, reminding him that Lilo hated his fucking guts.

There was more where that came from. Also bumped off during that time was a gambling operator called J. J. Frankel. Two stiffs were discovered in the Dyker Heights section of Brooklyn during the first week of October 1975, perhaps a message to Galante from Dellacroce. *Hate you, too.*

The corpses were found in an abandoned vehicle parked on 80th Street between Tenth and Eleventh Avenues. Each body was wrapped in a blanket and tied with a cord. They had each been shot in the head, no more than twenty-four hours before they were discovered. Police noted that the bodies were found just around the corner from Alphonse "Allie Boy" Persico, a Columbo captain, who police theorized was on Galante's side. The van had been reported stolen in easternmost Bath Beach, just south of Dyker.

The stiffs were identified as thirty-three-year-old George Adamo of Brooklyn and twenty-eight-year-old Charles LaRocca of Jackson Heights, Queens. Significantly, they were the guys suspected of tossing Carmine Consalvo off his balcony. They were both known cocaine dealers. And they had recently defected from Gambino and pledged allegiance to Galante.

The double-whacking in the Dyker Heights van was a not-so-subtle message from the rest of the underworld that Galante's plans to rule everything were not going to be achieved without opposition.

October 1976, significantly, was also the month that Gambino died and was placed in a $7,000 bronze casket at the Cusimano & Russo Funeral Home in Gravesend, Brooklyn, then transported to his well-attended funeral at Our Lady of Grace Church.

As far as the authorities could tell, no one knew who was running the Bonanno Family in 1976. Some informants were saying that Rastelli was still running things despite being in a fed pen. Others said that Galante was the boss, or acting boss, or whatever. It was enough to make cops wonder if the Bonannos were even a cohesive unit anymore but rather a split army, made of two (or more) factions that didn't get along.

In January 1976, Rastelli, already in prison, went to trial for the lunch-wagon conspiracy charges. He was tried with only two co-defendants, DeStefano and Gary Petrole, as nephew Louis Rastelli got juked. The trial took several months and all three were convicted. At his sentencing hearing, Rastelli was asked by Judge Thomas C. Pratt if he wanted to make a statement.

"Yes, Your Honor. At no time did I think I was doing anything wrong," Rusty said.

Judge Pratt didn't believe him and sentenced him to ten years, tacked onto the sentence he was already serving, and fined him $50,000. With Rastelli now off the streets for some time, Galante ally Nicky Glasses took charge of Rastelli's sewn-up-tight union, International Brotherhood of Teamsters Local 814.

CHAPTER TWENTY-SEVEN

Consorting with Joey Beck

BACK IN 1969, THE U.S. JUSTICE DEPARTMENT set up a "Strike Force" to direct the federal campaign against organized crime. That force was on its last legs in August 1976 (it would be closed down in November) but still active.

On August 2, Galante was subpoenaed by an attorney for the "Strike Force," Eastern District of New York, requiring that Galante appear before a special grand jury. Not again. As usual, he'd give only his name and age. And even the second question made him nervous. Give your age wrong and suddenly they want to deport you back to Italy, where running the Bonanno Family long-distance would be a pain in the ass.

Galante told the server that he understood the nature of the subpoena and would comply.

Getting out of prison after twelve years, there are a lot of loose ends to tie up. Even years after his release Galante was investigating and, when necessary, punishing everyone who worked for him when he moved to the Rock. Had they continued to do the right thing? If not, there was hell to pay.

Which brings us to the case of Andimo Pappadio, sixty-two years old, a Lucchese capo that ran the Manhattan Garment District, becoming an unofficial and reluctant acting boss while Tommy Three-Finger was in prison doing fifteen years for narcotics. That was in

1976. But back before Galante went away, Pappadio worked for him, in the junk business. Galante learned that Pappadio, himself with a record that dated back to 1935, exploited the fact that Galante went to prison. He used Galante's absence from the street as a ploy to move in on Lilo's gambling biz. Now Galante was back and Pappadio was toast.

On Friday, September 25, 1976, Pappadio and his wife returned to his Lido Beach, Long Island, home. They were in her Cadillac, getting back after a night out. As they pulled into the driveway, Pappadio spotted the maroon sedan parked across the street. Some boys were inside.

"What the fuck is this?" the bodyguardless Pappadio said.

If he thought of himself as a gangland target, he didn't show it. He told his wife to go into the house while he went to see who was watching his house. She did as she was told, and he crossed the street to confront the occupants of the maroon sedan.

But they confronted him first. A .38 automatic poked out the opened car window and a fusillade of shots dropped Pappadio, who was left dead in the middle of the street. As the car peeled out and hauled ass down Eva Drive, Pappadio's wife came running out of the house screaming her brains out.

A joint force of police from Nassau and Suffolk Counties interviewed Pappadio's friends and relatives, but no one had much to say. They were shocked: Pappadio was such a nice guy. He didn't have an enemy in the world.

A crime-scene investigator scanned the neighbor's lawn with a metal detector and dug up a .38 slug. The street was a madhouse. Neighbors were out watching the activity, and a steady stream of cars rolled by, people hoping to see some blood.

"We've talked to many people and, frankly, we're learning more from reading the newspapers," said the lead investigator, to a newspaper reporter. What the papers were saying was that Pappadio was caught in a "power play" between Galante and Dellacroce, involving a controlling piece of the Eastern Seaboard's heroin trade.

The murder of Andimo Pappadio remains unsolved.

*   *   *

On November 3, 1976, Galante struck again at Rastelli's army. He ordered a hit on Bonanno capo seventy-year-old Pietro Licata. Whacking made guys was supposed to be done only with Commission permission. Galante said fuck the Commission.

Licata was an old-time Sicilian mobster, whose trademark was that he always dressed in all white, a style that earned him the nickname the Walking Ghost. He was of the mind-set that organized crime should lay off drugs and stick to loansharking and gambling, which of course made him against everything Galante stood for.

A hit team staked out Licata's two-story brick home on 68th Road in Middle Village, Queens. When they got there, no one was home, so they waited. Just a few minutes before midnight, a 1974 Cadillac pulled to the curb in front of the house. Licata and his wife got out and were approaching an ornamental iron gate in front of the house when a man with a shotgun stepped out of the shadows and shot him at close range, killing him instantly.

Because the hit took place so soon after the natural-causes death of Carlo Gambino, police thought this hit might be part of a power-shuffle in the Gambino Family. A high-ranking police official, requesting anonymity, told a reporter, "Robbery was definitely not the motive. This appears to be a shuffle in the mob following Gambino's death."

Smarter cops thought the hit might have been connected to the Pappadio hit. The NYPD was also talking with New Jersey police about a possible connection between the Licata hit and a shooting on Route 80 near Danville, New Jersey, that took place that same night. Police investigated a car parked alongside the road and found two men inside, one shot in the neck.

The victim in the Route 80 shooting was forty-six-year-old John W. Carr of Maspeth, Queens, not far from Middle Village. Carr was taken to Saint Clare's Hospital in Danville and listed in satisfactory condition. Also in the car with Carr was thirty-one-year-old Vincent Santoto, also from Maspeth. The men told police they were driving along when a car pulled up alongside them and shot at them.

Not everyone agreed as to who Licata was and how important he was in the overall scheme of things. A second law enforcement official, possibly FBI, said that Licata was an associate rather than a capo and "hadn't done anything in years."

All that speculation was proof that law enforcement and the press were still not clear on what was going on behind the scenes in the American Mafia. You couldn't tell the players without a scorecard, and their last scorecard (Apalachin) was now more than a decade old.

(The campaign to annihilate the portion of the Bonanno Family that held allegiance to Rastelli would continue for years—even after Galante was gone. In September 1982, two of Licata's nephews, brothers, were bumped off in Ridgewood, Queens. They were forty-four-year-old Joseph Licata and his kid brother, twenty-eight-year-old Andrew Licata. The brothers were sitting in the family's café, Caffe Licata, in the Ridgewood section of Queens, only blocks away from Galante's turf along the Knickerbocker Avenue strip in Bushwick, Brooklyn. It was a Wednesday evening when three men wearing ski masks entered the café and opened fire with two shotguns and a handgun. The Licatas were pronounced dead at the scene. A third man, a customer in the joint, was wounded in the leg and taken to Wyckoff Hospital in stable condition. One investigator at the scene, confronted by a tabloid reporter, said, "There will be more killings unless they all fall in line and back Rastelli.")

In 1976, Galante listed as one of his legit businesses Safrajet Limited Incorporated at 80 Wall Street, but when FBI surveillance tried to determine what went on there they found that there was no Safrajet at that address.

The pattern seemed to be that Galante was winning the war with Rastelli. In February 1977, three of New York's daily newspapers ran articles discussing the growing power of Carmine Galante.

A few weeks later, *Time* magazine ran an article describing Galante as the "Boss of Bosses" on the New York crime scene. In reality, Galante could not be in charge of the system because he was functioning outside the system. If reporters had known that, they wouldn't have called him Boss of Bosses or even just Boss.

Truth was, Galante was persona non grata, not long for this earth.

On April 6, 1977, at 5:00 p.m., Joey Beck, described by the feds as Carmine Galante's "number-one man," was admitted as a patient at the Baylor University Medical Center in Dallas, Texas. Two days later, Galante flew to the Dallas–Fort Worth airport on American Airlines Flight 295. He visited the hospital and flew back to New York later in the day.

By this time, Galante was spending weekends in the Hamptons but staying in New York during the week. His new hangout was the Paris Bar and Grill, Cousin Moey's new joint on South Street in the fish district of the city. The joint was having problems. For no apparent reason, the Paris began to endure frequent visits from the city Health Department, threatening to shut the place down if this, this, and this—violations of the city health code—weren't fixed pronto.

Galante also hung out at the Crescent Lounge on Avenue U in Gravesend, Brooklyn.

While brooding in those joints, Galante and Cousin Moey thought up ways to expand the empire. Galante had heard that the Gambinos controlled all of the mozzarella in Pennsylvania but lacked the enforcement to prevent interlopers. Without the mootzarelle, you couldn't have pizza.

"You know, Lilo, that used to be Bonanno," Angelo said.

"Yeah," Galante said.

"You're away, Joey is in Tucson sipping espresso and reading a newspaper, Gambino moved in on the cheese."

"Yeah."

"We should take it back."

"Yeah."

So, Galante sent some boys to Pennsylvania to shake down pizza parlors.

"No, you ain't gonna get the mootzarelle from them no more; you gonna get it from us—or else something bad happens."

Now there were a few pizza makers who feared the Gambinos more than Galante, but they soon learned their lesson. During the evening of July 6, 1977, two youthful Bonanno hoods drove to Giuseppe's Pizza Restaurant in Ambler, Pennsylvania. The young men doused the joint with 210 gallons of gas, enough to blow up a city block.

Who knows what the arsonists' plans were?

What happened was that the whole thing went up with a terrific explosion, while the arsonists were still on the premises. One of them was blown to smithereens, leaving nothing large enough to even approach identification.

The other one, who was only in several pieces, was identified as the twenty-two-year-old nephew of Bonanno soldier Giovanni Fiordilino. The unexpected deaths didn't concern Galante. Now he didn't have to pay them.

More importantly, as far as Galante was concerned, many pizzerias in Pennsylvania decided they didn't want their cheese from the Gambinos anymore. That was what counted.

Years later, a Bonanno insider would testify that this time period was one of growing power for Galante, who was inducting new members into the fold, handing out buttons left and right to guys who were faithful to him and, in theory, enemies of Philip Rastelli.

In July 1977, Vincent Papa—the guy who went to prison after stealing $70 million worth of heroin from NYPD property clerk's office, the heroin that had been seized by police and became the MacGuffin for the movie *The French Connection*—was killed inside the federal prison in Atlanta, the same prison where Galante had recently fixed handball games.

On July 31, Galante fell down the stairs in his house in the Hamptons and had to go to the emergency room of Southhampton General Hospital, where he was treated for a pulled groin muscle and released.

*   *   *

On August 4, a special agent from the FBI served Galante a subpoena. At the time, Galante was home with Ann at his East 38th
Street address. The subpoena ordered that he appear before a federal
grand jury, Southern District of Miami, on August 8 at 10:00 a.m.

Galante complied, but when he got before the federal grand jury
he invoked his Fifth Amendment rights and zipped his lip. He was
granted limited immunity and ordered by a U.S. District Court
Judge to testify. Again, Galante refused, and this time he was cited
for contempt. Galante was arrested and freed on $50,000 bail.

Now, anyone who was around New York City during the summer of
1977 remembers it was different, weird. The back pages of the tabloids were dominated by the roller-coaster soap opera that was that
year's New York Yankees, with George Steinbrenner, Billy Martin,
and Reggie Jackson as the key players. And the front pages of the
tabloids were dominated by the Son of Sam, a group of weirdos who
were bumping off white kids in nice outer-borough neighborhoods
and then taunting the police and the press with well-written letters of
terror.

Galante didn't like that one of the hits was on kids who'd been
dancing at the old Humperdinck's. He put out an open hit on the Son
of Sam, and he didn't exactly keep it a secret.

"MOB JOINS HUNT," one tabloid headline read.

That prompted a comment from the mayor. As far as mob vigilan-
tism went, Mayor Abraham Beame wanted everyone to know he had
never encouraged that sort of thing. He had welcomed FBI opera-
tives who wanted to help out in his city. He was grateful for the state
police's assistance and the help from the various law enforcement
agencies in the metropolitan area, but he had asked politely that the
Mafia patrol stand down.

"We don't need the help of the mob," he said.

As it turned out, no one was accidentally shot and killed because
of the open hit, which was a miracle in itself. The police eventually
found David Berkowitz in possession of the killer .44 Bulldog.

Berkowitz took the rap for all of the Son of Sam shootings, allowing authorities to tie it up in a nice bow.

On August 24, Galante returned to federal court, where he for the umpteenth time refused to testify. This time, the federal judge told him that he would be committed to the custody of a U.S. Marshal until he decided to answer specific questions or until the termination of the grand jury, a period not to exceed eighteen months.

After that extensive investigation into Galante's movements, it was his lifelong friendship with Joey Beck that would do him in. It was a case the feds could prove through photographic surveillance. Beck was in the hospital. Galante went to visit him. Beck was a felon, so boom! That was a violation.

Most of the time, because Galante's life was in constant danger, his Zips kept his movements secret. But October 11, 1977, was different. There'd been a leak, and everyone knew where Galante was going to be. He was turning himself in to the U.S. Marshals office.

The sun had just come up but hadn't reached the tops of the buildings yet, and a crowd of people, there to see Lilo for a wide variety of reasons, was gathering, sleepy, with steaming coffee containers in their tight grip.

The location was Little Italy, Foley Square, just a block and a half west of Mulberry Street. Newspaper columnist Pete Hamill was there. He called Galante an "aging bum." Some of those in the crowd had cameras around their necks, not for taking snapshots, but pro boxes with long lenses that were easy to remove and swap out.

It was chilly. In the park a couple of fitness-minded New Yorkers did calisthenics. A group of Chinese senior citizens who met weekly at a nearby Catholic church were huddled for warmth waiting for someone to show up with a key. They didn't know from Galante. Their junkie kids were putting money into the man's pocket, and they were clueless as to who he was. "Mob." That was all they knew. You could tell by the car, the strut. Names didn't matter.

Galante of course had been causing mayhem in Manhattan for

decades, but his celebrity status was new. The crowd had largely been attracted by the series of newspaper and magazine articles written about Lilo, quoting inside sources saying he wasn't just a boss, but Boss of Bosses, a terrifying notion because of the blank swath of aggression that was Carmine Galante's dimly lit psyche. What was more fascinating than that? So much power in the hands of a barely human psychopath.

As the crowd waited, even more journalists arriving by the minute, rumors circulated that they shouldn't have to wait long. Officially, Galante was to arrive at nine o'clock, but the inside dope said he would come as early as seven thirty.

The inside dope was on the money. At seven thirty sharp a Mark V Lincoln Continental pulled up to the curb, New York plates 605 XUA.

The car's eight-track sound system was playing *Live & Love Italian Style*, by Jimmy Roselli. Many Italian Americans at that time liked Roselli better even than Sinatra. Sinatra pissed some off because he wouldn't sing in Italian. A cassette tape of Diana Ross songs was on the front seat.

The driver got out, circled around, opened the back door, and Galante emerged, a cold-blooded anachronism, wearing a fedora with the brim pulled way down. This was 1977. Businessmen had not worn fedoras in years. Right behind him was his daughter.

The pair walked efficiently to a door that had no handle on the outside. On the door was the sign: "AUTHORIZED PERSONNEL ONLY." As if by magic, the door opened just as Galante and his daughter got to it, let them inside, and then closed again.

Just like that, the show was over, and the crowd dispersed.

Inside the building, Galante was questioned by federal agents. At his side were his attorneys Roy Cohn and Michael Rosen. They told Federal Judge Robert J. Ward that Galante "regularly, religiously, and scrupulously adhered to the conditions of his parole." All he wanted to do was work in his daughter's garden out on Long Island. What was wrong with that?

The government begged to differ. They wanted to know about his relationship with Joey Beck. And, if somehow Galante managed to skate on the charges of consorting with Joey Beck, unlikely, the feds told a grand jury they were also able to establish that Galante had consorted with other felons since he was released on parole, those being Vito DeFillipo, Alphonse "Sonny Red" Indelicato, Cousin Moey, and "King of Porn" Mickey Zaffarano, who owned a strip of Times Square porn theaters and lived in an apartment above the Pussycat theater.

Now we know that Galante and Joe Beck had been friends since they were kids. One guy built like a fire hydrant and the other like a mini-giraffe. Joey Beck was now seventy-one years old, and his neck had grown no shorter, his head less bulbous, or his Adam's apple less intimidating. He remained a walking nightmare, just now an old one.

When Judge Ward asked about Beck, Galante shrugged his shoulders and said he didn't know the bum, which was the only answer. Forget the fact that they'd been seen together not just recently but going back to the days when they were teenagers in East Harlem.

Terms of Galante's parole said that he wasn't even allowed to be on the same side of the street as hoods like Beck, who was a felon with a capital *F*, having once done a federal stint for selling a million bucks' worth of counterfeit traveler's checks.

It didn't matter that Galante denied knowing Beck. The feds had photographic evidence taken at the Dallas hospital. Galante had been given a chance to explain himself and had lied instead.

The U.S. Marshal proclaimed him in violation of his federal parole and back to prison he went. By that night Galante was in the Metropolitan Correctional Facility, which was the federal prison in Lower Manhattan.

After his client turned himself in, Galante's lawyer Roy Cohn petitioned the Federal District Court to release Galante on bail pending a full bail revocation hearing. Judge Robert J. Ward scheduled a hearing to discuss the bail release question for October 14, 1977. This was denied and Galante sat in jail.

He was sent to a medium-security facility in Danbury, Connecticut. He was supposed to finish the narcotics sentence, which ran to 1982—although, as it turned out, Galante would not remain behind bars for nearly that long.

The investigation into Galante and his parole violation produced some uncomfortable truths. For one thing, it turned out that Galante's parole officer was on the Bonanno Family payroll, bought and sold.

The PO was forty-six-year-old James Gannon, whose title was chief of pre-trial services for the U.S. Probation Office. With the revelations regarding his corruption, Gannon was quietly fired. He made $28,600 a year as a probation official, and the Bonannos added to that about $1,000 a year for ten years to look the other way if Galante screwed up a little bit on his parole terms.

Gannon lost his job, but he was not arrested after he agreed to testify. He stunned the court when he said that one of the bribes was delivered on the steps of the very courthouse they were in, the U.S. Courthouse at Foley Square in the city.

Gannon didn't figure to skate. In addition to accepting bribes, he hadn't paid his taxes either. The feds had their hooks into him, and the feds never give up. He ended up doing six months.

It wasn't the first time that Lilo's jam evolved into a bribery scandal. It had happened after his upstate traffic ticket, and it happened here. The way Galante's power worked was always an eye-opener, and people's minds boggled at the notion that Galante had infiltrated the court system with a top probationary official in his hip pocket.

Also arrested and in deep shit was fifty-nine-year-old Joseph Kaufman, accused of being the guy who delivered the undisclosed amount of cash to Gannon on the courthouse steps. Kaufman gave a building on Prince Street as his home address, but that turned out to be the social club that Kaufman frequented. From then on, and for a long time, the detectives of the Manhattan District Attorney Robert Morgenthau's office kept a twenty-four-seven surveillance on the joint.

During the hearing, Galante's attorneys tried to associate the campaign to put him behind bars with the mob fever that had spread across America and the world following the release of Francis Ford Coppola's *Godfather* movies.

"All of those stories about the Mafia and the godfather are a creation of the media. . . ." That was their mantra.

On October 17, 1978, the *New York Post* ran a full-page headline that stated: "Galante Marked for Death in Prison: Feds Order 24 Hour Guard." According to the article, the chief U.S. probation officer, Morris Kuznesof, sent a letter to prison authorities recommending that Galante be placed in protective custody because "information has been received from a highly reliable source that an attempt to murder Galante is planned for Danbury."

The article also noted that Galante was not the only big-time mobster under federal custody who was getting extra security. Carmine Persico in Lewisburg, Pennsylvania, and John "Sonny" Franzese in Atlanta were also under special guard. The *Post* somehow got to Galante for a quote.

"Lilo, what do you think about reports that you are to be hit?"

"Baloney," Galante said, or a word to that effect.

The next day, Galante learned he was to be moved to solitary confinement.

"What the fuck for?" Galante balked.

"It's for your own good, Carmine," said Warden William Nelson.

The warden also dropped a press release that read in part: "Information has been received from a highly reliable source that an attempt to murder Mr. Galante will be made at my institution."

Galante was placed in solitary in a small cell and allowed only twenty minutes each day to exercise in a deserted corridor.

One of Lilo's most frequent visitors in Connecticut that October was Anthony Spero, Bonanno consigliere ever since Joe Bonanno moved to Tucson in 1968. Years before, Spero had been in Galante's crew, and they'd made a shitload of money together. Spero had visited Galante a few times at Lewisburg, too, so the suspicion was that

Spero was acting as a messenger, relaying Galante's orders to the troops.

Galante had dished it out and then dished it out some more, but he could read the writing on the wall. That baloney stuff, that was just an act. He knew there was a hit out on him. It was only a matter of time before he was taken off.

The following month, November 13, 1978, *Time* magazine ran an article about ongoing plans to have Galante whacked while he was a prisoner in Connecticut. The magazine also dropped the bombshell that, while Galante was incarcerated at the Metropolitan Correction Center in Manhattan during the spring of 1978 "two Mafia soldiers" were allowed to stand guard on a nightly basis outside Galante's cell. The MCC denied that anything resembling that had occurred.

"That's wrong," said MCC correctional supervisor Lieutenant Percy Pitzer. "We would never let something like that go on."

In Connecticut, Galante remained in isolation. Somebody told the *Post* that Galante had developed a bad case of nerves since he learned of the contract on his life. Again, a newspaper reporter got to Galante for a quote, this time offering a similar sentiment but not as euphemistic.

Galante reportedly said, "Bad case of nerves? Bullshit." He continued, "I begged the warden to give me an hour in the prison yard, but he said there's one of them out there that's going to kill me. Not here. Not in this place. Sure, these things happen. It's a way of life."

Galante said that the whole death threat bullshit had been manufactured by fed probation officials who wanted to damage his reputation so that the courts would not grant his appeal of his parole violation. During the interview, he denied being a part of the Mafia and denied that there was a Mafia.

As the autumn progressed, Galante became part of a tabloid scandal that involved mob bigwigs getting special treatment in federal facilities. Galante, along with Carmine "The Snake" Persico and Frank

Madonna, were said to have all sorts of goodies smuggled in to them, stuff that the average prisoner could only dream of, like meatballs and sauce, Italian cheeses and sausages, and cocaine. The drugs were not for consumption, not all of it anyway, but rather to pay off guards and otherwise earn favors inside the penitentiary. Guards were paid several hundred dollars apiece to bring in the contraband.

According to Assistant U.S. Attorney John Flannery, one of the guards, a twenty-six-year-old woman who lived on Avenue W in Brooklyn, took the extra income she made smuggling contraband to incarcerated mobsters and went on vacation in Aruba.

Prison officials first became aware of the steady stream of contraband being received by the top-echelon mob guys through a rat bastard squealer inside the pen, and they installed TV cameras and tape recorders to gather evidence against the guards. One day in late fall the party was over and a handful of prison guards were in deep trouble. And Galante had to do without his squeaky provolone.

On August 13, 1978, the *Daily News* reported that Lilo was still boss of the Bonannos even though he was away. Nicky Glasses his underboss. Who was Galante's consigliere? That depended on who you were talking to. The New York police said it was Joseph Buccellato, Galante's lieutenant who managed the Bushwick rackets, but the feds said it was Stefano Cannone, who hated Galante and backed Rastelli. (Cannone, in fact, would be one of the guys slapping backs at the afterparty following Galante's hit.)

From Connecticut, Galante was transferred to the fed pen in Michigan. No reason was given, but the move made it more difficult for Galante's messengers, like Spero, to get orders from him and deliver them to the streets of New York.

In December 1978, Galante was removed from his Michigan cell and transported to a courtroom in the Eastern District of New York to testify. The purpose was that same old wheeze: Galante was scheduled to testify before a federal grand jury.

Crazy is repeatedly trying the same thing and hoping the outcome would be different. The feds, when they called Galante into court, were crazy. What did they think was going to happen? Why they went through the motions was anyone's guess.

This time, just like always, he zipped his lips, and there was nothing for authorities to do but take him back to Michigan.

The transfer from Connecticut to Michigan had an unexpected benefit for Lilo. In Michigan, he befriended a lifer named Jerry "The Jew" Rosenberg, who'd been convicted of killing two during a holdup in 1962 and while behind bars earned two law degrees. He went to work on Galante's case. Rosenberg knew his shit. Lilo was as good as free.

Sure enough, on February 27, 1979, a federal judge decided that Galante had spent enough time behind bars and ordered him released. On March 1, Galante was released. Almost. There was some confusion about his sentence and the judge's order and Galante spent an additional week behind bars, finally emerging outside on March 7. He boarded a plane for Newark. As it turned out, Galante had seen his last of the inside of a prison, but he was to find out that things on the outside were even more dangerous. Galante was free to once again walk the streets of Brooklyn—but his hours were numbered.

On June 5, 1979, Nassau County investigators arrested a pair of Zips, two of Galante's bodyguards, The Tall Guy and Baldo Amato, as the men sat in a car outside the Greenhaven Mall in Massapequa. In the car, Nassau detectives found three loaded guns, a switchblade, two woolen masks, a plastic Halloween mask, two pairs of runner gloves, and a box of ammunition.

CHAPTER TWENTY-EIGHT

The Donnie Brasco Fiasco

WHAT WAS WRONG WITH THE BONANNOS? How did the family go from being an organized machine to the chaotic mess it became when Carmine Galante and Philip Rastelli were vying for control?

Well, there were two reasons:

One reason was Joe Bonanno's loss of control. Both before and after his exile to the Southwest, he was done as a boss, which left a power vacuum. The other reason, more subtle and insidious, was the work of one undercover FBI agent who knew how to walk the walk and talk the talk and got inside.

FBI undercover agent Joseph D. Pistone must have had gonads of steel. He volunteered for the most dangerous job in law enforcement. He was going to be a mole, working his way inside a pack of killers.

It would be more than a nine-to-five job. It meant that Pistone would have to practically change his identity. For the length of the mission, he'd no longer be himself. In many ways, it was more like being an actor than being a cop—an actor who could never leave the stage.

It was more like being a wartime spy than being a cop, and the chances were good that instant death would be his fate if the wire he wore under his clothes was discovered.

Pistone had no idea how long the job would last, maybe a week, maybe a year, maybe many years—but whatever the length, he could never relax. He could never let down his guard.

Along with new laws like RICO, the most effective tools the FBI used to combat organized crime were tax audits and undercover agents. Of the latter, none got further inside than Pistone.

Even before his mission began, Pistone had to study, so that he could react to all situations just as a real street kid might, a street kid mob soldier wannabe. There were a million ways in which something could go wrong, and it only took one to fuck up the mission and, perhaps, end Pistone's life.

Pistone ceased to exist. He was now Donnie Brasco, and he played the eager kid part perfectly and was given the usual starter job, which is hijacking trucks and stealing their contents. Trucks filled with dresses or furs were the best because the items were easily sold, despite being hot. If a guy wanted to give a fur to his goomara she didn't need to know it fell off a truck.

Brasco executed these crimes without a crack in his performance and earned trust with each job. Eventually he rose to the point where he had accrued firsthand knowledge of negotiations between the Bonannos and other crime families in New York and elsewhere.

Brasco became privy to the machinations of the massive heroin-importing system set up by Galante and others, and he survived to testify at the trial that brought a lot of guys down.

During Pistone's infiltration into the Bonannos, he often wore a wire—and even when he did not he'd write down the conversations he'd heard at night so he'd later be able to accurately testify about them in court.

One of the most memorable quotes Brasco recorded was by Benjamin "Lefty Guns" Ruggiero, who explained to Donnie why it was such a great thing to be a made man and an official member of the American Mafia.

Ruggiero said, "As a wiseguy, you can lie, cheat, and steal, all legitimately. You can do anything you want, and no one can say anything about it. Who wouldn't want to be a wiseguy?"

Brasco got to the point where he was ordered to "make his bones" so he would qualify to get a button. It was then that the feds called the mission off. Stealing dresses was one thing, but the feds couldn't be part of a murder, so they pulled the plug on the Donnie Brasco project.

The FBI knew that, even after the evidence was gathered, their case against the Bonannos would disintegrate if something happened to Joseph Pistone. To make sure nothing did, the feds handled it in a way the mobsters could understand. Two special agents visited the home of Anthony "Fat Tony" Salerno and said that nothing was to happen to Joseph Pistone or members of his family or else there would be "massive retaliation."

"You guys have a job to do," Salerno said. "You have my guarantee."

Salerno sent the word out. Pistone and his family were "off-limits"—and no harm did come to Pistone or his family.

As we'll see, much different treatment was in order for the Bonannos who were duped by Brasco's act and allowed him access to the information he testified to. Guys got whacked. Some guys got kicked out. Lefty Guns and his hijackers were arrested. As it turned out, Pistone didn't get a chance to testify against the Bonannos until 1981, by which time Carmine Galante was dead and Philip Rastelli in prison. Not only was the Bonanno the smallest and weakest of the Five Families by that time, but its failure to hold at the center was an argument that it had ceased to exist.

The Donnie Brasco case became famous when Pistone wrote a series of best-selling books: *Donnie Brasco: My Undercover Life in the Mafia* (1987), *Donnie Brasco: Deep Cover* (1999), *The Way of the Wiseguy* (2004), and *Donnie Brasco: Unfinished Business* (2007).

CHAPTER TWENTY-NINE

Dope War

A WAR IN THE BRONX RAGED during the spring of 1978, a war for control of a dope empire between Carmine Galante's crew and Vito Genovese, a guy who used to give Galante his orders—like whacking Carlo Tresca, for example. But that was thirty-five years earlier. During March and April 1978, a dozen New York goons were iced, and cops said at least seven of them were tied in with the Galante-Genovese conflict.

On April 21, 1978, the bullet-riddled body of twenty-five-year-old Louis Gioia was found in a black steamer trunk in a garage at 161st Street and River Avenue, within spitting distance of Yankee Stadium. Police were familiar with the garage, as it had been used in the past as a drop for stolen cars. Gioia, investigators learned, lived on Mulberry Street in Little Italy and moonlighted as a hit man for Joey Beck, Carmine Galante's most trusted partner. Folks from the neighborhood remembered Gioia as a wiseass kid, a tough kid, a kid who dreamed of making it big.

Of course, the authorities were on the outside looking in, but it seemed to them like the war began in March when feds seized more than a ton of weed in Florida. The bust burned Pasquale "Paddy Mac" Macchiarole, a fifty-eight-year-old captain in the Genovese Family, who had operations running in New York, New Jersey, and

Miami. Paddy Mac's New York rackets were operated out of the back room of his legit liquor store. He always had a variety of irons in the fire: freight, loans, nightclubs, gambling.

The bust was based on a phone tip from a top-echelon gangster, a guy who was "with" Carmine Galante. Paddy Mac ordered violent retaliation for Galante's sabotage—but he moved too slow and Galante got in the first shot.

Paddy Mac was quite the earner, with powerful friends. He was a friend of gambling czar Jimmy Napoli, who also had a piece of many rackets: gambling, shylocking, extortion, and dope.

Macchiarole got in bad trouble once, in the early 1970s. Among the joints he was shaking down was a nightclub near LaGuardia Airport called the Cloud Room. That earned him a beef with a thirty-nine-year-old African American named Conrad Greaves, who ran a series of nightclubs, including the Cloud Room and the Stadium Lounge near Yankee Stadium in the Bronx. The clubs were pulling in tens of thousands of dollars a week. Paddy Mac wanted some. Greaves paid once. The second time he said no. So Paddy Mac whacked him.

Paddy Mac was busted but ended up skating on the Greaves murder. Soon thereafter he made a fatal mistake when he tried to deal dope on the staked-out turf of Carmine Galante. It happened on one of those beautiful spring days that make you glad to be alive. Paddy Mac left his Queens home and disappeared. He was found three weeks later, hogtied, stabbed, thoroughly ventilated with hot lead, wrapped in plastic, and rolled inside a canvas tarp in the trunk of his new Lincoln Continental in a supermarket parking lot on Rockaway Parkway near the Canarsie Pier.

Paddy Mac's kid, John Macchiarole, a grown man, really, thirty-three years old, started mouthing off to anyone who would listen that he was going to avenge his father's death. He wasn't going to do shit. A few weeks later, John Macchiarole was also killed.

On April 14, an eight-member U.S. Parole Commission reduced Galante's penalty for "associating with known criminals" and ordered he be released in sixty days.

Galante's attorney Roy Cohn said, "It shows that this is still a government of laws and not men."

Galante was released in June 1978 but remained under the supervision of the Parole Commission.

On the same day that Paddy Mac's body was discovered, March 23, 1978, a forty-eight-year-old ex-con named Americus Scotese was whacked near his Brooklyn home. Scotese went out to walk his dog first thing in the morning and didn't come back. His body was found at 6:30 a.m. near his house.

Investigators quickly learned that Scotese had your proverbial arm-long record, with twenty arrests dating back to 1945 for burglary, possession of stolen property, grand larceny, and assault. He'd also botched a one-ton marijuana shipment.

Scotese was blown away by a pair of assassins, one firing a shotgun, the other a revolver, wounding Scotese in both the stomach and the head. A guy I know made his bones with the Scotese hit and got his button later in 1978.

It didn't stop there. During the same hour that Scotese was getting his, thirty-three-year-old Patrick Presenzano was whacked. Patrick was Cousin Moey's son. His throat was slit, he was shot three times, his pants were pulled down, and he was dumped from a moving car on Avenue X and Boynton Place, a desolate spot at the edge of the subway train yards just north of Brighton Beach.

When Patrick's stiff was searched, police found papers indicating that Patrick owned homes in Staten Island and Miami. Scotese and Presenzano, investigators learned, had a lot in common. They were both involved in large-scale dope smuggling, and they both maintained wildly luxurious pads in Florida.

The hits just kept coming. The day after Presenzano and Scotese were killed, the body of forty-two-year-old Leopold Ladenham, a known collector for Cousin Moey, was found in the trunk of his car in a parking lot at JFK Airport. He'd been shot multiple times in the head.

A week later, there was a twofer: Police got a call about a foul odor coming from a car out in Canarsie, which is the neighborhood in Brooklyn farthest from Manhattan. It used to be the butt of jokes because it was considered hard to get to and out of the way. "What did you do, come by way of Canarsie?" folks on TV shows would quip. It was an automatic laugh. And Canarsie really was out of the way and hard to get to, which is why many hoods chose it as a dumping ground.

Investigating the odor, cops discovered thirty-eight-year-old Nino Martini and thirty-seven-year-old Michael Mandolino shot to death in a car trunk wrapped in black plastic. The authorities didn't link the men with the war, but the killing style was familiar. By this time, homicide cops recognized the MO. Mandolino had been arrested once in 1975 on a burglary charge out on Long Island. Martini was the owner of an auto body shop on Nostrand Avenue in Midwood, Brooklyn. Both men had been shot in the head.

One of the victims was wearing only underwear. The other had on socks and pants. The medical examiner estimated that Martini and Mandolino had been in the trunk of that car for about a week. Police theorized that Mandolino was the target and Martini was in the wrong place at the wrong time.

The combination of auto shop, dump site in the trunk of a car, and the Canarsie location made many feel this was the work of Roy DeMeo's crew, which functioned as a modern-day Murder, Inc., carrying out hits for anyone willing to pay.

The DeMeo crew carried out business differently than other professional killers. For them, murder was the first choice. They didn't just kill men who had somehow wronged them or failed to pay back a debt: they killed anyone who was viewed as "bad for business." The term was very loosely defined.

In addition to the frequency of the violence, there was also a new level of calculation to the *method* these men used to dispatch their victims. DeMeo's crew had complete control in situations where other gangs largely left matters to the fates.

Traditionally, the boss of a crime family would order a hit and send out gunmen to hunt down the subject, fill him with lead, and run away. There was often a jumble of chaos as murder scenes played out in a splattery slapstick of uncontrolled elements. Bodies were left where they were. Take the cannoli.

But the DeMeo crew didn't do it that way. They did the deed in private and made all evidence extremely difficult to find. The murders took place in several indoor locations: in an apartment behind a bar, in the butcher's area at the rear of a supermarket, in automobile chop shops where the automobiles weren't the only things being reduced to parts.

The boys distributed the remains of their victims in various hard-to-search places: off the end of the Canarsie Pier, in the Fountain Ave. landfill, hidden among illegally disposed of medical wastes, or out at sea miles off Long Island's South Shore.

When a DeMeo victim was found, as occurred when bodies were left in trunks of cars, it meant that a message was being sent.

Police were also looking for links between these crimes and the murder of fifty-year-old Steven Casale, whose body was found on April 23, 1978, wrapped in a plastic bag in the trunk of a gold-colored 1969 Cadillac parked in a supermarket parking lot at 84th Street and New Utrecht Avenue in Bensonhurst.

CHAPTER THIRTY
The Men Who Would Kill Galante

THE PLAN TO HIT GALANTE was messengered to the Commission by thirty-six-year-old **Joseph Charles Massino**. Joe Massino was a protégé of Philip Rastelli, a guy who took his orders directly from the boss, who was away in Pennsylvania at the time.

Massino started out like so many hoods as a truck hijacker, paying his dues on the streets right around the same time as his friend John Gotti, then graduated to tougher assignments, earning himself the position as Rastelli's right-hand man. Massino grew up, if that's the right term, in Maspeth, Queens, a juvenile delinquent who somehow managed to stay in school until the tenth grade. He married a woman named Josephine and had three daughters, interesting to us because Josephine's brother was Salvatore "Good-Looking Sal" Vitale, who would work side by side with Massino, become a trusted friend, and then, like Judas, betray Massino when the chips were down.

Massino kept in shape as a young man, but like a lot of guys, he loved to eat and eat and eat, until by the 1970s he was known as Big Joey for his packed-on poundage. He came down with fat-man diseases like hypertension and diabetes.

In 1975, he was still working on occasion side by side with John Gotti, as both were on the 1975 hit team that whacked Vito Borelli, fulfilling a contract put out by Big Paulie Castellano, the ill-fated Gambino boss.

That year, Massino was caught by cops in possession of stolen goods, but, in one of those cases that drives people nuts, the charges were dropped because he hadn't been properly Mirandized.

Massino was made in 1977 in a ceremony conducted by Carmine Galante and went to work on Phil "Lucky" Giaccone's crew. Giaccone was also in the backup car on Knickerbocker Avenue.

Massino had been worried about Galante, afraid that Galante wanted him dead for too much ambition, so he turned the tables. Rastelli said OK, so Massino relayed the request to whack Galante to the Commission, who thought Galante was a pain in the ass with all of his "Boss of Bosses" talk, and got permission to whack Lilo. There would always be guys who didn't want to share the pie, and it was the Commission's job to make sure the Five Families all got a piece.

Those plans were approved by the Commission, working through Gambino underboss Aniello Dellacroce, and Stefano Cannone, Bonanno counselor. The vote took place at Jerry Catena's house in Boca Raton, Florida. Catena had been one of the men arrested in Apalachin.

The voters, according to legend, were Santo Trafficante, Florida boss, Aniello Dellacroce and Big Paulie Castellano of the Gambinos. Frank "Funzi" Tieri, Anthony "Tony Ducks" Corallo, and others. As a gesture of respect, they reportedly called Joey Bonanno long-distance in Tucson to get his stamp of approval, which he gave.

Galante had to go.

The writing was on the wall. Galante was a dead man walking. In this chapter, we'll introduce you to the team of men who would carry out the hit on Galante. And Joe Massino made sure he was part of the hit team. He badly wanted to be there when Lilo breathed his last.

Some of you have read my book *Mafia Hit Man*, about the hood Carmine DiBiase, aka Sonny Pinto. If you did, then you remember there was a character in there named Alphonse "Sonny Red" Indelicato. Indelicato was a Little Italy guy. He was on the scene, and according to one account fired his weapon, when DiBiase shot and killed Mikey Errichiello on Christmas Day 1951 in a Mulberry Street social club called the Mayfair.

Sonny Red got his nickname because he had a fondness for red cowboy boots. In 1954, Indelicato went down for the Errichiello hit while DiBiase went on the lam.

A first trial ended in a hung jury, but a second jury convicted Sonny Red of Murder Two and sentenced him to twenty years. When Indelicato got out, twenty full years later, he worked for Joseph "Joe Yak" Yacovelli, and even had Yak as his houseguest during the time when Yak was plotting to whack all the President Street Boys, starting with Joey Gallo. Now the reason I bring him up is that Alphonse had a son in 1947, named Anthony, who grew up to be one of the men who shot Carmine Galante.

Anthony Indelicato was sometimes called Bruno, which might've been his actual middle name. He was also called Whack-Whack, which was what he did for a living. He had a well-deserved reputation for brutality. He didn't just dispatch victims as another hit man might. He tortured his victims. You've heard of guys getting their armpits blowtorched? That was Whack-Whack. He also had a thing for acid, using it on his victims' faces, hands, and feet. Psychiatrists said that Whack-Whack, had he not been a pro killer, would have killed anyway. He had all the traits of a serial killer, a person who enjoyed killing (and torturing), a psychopath's psychopath.

Whack-Whack was also ahead of the curve when it came to cocaine addiction. It was the 1980s when the drug became popular and many thousands went into debt to their coke dealers. Indelicato was a cocaine addict in the 1970s. He went into rehab a few times but always started using again as soon as he got out, and the more snow that went up his nose, the more paranoid he became. The joke was that, when he was all wired up, he was even suspicious of himself. Under these circumstances, Whack-Whack could not be trusted to do as he was told. He was supposed to only hit Commission-approved wiseguys, but he'd go rogue and kill whoever happened to be bothering him at that moment. There was talk of bumping him off because he was a loose cannon, but when it came time to ice Carmine Galante, Whack-Whack was first to be named to the hit team.

Also in on the initial plans was **Dominick "Big Trin" Trinchera**, a Bronx-born hood, whose parents came over on the boat, dad from Rome, mom from Naples. Trinchera had been among those indicted, but never adjudicated, for the hit on Joey Gallo. Of the conspirators who whacked Galante, he was the largest. "Big Trin" might as well have been called Fat Trin, as he tipped the scales at 350 by the time Galante's fate was decided and would sit in the backup car, where he took up more than his share of the back seat.

According to the feds, who were listening in, there was a meeting during the late spring of 1979 between Trinchera, Indelicato, and a **Louis Giongetti**. Trinchera introduced Indelicato to Giongetti. Whack-Whack asked Giongetti if he had ever "hit anyone." Giongetti assured Indelicato that he was experienced and well trusted. In July, again according to fed surveillance, Trinchera sent Giongetti to what was referred to as a "safe house," to pick up shotguns and other weapons to be used in the Galante hit.

Galante's personal bodyguard, ever since he got out of prison five years earlier, was Cesare Bonventre, The Tall Guy. He might've been on Galante's side when the shooting started, but as we'll see, the second his boss was dead, he demonstrated his allegiance to Rusty Rastelli on the spot.

Santo Giordano, who would stand as armed guard outside while the hit team went in, had several skills that made him a successful gangster. He could strip a car in less than ninety seconds, and he could in a pinch fly an airplane. This made him a natural for smuggling operations, both in the air and on the ground.

* * *

Russell Mauro was a major heroin dealer and Bonanno gun. Mauro first came under police radar at age twenty-eight in February 1967 when two cops in a patrol car—NYPD patrolmen Ronald Abolt and Theodore Warren of the Snyder Avenue station—spotted Mauro and another man trying to force their way into a physician's home on Ocean Avenue at 6:55 p.m. in Flatbush, Brooklyn.

The home belonged to Dr. Nathan Spector. Mauro's accomplice was Salvatore Fanale of Staten Island, who identified himself as an out-of-work cabdriver. Dr. Spector told the police that he answered his doorbell just before seven o'clock and was confronted by Mauro.

"I need to make an appointment for my wife," Mauro said.

At that point, Finale appeared at the door and the two men tried to push their way inside by force. The doctor resisted vigorously and tried to slam the door closed on them.

The robbers were persistent, however, and eventually managed to kick the door open. They forced the doctor into his office and made him lie facedown on the floor. The doctor's wife and housekeeper were in another room in the house.

Unfortunately for the criminals, just as they were kicking down the front door to the house a patrol car cruised by. The cops made a hasty U-turn, pulled over the curb, and ran into the house with guns drawn.

The robbers chose wisely and did not fight the police. Cops pulled a .22 revolver off Mauro. Fanale tried to make a run for it but was nabbed and disarmed of his .38 revolver by Patrolman Abolt.

Mauro and Fanale were taken to jail and, the next day, were brought to Brooklyn Criminal Court. Mauro said he was a truck driver and gave his address as a home on East 8th Street in the Homecrest section of Brooklyn.

In court, the men stood before Judge Morton Tolleris, and were charged with assault, robbery, and violation of the Sullivan Law (weapons violation). They were granted $10,000 bail each.

Mauro did a stint for the robbery but evolved into a major heroin dealer for the Bonanno Family. And, as we shall see, he might've been the last person Carmine Galante would ever see.

Phil "Lucky" Giaccone was born in Ridgewood, Queens, in 1932 during the Great Depression. As a kid, he was an angel, an altar boy, did well in school, finished even. By the time he graduated from high school he was smart enough to know that going to work in the legit world was a sucker's bet and found himself under the wing of Bonanno bigwig Giovanni Bonventre. Officially, Giaccone ran a trucking firm in South Ozone Park, and his garage served as a clubhouse for his crew. When it came time to rid the Bonanno Family of its animalistic boss, Philly Lucky was in.

J. B. Indelicato, Sonny Red's older brother.

In the meantime, as the hit was planned, Galante continued to behave as if he did indeed rule everything. He strutted on short legs, chin up like Mussolini, into new restaurants in Little Italy and announced that he oversaw all crime in the world. Had he lost his mind? Did he believe it? He was a powerful man, but not all-powerful, a distinction he may never have grasped.

It wasn't like Galante was reckless. He knew it was a wild world out there; he'd been a major force of wildness—so Galante kept a couple of Zips with him for protection whenever he was out. Galante tried to be careful, and he tried to carry on as a free man should. Eventually that was going to catch up with him, he knew, and during his last days he was prone to wistful nostalgia, sullen as he pondered the sacred twilight.

CHAPTER THIRTY-ONE
Death of Galante

ON THE DAY CARMINE GALANTE died, July 12, 1979, the top stories in the city were: a Pan American Boeing 747 jet had been grounded at JFK Airport because cracks were found in its fuselage; the defunct space station Skylab broke up and scattered debris on Australia; crisis scapegoat Energy Secretary James R. Schlesinger was on the verge of resignation; a twenty-four-year-old nurse's aide named Sharon Anglin was found dead in her apartment on East 91st Street, a victim of a sexual assault; a new baby gorilla was born in the Bronx Zoo; 353 corrections officers on Rikers Island were suspended after they walked off the job protesting a new ruling that would have them working longer hours so that inmates wouldn't have to go to bed early; yellow taxi rates went up fifteen cents per mile; merchants throughout the city refused to accept the new Susan B. Anthony dollar coin because they felt it was too small; Gary Burghoff, the guy who played Radar O'Reilly on the TV show *M*A*S*H*, announced that he was leaving the show; a feud was brewing between New York Yankee "Sweet Lou" Piniella and another team's mascot; Indiana basketball coach Bobby Knight was arrested for assault in an incident with a police officer in Puerto Rico; and the Mets beat the Dodgers in extra innings on a game-winning hit by catcher John Stearns. It was a typical array of news stories. Twenty-four hours later, the tabloids were going to be all about Carmine Galante.

* * *

Typically, New York City's hottest days are in the first half of July, and this year was no different. This was a day so hot that you could see the air shimmering as heat rose from blacktop, a day so humid that many men could sweat through their shirts walking from their front doors to their cars.

As the clock struck noon, Galante was being driven by his nephew James Galante in a brown Lincoln limousine to Joe and Mary's Italian-American Restaurant on Knickerbocker Avenue between Troutman and Jefferson Streets in the Bushwick section of Brooklyn, driven to what would be his final meal. The sign above the restaurant's entrance read: "We Give Special Attention to Out Going Orders."

Bushwick was on the slide. Middle-class Italians were moving to Staten Island and being replaced by impoverished Puerto Ricans. Despite the shifting demographics, there remained in Bushwick islands of Bonanno turf. One such oasis was Joe and Mary's.

As he'd done dozens of times before, nephew James waited until his powerful uncle was safely inside the restaurant, and drove off.

Giuseppe "Joe" Turano, the Joe in Joe and Mary's, was Galante's cousin. He and Mary didn't care what their customers did for a living. They only knew that they were all homesick for the old country, and when lunch was served it was Sicilian down to the bread crumbs. Turano's joint was friendly, and the food was good, but it didn't look like much from the outside. The front windows wore yellow curtains, once vibrant, now sun bleached.

Turano, the story goes, was planning a trip to Sicily. Mary, his wife, was already on vacation in Sardinia, and he was to join her. This was Thursday. He was leaving on Saturday. This was to be a family get-together at Joe and Mary's to say farewell. The going-away party filled a large table in the back, on the outdoor patio.

Now maybe there was a little breeze, but indoors there were fans blowing and of course it was in the shade. The choice to eat outdoors had to be for security reasons. You couldn't bug the sky. When the men sat down, it was eighty-eight degrees in the shade—with an excruciating eighty-percent humidity. The men were in the direct sunlight, and the patio held the heat nicely. They must have been broiling, soaking three times over through their polo shirts.

Constanza Turano, Joe's teenaged daughter, was in the restaurant's kitchen when Galante arrived. She overheard Galante talking to her grandmother, discussing old times. Galante was practically maudlin. Part of him saw it coming.

Also attending the celebration was Cousin Moey. Early in the meal, however, Moey said, "I don't feel so good. I think I go for a walk."

"Go for a walk," Galante said with his mouth full.

Moey, who'd been at Galante's side all along, now left that side forever. He excused himself and left the table. He didn't come back.

Minutes later three men arrived. They were drug dealer Leonardo Coppola, thought to be loyal to Galante, and two Zips: Galante's bodyguards Baldassare Amato and his Sicilian cousin Cesare "The Tall Guy" Bonventre. Turano, whose party it was, didn't like Coppola and was clearly irritated when the guy showed up at his joint.

"Don't worry, Giuseppe," Galante said. "Coppola is my friend. Have some wine. Soon we will all be friends."

Turano still didn't like it, but three setups were prepared, and the newcomers sat at the table. Galante sat at the head of a long table, facing the back of the restaurant. His bodyguards flanked him, Amato on his left, Bonventre on his right. Coppola sat opposite Bonventre, and Turano sat at the other end of the table with his back toward the building.

At about 2:45 p.m., the party was between courses; the main meal had been eaten and everyone was waiting for dessert to be served. Just then four men got out of a Mercury sedan on Knickerbocker Avenue.

Three of them, armed with handguns and a shotgun, their faces obscured by ski masks, entered Joe and Mary's through the front door. The fourth was the driver, Santo Giordano, who held a rifle and stood guard on the sidewalk as the others entered the restaurant.

Turano's son John shouted out a warning from the storeroom.

John made eye contact with one of the masked men, who said, "Don't move."

While two of the gunmen moved swiftly through the restaurant and burst into the outdoor patio, the third, Dominick "Big Trin" Trinchera stepped into the storeroom and shot and wounded John Turano. He then joined the other two on the patio.

"What are you doing?" Turano managed to say, looking back over his shoulder, before all hell broke loose.

At the sound of the gunshots, in the kitchen a hysterical Constanza Turano hid behind a refrigerator.

All three gunmen then turned to the men at the table. There was a fusillade of shots and Galante, Turano, and Coppola all went down. Russell Mauro concentrated his attention on the primary target, Carmine Galante.

Galante was lighting his cigar when he took Mauro's shotgun blast point-blank to the upper chest. The blast knocked him onto his back to the patio floor, killing him instantly. A subsequent .45 shot to the left eye put an exclamation point on the hit. Blood soaked Galante's shirt and pale blue knit slacks.

Bruno "Whack-Whack" Indelicato shot Turano. Galante's bodyguard Cesare "The Tall Guy" Bonventre stood up, all six-foot-seven of him, and instead of defending the man he was supposed to guard joined the hit team. He shot and killed Coppola and then fired two shots into his ex-boss's dead body.

Either Bonventre knew the hit was coming and was in on it all along, or he made a quick, dramatic, and no doubt lifesaving shift of allegiance. Mauro and Indelicato each had a shotgun shell left. Mauro fired his into Galante, just to make sure, and Indelicato fired into the head of Coppola, who by this time was stretched out on the floor.

The noise had been deafening, and just like that it was over, silent except for the ringing in the ears. The men in the ski masks retreated through the restaurant and out onto the street. Bonventre followed them and four men piled into a blue Mercury sedan.

When the sound of the gunshots ended, Santo Giordano left his post at the restaurant's front entrance and got back behind the wheel of the getaway car. Resisting an urge to peel out, Giordano drove the speed limit, twenty-five miles per hour, down Knickerbocker Avenue, blending with traffic in seconds. (The Mercury had been stolen from one Hermelo Blen of Ozone Park, Queens. He reported it missing to the police of the 106th Precinct, and it was found abandoned not long after the hit on Galante.)

While the killing was going on, there was a car parked out on Knickerbocker Avenue, not the getaway car, but another, the backup, a crew of observers, cagey veterans, making sure everyone did what they were supposed to do, and to clean up the mess if they didn't. Now this car moved into the center of the street and formed a sort of roadblock to make sure the getaway car could get away without traffic getting in the way.

The men in the backup car were Alphonse "Sonny Red" Indelicato, Anthony's dad and a stone-cold killer since the 1950s; and Joe Massino, who was largely responsible for putting the hit together. Sonny Red's older brother Joseph "J. B." Indelicato was in the car also, as was Phil "Lucky" Giaccone.

When Constanza Turano came out from her hiding spot in the kitchen, she saw Coppola and Galante on the floor, and Amato crouching behind a table with a gun in his hand. Her brother, John, in the kitchen at the time, later recalled that he thought it was odd that Amato and Bonventre arrived wearing leather jackets despite the heat.

Most famously, when the police arrived on the scene, as usual with a photographer from the tabloid press in tow, they found Galante sprawled out on the patio with a cigar still clamped in his jaw. His hand was positioned as if he were about to relight his stogie, and his blood seemed to be pumping directly from his blasted heart into a river flowing down a large metal drain at his side.

His life had gone down the drain. The symbolism was rife with meaning.

A police officer reached down and took the fallen Turano by the wrist.

"This one's still alive," he said. But Turano died in the ambulance on its way to Wyckoff Heights Hospital.

The cops wouldn't allow the photojournalist to enter the patio, so he instead ran up the stairs and bullied his way to a rear window where he could look directly down upon the crime scene. There he captured the photo that would grace the front page of the next day's *Daily News*, a photo that would become one of the most famous in organized-crime history, forever making Carmine Galante more famous in death than he ever had been in life.

And just like that, Galante's power was gone. He had positioned himself perfectly to rake in the dough, head collector and bagman for the Commission's cut of the Sicilian heroin racket, but he forgot he was a middleman, a very rich and powerful middleman for sure, but a middleman, nonetheless. He wasn't the Boss of Bosses, indeed not even really a boss. He wasn't the winner of all competitions. Unlike the handball games in prison, there were real-life games that Galante lacked the juice to fix, and finally, in the game of life, he'd lost.

When he decided that he was going to siphon more money for himself from the Big Dope Machine and leave less for commissioners, it was only a matter of time before they turned on him.

The hit was preventive as well. The Commission didn't know Galante's plans, but they assumed his power hunger would continue to make him a pain in the ass. If he was disrespectful enough to steal from commissioners, then he might try to hit one or more of them, too, right? Better to take him off.

Both Zips at Joe and Mary's, Bonventre and Amato, were with Salvatore "Toto" Catalano, the head of the Zips, who was initially sent to the United States to keep an eye on Galante and be his brains if any thinking needed to be done. Galante was whacked with two Zips at the table, both of whom walked away without a scratch, at least one of them making a getaway with the assassins.

And Bushwick, a neighborhood already on the steep slide, found itself with another gaping void with the senseless murder of the beloved Joe Turano, restaurateur, tragic collateral damage from the hit on Galante.

Joe Bonanno had once suffered the pangs of that same kind of hunger, of ultimate power, a guy who dreamed of wiping out the Commission so that there was only one seat at the table, his. But Bonanno was a smart man. He knew when the jig was up, when it was time to go away and leave the crime life behind, to enjoy his later years.

Galante was like Bonanno in the sense that he had great ambition, but he wasn't a smart man, and he didn't know when to stop pushing. He'd walked into a trap, and he didn't even see it coming. Galante, of course, knew that he was on the short list of men to be hit but must have felt safe at Joe and Mary's. It was home, but even homes can be invaded.

He clearly had no idea that his bodyguards had turned on him. Coppola was loyal to Galante and thus was taken out by the gunmen. The idea of taking out a boss's guards along with the boss made sense, as it limited the chances of competent blowback. Much has been said about Bonventre's gesture, putting slugs into an already-dead body, unnecessarily connecting his gun with the crime. It could have come back to bite him, but as it turned out it did not.

And what about Cousin Moey? Angelo Presenzano's role, if any, in the hit is a mystery. Certainly, the fact that he left the meal early is suspicious. But Moey? Galante's best man at his wedding, the guy who'd been whispering in his ear and helping him think things through since they were kids? Would he turn on his beloved cousin Lilo?

Maybe he had no choice. What we do know is that, without Lilo, Moey didn't have much of a mob career left in him.

There is evidence that Cousin Moey's indigestion was real, as FBI surveillance recorded evidence at the Ravenite Social Club that the Galante hit team was supposed to take out Angelo Presenzano along with Galante and was surprised and disappointed that Moey wasn't on the patio when the shots rang out.

Within hours of Galante's death, Big Paulie Castellano, himself not long for this earth, sat down with Salvatore Catalano and a few other Zips at Martini's restaurant in Bay Ridge, Brooklyn. It was a seafood joint on Fourth Avenue and 86th Street, a major commercial intersection. It had been open since Christmas 1974.

At Martini's the men discussed what to do with the piece of the heroin-smuggling pie that had been vacated by Galante's exit. Paul Castellano—a guy who'd once threatened to kill anyone in the Gambino Family, and possibly anyone, period, whom he caught selling heroin—told the Zips that from now on the money previously given to Galante was now to come to him. (Martini's is long gone. There's a sushi place there now.)

The first guy to put his hands in the stiffs' pockets was a cop. While police tape was still being put up, Galante's pockets were searched. There was discussion. Should they remove the cigar from Galante's lips? Eventually, they left the cigar alone. The medical examiner might want to see the stogie in situ. Galante had $860 in cash on him. He had a Medicare and Social Security card. Forensic scientists and the medical examiner showed up and went through the slow process of figuring how many guns were fired and which weapons were responsible for which wounds. They discovered shell casings from a .45 semi-automatic, two .38 semi-automatics, and shotgun shells.

Galante's body was carried through the restaurant to the street, where it was loaded into a police hearse. As a reporter watched, a man named Joseph Bricolli spat on the hearse.

Asked why he had disrespected the dead, Bricolli replied, "It was during the war and I was working very hard against the Fascist Mussolini with my friend and hero Carlo Tresca. Galante was the man who killed Tresca. Garbage is what he was. He killed my hero—and then he sold heroin to children."

* * *

In Little Italy, there was a celebration of Galante's death in the Ravenite Social Club, the first floor of a five-story brick building on Mulberry Street. It was an interesting place to hold the "wake."

The Ravenite had been a mob hangout since its inception in 1926, when it was known as the Alto Knights Social Club and Lucky Luciano came in for his espresso. It became HQ for the Gambinos, and it was Don Carlo himself who in 1957 renamed the club the Ravenite, in honor of his favorite poem, "The Raven" by Edgar Allan Poe. Gambino, and then Aniello Dellacroce and then John Gotti ran the family out of the Ravenite. And now, Galante dead, there was a party going on there.

This we know because the NYPD had the joint under surveillance. An hour after the hit in Bushwick, Bruno and Sonny Red Indelicato, Phil Giaccone, alleged consigliere Steve Cannone, and other wiseguys were out front of the Ravenite, and were filmed as they celebrated like it was New Year's. Inside the club, Gambino underboss Aniello Dellacroce sat, celebrating in a quieter manner. The men believed that the hit on Galante would bring peace not just to the Bonanno Family but to all of the families. Galante had represented chaos and there was a strong sense that order had been restored now that he was gone. Of course, it didn't work out that way.

The film of the Ravenite celebration would one day be shown to the jurors at the so-called Commission Trial, evidence under the RICO laws that all of New York's bosses were culpable in Galante's death.

Whack-Whack, Big Trin, and The Tall Guy were all promoted to capo following the Galante hit.

Police were interested in reports that Cousin Moey had been at the lunch but left early because of a "stomachache." He walked out into Bushwick and didn't return, interesting because he was one of the men in the car when Galante received his infamous upstate speeding ticket. They didn't find him, and for all we know the stomachache was real. Moey didn't have long to live, dying of natural causes on July 20, 1979.

With Galante gone, Rusty Rastelli was firmly in charge of the Bonannos, calling the shots from behind bars.

Some mob funerals are spectacles, ostentatious affairs, celebrations of ill-gained power—hoodlum pomp, it's called. But not Carmine Galante's. His final services were modest. Because he had been the victim of a homicide, an autopsy was mandatory and performed by the Kings County Medical Examiner. After the postmortem procedure, Galante's body was embalmed at the Provenzano Lanza Funeral Home on Second Avenue in the crumbling ruins of the Lower East Side of Manhattan.

The story goes that the guy who embalmed Galante's recently autopsied stiff was also the maître'd at Lanza's, one of Galante's favorite restaurants, at 10th Street and First Avenue. After embalming, Galante was laid out in Chapel B.

Buildings on both sides of the mortuary were abandoned and graffitied. Down the block the rusting and charred hulk of an abandoned car sat curbside. It was bleak, as was much of New York City during the late 1970s, suffering both a fiscal crisis and a crisis of the soul.

The Roman Catholic Church denied Galante a funeral mass.

The ceremony was modest, but it was still a great place to mob watch. There was a limo parked outside with a pair of men in the back, invisible due to the tint in the windows. Other men took turns getting into the limo, meeting with its occupants, and then getting out, making room for the next. Each time the door opened there was a glimpse of the limo's interior, pure silver opulence, a fully stocked bar, and a telephone (in the days before cell phones an extravagant luxury).

Two man-mountains stood on either side of the funeral home door, checking everyone out before allowing them inside. The usual assortment of law enforcement (city and fed) was outside, some photographing all comers and goers, others jotting down license-plate numbers. A contemporary report said that Galante rested in an open casket, hard to believe considering the way he died, shot in the face by a .45, his left eye knocked out.

The largest flower display came from Galante's estranged wife, Helen. It was a white carnation heart with a gash of red. On it was spelled out "Alter Ego Per Semper," which means "I will be his forever, he will be mine forever."

When reporters got attendees to talk at all, they asked who whacked Carmine. It was as if they had all rehearsed their lines. It had nothing to do with the mob, they said. Some Puerto Ricans had gone in there to rob the place, panicked, and ended up shooting some people.

"We live in a jungle," they inevitably concluded.

No one believed the story.

Galante was buried in St. John Cemetery in Middle Village, Queens, in a row's end grave near the southeast corner of the cemetery. There were fifty-nine mourners on hand, including his last lawyer, Roy Cohn, his wife, Helen, and his daughter Nina from his second family in a black dress. As per tradition, the goomara, Ann, despite being Nina's mom, stayed home to avoid an unsightly catfight.

(Today there is perhaps no other graveyard in the world with more big-time hoods buried there than St. John. In addition to being Lilo's final residence, there are also the nearby graves of Lucky Luciano, Joseph Profaci, Joseph Colombo, Carlo Gambino, John Gotti, and Vito Genovese.)

During the graveside ceremony, the rogue priest who agreed to lead the ceremony struggled, finally saying that he would leave the fate of Carmine Galante's soul to the "judgment of God," as Nina placed a red rose on her father's coffin.

An FBI guy who kept the scene under surveillance, and from whom we get these details, commented on the sparse crowd, "Galante was so bad that no one even wanted to be around him when he was dead."

Galante had only been dead for a couple of years when many of the men involved in his death were themselves killed.

On the morning of May 5, 1981, Trinchera told his wife that he had to go to a meeting, kissed her goodbye, and she never saw him again. Trinchera's meeting was in a Brooklyn social club, the 20/20 Night Club in the Clinton Hill section of Brooklyn.

When he got there, Alphonse "Sonny Red" Indelicato and Phil "Lucky" Giaccone were already there.

Trinchera asked where the meeting was and was told that it was in the storeroom. The three men were allegedly led into the storeroom by Gerlando Sciascia and Frank Lino, where Joe Massino waited. The men weren't given much time to look around, so they might not have noticed that there were tarpaulins on the floor, suitable for wrapping up bodies.

Earlier that day, while setting the trap, Massino had urged his hit team to avoid shooting because he didn't want to have to explain a lot of bullet holes in the room. As the victims entered the storeroom, they nodded their nervous greetings.

A small group of gunmen burst into the room in ski masks looking like the minions of the Grim Reaper himself.

For reasons unknown, one of them yelled, "It's a holdup!"

Maybe he wanted the men to reach for the sky rather than for their own heaters. (You weren't supposed to bring a weapon to a peace meeting, very bad form, but you never knew.)

Massino savagely turned on Phil Lucky and punched him in the jaw. Lucky collapsed to the floor. Sonny Red made a break for the door, but it was Massino again, knuckles still stinging, who blocked his path.

Trinchera, who didn't move too fast but had a lot of bulk, made for the door.

Massino realized that his instruction to not use bullets wasn't going to work. He gave the OK to finish it, and one of the masked men produced a submachine gun and efficiently took out Trinchera, Sonny Red, and Phil (Not So) Lucky.

A later federal indictment claimed that J. B. Indelicato was also on the hit list for this day but somehow evaded his killers. Reportedly, J.B. took over his dead brother's crew, which included his nephew Bruno as a soldier.

Also shot that same day in Bushwick was Bonanno associate Santo Giordano, the Knickerbocker Avenue lookout, who at 10:50 p.m. was wheeled into the emergency room of Wyckoff Heights Hospital on the Brooklyn-Queens border, with a hole in his back and a bullet lodged against his spinal cord. He told police his name and then zipped his lips. They told him he was never going to walk again.

Back in the 1950s, mobsters would be whacked and the Law would have no idea why. Maybe it was a war between families; maybe it was a civil war within a family. They didn't know. But, by 1981, enough wiseguys had ratted that the authorities understood who belonged to which family and who was whacking who and why. The shooting at the 20/20 was correctly seen as one faction of the Bonanno Family cleaning house of powerful men who wouldn't fall in line.

One FBI agent said, "It was an especially neat spring cleaning."

Allegedly one of the hooded men was Massino muscle Sal Vitale. Another was Vito Rizzuto, who came down from Montreal to be in on the action. Rizzuto was the one reported to have yelled, "It's a holdup!"

Weeks after the triple hit, children were playing in a vacant lot in Ozone Park, Queens, on Ruby Street south of Blake Avenue. The kids were playing in a pile of dirt when they inadvertently excavated the body of Sonny Red, which was wrapped in a blanket and pretty ripe, partially decomposed and crawling with insect activity.

Over the years that Ruby Street lot would build a reputation as a popular dumping spot for killers following the orders of John Gotti. It would be twenty-three years before the remains of Giaccone and Trinchera were found on that same lot not far away.

After his father's murder, Anthony "Bruno" Indelicato went into hiding in Fort Lauderdale. Luckily for him, the guy who was assigned to whack Anthony was Donnie Brasco, who couldn't do the job on account of he was an undercover FBI agent. Bruno would eventually be arrested and tried as part of the Commission Trial.

During the summer of 1982, five racketeers were on trial in a Manhattan court: Benjamin "Lefty Guns" Ruggiero, Anthony "Mr. Fish" Rabito, Nicky Santora, John "Boobie" Cerasani, and Antonio "Boots" Tomasulo. This was the big-time trial caused by the Donnie Brasco fiasco.

We discuss it here because Santo Giordano, the man who stood guard on the street while Galante was whacked, was called to testify for the prosecution. Giordano, still paralyzed from the bullet lodged in his spine, testified from a wheelchair.

Officials were hoping that, once the men were under oath, they would get the details of the shooting that took away Giordano's legs, as well as the shootings that disappeared Sonny Red, Phil Lucky, and Big Trin. They were to be disappointed.

Giordano, identified by the prosecution as an unindicted co-conspirator, told the court that he was thirty-nine years old and lived in Middle Village, where, before he was shot, he made a living as an auto mechanic.

He testified with a straight face that he had been shot in an altercation stemming from a traffic incident.

"It had nothing to do with the mob or anyone getting rubbed out," Giordano said. "I was in Bensonhurst, on Eighty-Sixth Street near Bay Forty-Sixth Street, and my car was blocked in by someone who double-parked. I honked the horn to get the attention of the car's owner. But when he came out, he didn't move his car; he punched me. I punched him back, knocked him down, and he came up with a gun and shot me."

It was unlikely, just about everyone realized, that Giordano had been shot in Bensonhurst and taken to a hospital in Bushwick. Both locations are in Brooklyn, but opposite sides of the borough, fifteen miles and a forty-minute drive away.

Giordano admitted that he'd never reported his shooting to the police and then he'd refused to talk to police who came to visit him in the hospital.

"I didn't talk to them because I wasn't feeling too good," Giordano said.

The frustrated prosecution called to the stand the doctor who had treated Giordano after he was shot. They asked if Giordano ever told him about the circumstances behind his shooting. The doctor was smart. He said he never asked.

The message was clear. If you were a Bonanno and you weren't doing the right thing, your life expectancy was yesterday. The dead hoods kept piling up. Thirty-five-year-old William "Cappy" Capparelli of Astoria, Queens, and forty-year-old Thomas Genovese of Staten Island were next, their bodies discovered on May 15, 1981.

Cappy was found shot twice in the head and once in the neck in a car parked at Cherry Street and Mechanics Alley on the Lower East Side of Manhattan, and Genovese was discovered in a car parked in Bay Ridge, Brooklyn, with three bullet holes forming an equilateral triangle in the back of his head.

The FBI went on the record saying that the two killings were not connected, as if they had a clue. The feds did admit, however, that members of the Bonanno crime family were dropping or vanishing at a significant rate. Four upper-echelon members of the family, the FBI said, were missing and presumed dead, all part of a power struggle orchestrated by Phil Rastelli from his Pennsylvania jail cell, as usual using Joe Massino as his legman, putting the hits together.

On August 17, 1981, another Bonanno rebel, Dominick "Sonny Black" Napolitano, was killed under Massino's orders. Sonny Black got his nickname when he began to dye his hair when he was still in his twenties. Sonny Black, who ran his rackets—gambling, shylocking—out of the Withers Social Club at the corner of Withers Street and Graham Avenue in Greenpoint, Brooklyn, was the scapegoat for the Brasco disaster.

Napolitano was the one who befriended Brasco, took him under his wing, and brought him around, introducing him to the boys. Not only did Napolitano present Brasco as trustworthy; he also blabbed in front of him, telling him inside stuff, how there was a commission and they would meet to see who would and wouldn't get whacked, how the Commission decided that Funzi Tieri needed to be taken down from his perch and replaced by Big Paulie Castellano, how some guys were good earners and others not pulling their weight financially. Sonny Black could see opportunities where others saw only a wall.

Brasco got so far inside that the Commission voted at one point to eliminate the Bonannos as one of the Five Families, since they lacked the good judgment to keep undercover FBI agents out of their meetings—and word was it was all Napolitano's fault.

Napolitano once learned that a portion of the Shah of Iran's art collection was being housed in New York and stole it, scoring five paintings and twenty-seven sculptures. The stuff turned out to be lucrative but complicated to unload, as investors willing to pay big for stolen art meant finding a fence who could handle himself in both the underworld and the art world. That turned out to be Stephen Salmieri, a "cat burglar" who could help locate buyers for the Shah's art. Salmieri turned out to also be an undercover FBI agent. These kinds of errors on Napolitano's part were his fatal flaw.

In addition to being a cold-blooded killer and a powerful captain, with a crew that numbered upward of five hundred soldiers, in a New York crime family, Napolitano was a breeder and racer of racing and homing pigeons, which he kept in coops on the roof of his Brooklyn apartment building.

In a world of slobs, Napolitano was said to be a polite man, a gentleman, who remembered his pleases and thank-yous right up until the instant he squeezed the trigger.

Tragically, the fifty-one-year-old Napolitano knew that his time had come before he was whacked. He gave his jewelry to his favorite bartender, at the Motion Lounge. He also gave the barkeep the keys to his rooftop pigeon coops.

Sonny Black went missing in action during the summer of 1981.

One day, in a thoroughly professional and efficient way, Napolitano was picked up by Bonanno capo Frank Lino and Steve Cannone. He was taken to a house, thrown down a flight of stairs to a basement, and shot with .38s. According to legend, the first shot didn't kill him, making Napolitano's last words, "Hit me one more time and make it good!"

So, they shot him more. Twenty-two times more.

Napolitano was missing for a year. After his decomposed body was discovered looking like bad Swiss cheese, the medical examiner counted twenty-three bullet holes in him. The hands had been cut off the body, a silent warning that all wiseguys should be more careful when choosing friends.

A soldier named Anthony Mirra, another guy who initially brought Brasco into the fold, was also slated for execution the same day as Napolitano but had the good fortune to be arrested by police on his way to his own hit.

Napolitano was indicted by the feds after he was already dead.

CHAPTER THIRTY-TWO
Commission Trial

MAKING FULL USAGE OF THE NEW RICO laws, on February 25, 1985, the feds busted just about all of the mob bosses and underbosses from New York's Five Families. RICO stated that if you belonged to an organized-crime group that committed a crime, then you too are guilty of that crime. The crimes involved not just guys getting whacked but also systemic narcotics trafficking, loansharking, gambling, labor racketeering, and extortion.

The case against the Five Families began in 1983 when the feds wire tapped the offices of Ralph "Little Ralphie" Scopo and gathered evidence of him extorting money from contractors. As president of the Cement and Concrete Workers District Council of the Laborers' International Union of North America, it was his job to make sure the Commission got their tribute, a process that brought in the bosses or those who sat in their place at Commission sitdowns. The feds also learned many of the details about how the Commission worked from an electronic bug placed in the car, a Jaguar, of Salvatore Avellino, and listened in as Avellino discussed the history and roster of the Commission, as well as the relationship between the bosses.

On October 8, 1986, in Federal District Court in Manhattan, the huge, sprawling "Commission Trial" got around to the hit on Galante. The trial had a dozen big-time defendants: Big Paulie Castellano, Gambino boss; Anthony "Fat Tony" Salerno, Genovese boss (well, pretending to be the boss anyway, standing in for The Chin, whose cover story was that he was too mentally ill to possibly rule a crime gang); Anthony "Tony Ducks" Corallo, Lucchese boss; Philip Rastelli, Bonanno boss; and Carmine "The Snake" Persico, Colombo boss, not to mention an array of underbosses, consiglieres and officers of the Five Families, Aniello Dellacroce, Gambino underboss; Gennaro "Gerry Lang" Langella, Colombo underboss; Salvatore "Tom Mix" Santoro, Lucchese underboss; Christopher "Christy Tick" Furnari, Lucchese consiglieri; Ralph Scopo, union leader and Colombo soldier; Stefano Cannone, Bonanno consiglieri—and last but not least Bonanno soldier Anthony "Bruno" Indelicato, who was in on the Galante hit. A couple of the defendants didn't make it to the jury's decision. Dellacroce died of cancer on December 2, 1985, and Castellano was whacked in Manhattan on December 16.

Indelicato was charged with participation in the Galante hit, and it was during the prosecutor's case against Indelicato that Galante's murder became the focus of testimony.

On that day two of the children of the owner of Joe and Mary's Italian-American Restaurant testified as to what they saw and heard on that fateful day back in 1979.

First on the stand was Joe and Mary's daughter, Constanza Turano.

"Miss Turano, where were you when Carmine Galante entered the restaurant?" asked U.S. Attorney Michael Chertoff.

"I was in the kitchen," Constanza said in a whispery voice. The judge asked her to speak up so that the jury could hear, but her voice never did get much louder. Luckily for us, the court reporter heard her just fine.

"You are related to Mr. Galante in some way, Miss Turano?"

"Yes, he is my grandmother's cousin. My grandmother was there, and I heard Mr. Galante speaking with my grandmother briefly. They discussed old times."

"What did Mr. Galante do after he spoke with your grandmother?"

"He joined my father in the back patio for lunch."

"Your father is Giuseppe Turano?"

"That's right."

"Just the two of them?"

"At first. They were soon joined by three other men."

"Did you know the men?"

"I knew Leonardo Coppola. He was a family friend. I later learned that the other two were Baldassare Amato and Cesare Bonventre."

"Do you know what the men were discussing as they ate?"

"No. I could hear them having conversation, but I couldn't tell what they were saying. I didn't pay any attention. It was no business of mine."

"What happened next?" Chertoff asked.

"Well, it was about a quarter to three in the afternoon when I heard my father's voice. It was loud and urgent."

"What did he say?"

"He said, 'What are you doing?' Just then I heard gunshots."

"What did you do?"

"I hid behind the refrigerator."

"Could you see anything?"

"I just saw people running. They had ski masks on, and they were carrying guns."

"What did you do after you came out from behind the refrigerator?"

"I went out back and I saw my dad, Mr. Coppola, and Mr. Galante all lying on the floor. I saw Baldo Amato crouching behind a table with a gun in his hand."

The woman, despite the intrinsic quietness of her voice, had been a clear and coherent witness. Her brother did not handle himself nearly as well. His memory was poor. He couldn't remember details. The prosecutor, clearly frustrated, told Judge Richard Owen that earlier the witness had told him that he was afraid to testify. The witness did offer some details, however.

"What was the weather like that day, Mr. Turano?" Chertoff asked.

"It was hot."

"And what were Mr. Amato and Mr. Bonventre wearing when they arrived?"

"Leather jackets."

Chertoff managed to get Turano to talk about the gunmen.

"There were three of them and they were wearing masks. They all came into the restaurant at the same time." The witness lowered his head and mumbled. Judge Owen made him repeat his statement.

"Where were you when they entered?"

"I was in the restaurant."

"Did they notice you?"

"Yes. One of them pointed a gun at me and told me not to move."

"What did you do?"

"I remained motionless. The three men went out back and I shouted a warning to my father. Then I heard shots going off."

"What did you do then?"

"I don't remember."

"Did you eventually go out onto the patio?"

"Yes, sir."

"And what did you see?"

"Just bodies. Just the bodies."

At the same time as the Commission trial, in the same courthouse, the "Pizza Connection" drug case was being tried. Amato was a defendant in that trial.

On the same day that the Turanos testified about the Galante hit, which also killed their dad, the prosecution also called to the witness stand Joseph D. Pistone—Donnie Brasco. Pistone told the jury, and the world, a fact about organized crime that had been previously unknown to all but a choice few insiders, the fact that there was a mob rule against killing a made guy without the Commission's approval.

The trial lasted from February 25, 1985, on to November 19, 1986, at which time a federal jury convicted the defendants. Salerno, Corallo, Santoro, Furnari, Persico, Langella, and Scopo were each sentenced to one hundred years in prison. Indelicato got off easier, sentenced to forty years.

CHAPTER THIRTY-THREE
The Galante Blood

WHILE MOST OF GALANTE'S DESCENDANTS have been law-abiding citizens, he did in one case pass down the criminal gene. Carmine's nephew also named Carmine Galante knew his share of trouble when he was a kid.

This Carmine was the son of the Cigar's younger brother Peter, who had driven a *Daily News* truck his whole life but had passed away by 1999, the year his son got in trouble.

On April 4, 1999, young Galante, then twenty-two years old and working as a pizza deliveryman, received a phone call from a bar. It was three o'clock in the morning.

It was a friend, nineteen-year-old Rocco Castellano of Gravesend, Brooklyn, saying, "Hey, you better get down here. Some college jerk-off is talking to your girlfriend."

The bar was the Bee-Kee-Nee Bar at 9060 Fort Hamilton Parkway in Bay Ridge, Brooklyn, and the college kid was eighteen-year-old Bill Manolis, a freshman at St. John's University in Queens. Manolis, who was only a block from the home in which he grew up, was out celebrating his birthday with friends and having a pretty good time.

Galante stalked into the bar at 3:45 a.m., fifteen minutes before closing time, and didn't waste a minute. The punishment for talking to his girl was death. He pulled a knife and, with witnesses looking on, plunged it into the teenager's chest. Manolis was taken to Lutheran Medical Center, where he died at five o'clock that morning.

Galante and Castellano bolted from the bar, jumped into a dark Toyota Camry, and zoomed off into the inky Brooklyn night, around Dyker Park and into Bath Beach, where they could breathe. They abandoned the Camry a mile and a half from the bar and disappeared. Castellano was arrested two days later. Galante remained a wanted man for two years.

During the spring of 2001, the *Daily News* put young Galante's mug shot—from a 1996 drug-possession charge—in the paper as part of a rogue gallery of "worst of the worst." In addition to the drug charges, he'd also been arrested twice for petty larceny. Pesky journalists inquired, but officials were at a loss as to why Galante had, despite his record, never done any jail time. He was arrested twice while on probation for drugs and yet his probation was never revoked. Sometimes that means it's a who-you-know world.

The headline in the paper read: "Have You Seen This Man?" Well, many readers thought they had. After assuring confidentiality, the tabloid was flooded with tips as to Galante's whereabouts.

On Monday, April 16, 2001, a team of law enforcement, made up of members of the NYPD, the Drug Enforcement Administration, and Suffolk County cops, converged on a house on Pole Drive in Mastic, Long Island. Galante, it turned out, had been living in a basement apartment with a stray pit bull he'd picked up.

"Where you been, Carmine?" a cop asked.

"Here and there," he replied.

About the teenager he'd killed, Galante said, "I wanted to stab him. But I didn't want to kill him."

Police learned that Galante had left the country for Italy initially after the murder but had returned and lived under the names Bono Vinestro and Vincent Bono.

After Galante's arrest, Manolis's mother, Maria—a Greek Orthodox parochial schoolteacher in Park Slope, Brooklyn—said, "Thank God they finally got him. I feel this is the beginning of peace. The real closure will come when I see this man behind bars so he can't do this to someone else."

On April 17, 2001, Galante was charged with second-degree murder and criminal possession of a weapon. To get by while on the lam, Galante said he'd worked part-time construction and landscaping jobs. But, he admitted, he spent most of his time eating and watching television, a truth demonstrated by the fact that Galante had packed eighty pounds onto his five-seven body while "on the run" from the Law.

Neighbors had no idea he was a fugitive and barely noticed him. They'd see him walking his dog. Sometimes a woman came to visit him. He wasn't friendly; they all agreed on that. He walked around with a leave-me-alone scowl on his face, and the neighbors did. None knew his name.

"He was not a nice person. You could just tell," one neighbor commented.

Local cops remembered young Carmine being trouble while growing up in Bensonhurst. His parents were legit. They'd tried to keep their son out of trouble and had warned him not to hang around with gangsters. But it didn't take.

Young Carmine was determined to take after his uncle Lilo. Even the Bonanno Family was on dad Peter's side and refused to allow the young Carmine into their Bath Beach social clubs. So Carmine switched families and began dating the sixteen-year-old stepdaughter of Joseph "Joey Flowers" Tangorra. This was the girl Manolis was talking to on the night Galante stuck a knife in his heart.

On June 7, 2002, Galante pleaded guilty to killing Manolis. The plea bargain meant that Galante was finally going to see jail time— to the tune of at least eighteen years. At the sentencing hearing, Galante addressed the Manolis family.

"I hope and pray for your forgiveness," he said. "Never in a million years did I think that death was going to be the result."

New York State took charge of Galante on July 8, 2002, and have yet to give him up. As of 2022, Galante remained behind bars at the Woodbourne Correctional Facility in Sullivan County.

Epilogue

COUSIN MOEY MIGHT OR MIGHT NOT have known Carmine was going to be whacked when he excused himself from the table at Joe and Mary's with a tummy ache. If he did know and he left to avoid death, he didn't delay the Grim Reaper by much. Eight days, to be exact.

After Galante was hit, Moey went into hiding, holed up in the Raleigh Hotel up in the Catskills in a town called South Fallsburg, New York. According to the official record, Moey suffered a heart attack at 2:30 a.m. on July 20, 1979. He was rushed to a hospital where he soon died quietly.

On President Street we were more concerned, in a celebratory way, with another death that same day. That cheating rotten no-good lawyer who'd burned Joey Gallo and deserved to die, forty-six-year-old Robert Weiswasser, was found on July 20 in the back seat of his rented car on 86th Street in Manhattan, shot twice in the back of the head by someone who did the world a favor.

John Bonventre, Joe Bonanno's uncle who was in the car during Carmine Galante's controversial traffic stop, returned to Sicily in his old age, but continued his criminal activities. In May 1971, Bonventre was one of fifteen Mafiosi to be banished by Italian Carabinieri police to a three-mile island off the coast of Sicily called Filicudi.

* * *

Andrew "Andy Curly" Bucaro, the hood who went down with Carmine Galante for the 1930 botched payroll robbery and shootout with Detective Joseph Meenahan that resulted in the wounding of a six-year-old girl, was by all accounts a lifelong criminal, frequently caught but seldom convicted.

Bucaro spent World War II hiding from the draft board and helping Carmine Galante run more than a dozen stills on Long Island, including Brooklyn and Queens. He was arrested by feds in 1944 along with forty-two others. The operation was so big that a judge compared the outlets to buy the tax-free booze to "chain stores."

At age fifty-seven, Bucaro was participating in a floating craps game, busted in January of 1963 on Herkimer Court in Bedford-Stuyvesant, Brooklyn. For what it's worth, it was one of the fancier craps games that New York police had busted. It included a professional-looking gambling layout with an expensive collapsible dice table made of quality carpentry. The charge against Bucaro was "being loud and boisterous while engaging in a game of dice."

But, as we've seen, Bucaro might've never outgrown the simple pleasures of rolling bones and smash-and-grab, but he also made his bones at an early age and traveled regularly to Sicily on business. Some say he quieted down in his later years, made appearances at mob funerals, and passed away himself in 1980.

The Ravenite Social Club, the storefront on Mulberry Street where the celebration was held just minutes after Carmine Galante was whacked, went on to become John Gotti's headquarters. It was here that men stood in line to shake hands of congratulation with Gotti after Big Paulie was whacked. It was here that they celebrated long into the night when Gotti beat an assault rap in 1990, and here where they put yellow ribbons on the front windows when Gotti was convicted of racketeering in 1992. We know because the place was almost always bugged by the government. Conversations that would contribute to putting Gotti behind bars, conversations with Frankie "Locks" Locasio and Sammy "The Bull" Gravano, were held in the Ravenite.

Gotti knew that there were feds always watching the place. He'd go talk to them: "Hey, next time you bust me, don't make so much noise. It bugs the neighbors."

But Gotti apparently didn't know the walls inside the Ravenite had federal ears. He knew that there had been one failed attempt to bug the Ravenite in 1979, when the joint was still Aniello Dellacroce's headquarters. The caretaker and gatekeeper of the Ravenite, a guy named Michael Cirelli, caught a detective trying to place surveillance devices in the club. Cirelli grabbed a baseball bat and chased the guy out.

Told about the break-in, Gotti said, "Next time the fucking cops break in, shoot 'em and say you thought they were burglars." As far as Gotti knew, they didn't come back. But they had, and they were listening to every word.

Feds recorded Gotti in the Ravenite, losing his temper, saying things like, "You tell this punk, I, me, John Gotti, will sever your head off!" About lawyers, he said, "They're overpriced, overpaid, and underperformed."

On October 15, 1997, the Ravenite was raided and closed by federal agents. Eight marshals raided on a Wednesday morning and declared that they were seizing the property because it had been "forfeited and condemned" by U.S. District Judge I. Leo Glasser because it was used as John Gotti's criminal headquarters.

The site is now used as a shoe store.

On March 29, 1953, the *Brooklyn Daily Eagle* published a feature celebrating Joseph Meenahan's thirty-two-year career as a New York policeman. The man who shot Galante, and who was shot by Galante in return, rose to the rank of captain in 1944 and was in command of the Brooklyn Homicide Squad West.

For years he had overseen all of Brooklyn, but the borough was divided into east and west in 1950. Meenahan told the guy from the *Eagle* that most murders were easy to solve. They were hot-blooded: lovers' quarrels, drunken brawls, guys who just snapped. These cases tended to break in the first two days. The toughest ones were the gangland murders, he said. Professionals knew what they were doing. They knew how to avoid leaving bread crumbs for detectives to follow. His most difficult case was trying to determine who whacked the young man, Arnold Schuster, who dropped a dime on bank robber Willie Sutton. (Meenahan had no way of knowing that "Mad Hatter" Albert Anastasia ordered the hit on Schuster, just because he hated squealers.) Meenahan's best bust was in 1948 when he caught the twenty-one-year-old animal who raped and murdered an eighty-year-old spinster named Mary Gray in her third-story apartment on Madison Street in Brooklyn.

Meenahan called the shootout with Galante in 1931 his first "battle scar." He lived in Jackson Heights, Queens, with his wife and three kids, who were used to him being called in the middle of the night because someone discovered a stiff.

In 1953, Meenahan was honored by the Flatbush Chamber of Commerce and given the Gold Medal of Valor as the "worthiest cop" in Brooklyn. He retired in 1961 and died in 1971 at his home on Kildare Walk in Breezy Point, Queens, at the age of seventy-one.

Judge Albert Conway, the man who sentenced Galante to twelve and a half years in prison in Kings County Court on January 8, 1931, continued to climb the judicial ladder, serving for decades as a judge of the New York Court of Appeals. He died in 1969 at age eighty at the Methodist Hospital in Brooklyn.

Anthony "Whack-Whack" Indelicato was the only member of Galante's hit team to go to trial for the crime, although it was hard to tell. Killing Galante was just one of the charges against Indelicato, and Indelicato was just one of the defendants in what became known in 1986 as the Commission Trial.

Evidence introduced by the U.S. Attorneys against Indelicato at the Commission Trial included ballistics, medical evidence, and eyewitness evidence. Indelicato's palm print was found on the inside of the getaway car's door.

Indelicato was sentenced to forty years, fined $50,000, and sent to the fed pen in Lewisburg, Pennsylvania. While incarcerated, Indelicato found romance. There he met Cathy Burke, who was in the prison visiting her inmate father. Romance bloomed and in 1992, after Indelicato was transferred to a fed pen in Terre Haute, Indiana, he married Cathy.

He was released in 1998, and moved with his wife to Howard Beach, Queens, where he joined the crew of Bonanno capo Vincent Basciano and re-started his career as a dispatcher of souls. He had to go back to prison for a short stint because of a parole violation (consorting with felons).

In 2001, back on the streets, Indelicato was getaway driver during the hit on Bonanno associate Frank Santoro, who was shot by Basciano while Santoro was walking his dog.

In February 2006, Indelicato was charged with murder and racketeering in connection with the Santoro murder. He cut a deal and on December 16, 2008, was sent away for twenty years to the Fort Dix Federal Correctional Institution. He is scheduled for release in 2023, when he will be seventy-seven years old.

Sometime during May 1991, fifty-three-year-old Russell Mauro, perhaps the man who actually killed Galante, was himself taken off the board by Bonanno soldier John Palazzolo. And three others.

On May 29, police got a call from a resident in Astoria, Queens, saying that there was a Lincoln Town car parked on 34th Street in that neighborhood and it was stinking to high heaven. Police reported to the scene and opened the car's trunk. The stench was enough to blast them backward. In the trunk was a stuffed green plastic bag—stuffed with the remains of the fifty-three-year-old Mauro.

The green bag was taken to the Kings County Morgue, where the medical examiner determined that the cause of death was multiple gunshot wounds to the head, neck, and legs.

Determining the time of death when a body has reached such a state of decomposition is imprecise, but the medical examiner said that Mauro had been dead for "about a week."

Mauro's relationship with the Bonannos had been tumultuous. He'd been promoted to capo and given his own crew during the mid-1980s. In 1987, however, Mauro failed to do the right thing and, though allowed to continue breathing, was busted back to soldier.

Mauro owned the Catherine Social Club on Mott Street in Little Italy. He lived in an apartment building around the corner on Mulberry Street. Police said that Mauro was last seen on May 20 standing in front of his club dressed in a blue-and-gray warm-up suit. On May 22 he was reported missing by his brother Robert.

The Lincoln Town Car, which threatened to reek forever, was registered to Mauro's girlfriend's mother.

In 2016, at a mob trial in Manhattan, it was revealed that one member of the team that whacked Mauro was James "Louie" Tartaglione, who admitted to walking Mauro into the 20/20 Night Club so that he could be shot. Tartaglione, by this time a seventy-eight-year-old man, admitted that he also hung around after the multiple hits that day and helped "clean up."

Tartaglione's admission came in a crowded courtroom during the trial of Anthony Santoro, Vito Badamo, and Ernest Aiello, who were charged with loansharking, gambling, and narcotics. There were fireworks in the courtroom when Badamo's defense lawyer cross-examined Tartaglione the day after the witness admitted to participating in the whacking of Russell Mauro.

"You've admitted to the murder of Russell Mauro?"

"Yes."

"He was your longtime pal and you walked him into that social club in 1991 knowing he was to be killed."

"Yes."

"And you stuck around afterward and helped clean up your longtime friend's blood?"

"Yes."

"You've said you never apologize for people whose murder you participated in, like Russell Mauro?"

"Did I apologize? As a person involved with the crime, if I were to approach a family and say I apologize, wouldn't I be indicting myself?"

"Well, Russell Mauro's brother is in the courtroom right now. You want to explain why you killed him?"

Mauro's brother stood up in the gallery and said, "Why? Why? You piece of shit!"

"Calm down, calm down," Justice Mark Dwyer said, rapping anxiously with his gavel.

Looking around, every security guard in the courtroom was on his toes and had his hand on his gat.

But Mauro's brother wasn't done. "Judge, I waited twenty years to find out why?"

The answer was because he was in the Life and that's what happens, but Mauro's brother didn't want to hear that.

Cesare "The Tall Guy" Bonventre, who had pumped bullets into Galante's dead body to prove he was hip to the way the wind was blowing, was arrested by the feds after the Galante hit, denied knowing anything about it, and was released without being charged.

Somebody said once that Bonventre killed twenty guys, but who knows? No one was keeping score. We do know that he was promoted to capo following the hit, making him, at twenty-eight, the youngest capo in the family's history.

Bonventre's crew was made up of Knickerbocker Zips from Sicily, the Bonanno Family's designated killers.

Bonventre hung out in the city, at Second Avenue and 84th Street, where his cousin Baldo Amato, with whom I once ate cannoli, had a deli. In the early 1980s, the deli burned down and, with the insurance money, a fancy apartment building with a built-in Italian café was built in its place.

The mid-hit switch on Joe and Mary's patio wasn't the first or last time that Bonventre changed allegiances midstream to stay on the pathway of health and prosperity. It was only a matter of time before he got the direction of the wind wrong and found himself facing a gale force of hot lead.

The fatal mistake came when he switched from the side of three Bonanno capos—Alphonse "Sonny Red" Indelicato, Phil "Lucky" Giaccone, and Dominick "Big Trin" Trinchera, who were planning a coup in the Bonanno Family—to the side of Rusty Rastelli.

Rastelli was in prison at the time, and underboss Joseph Massino was carrying out his orders. Giaccone, if you remember, was sitting in the backup car during the Galante hit, and Big Trin was a shooter.

But Bonventre, true only to himself, decided to turn his back on them and pally up with Massino. Trouble was, Massino didn't trust Bonventre. Massino didn't trust any of the Zips, for that matter.

Massino was a man of iron constitution, but even he was a little afraid of Bonventre. The guy was "sharp." Around him you "needed to be careful." Plus, Massino knew The Tall Guy was a horse of changing colors. He was power hungry in that dangerous way. Massino decided he didn't want Bonventre to be his friend. In fact, Massino didn't want Bonventre to be on the earth.

In April of 1984, two Bonanno hoods, Sal Vitale and Louis Attansio, put The Tall Guy in a car. Vitale drove. Bonventre got in the middle of the front seat, and Attansio took shotgun.

"Where we going?" Bonventre asked.

"Meeting with Mr. Rastelli," Vitale said. Rastelli had been released from prison on April 21, 1983.

"Where's the meeting?" Bonventre asked.

He was told they were going to a glue factory in Wallington, New Jersey. Bonventre didn't much like the sound of that. It didn't make any difference what they told Bonventre because Attansio shot Bonventre twice in the head right there in the car.

It wasn't a smooth hit, though, because the bastard didn't die. In fact, he stayed conscious and strong enough to fight. He must've had a steel skull. Bonventre grabbed the steering wheel and tried to crash the car.

Attansio had to pull Bonventre off the steering wheel. The Tall Guy was losing strength quickly. The men drove into a garage and got out. They ordered Bonventre to get out of the car, and he did so, on his hands and knees, barely conscious now. Attansio put him out of his misery with two more shots to the head, at which point The Tall Guy was disassembled into many parts, not so tall anymore, and stuffed into three fifty-five-gallon drums, which were left upstairs in a Garfield, New Jersey, warehouse.

Unaware that Bonventre was dead, the feds named him in a grand jury indictment in what would be called the Pizza Connection case, distributing heroin through pizzerias, in pizza boxes. Vitale made his bones with The Tall Guy hit and received his button later that year.

Bonventre's jellified remains were discovered a few weeks after his indictment and poured into a grave in Saint Charles Cemetery in Farmingdale, Long Island. His murderers were brought to justice in 2004 when now government witness Sal Vitale told the story in court, which is why we know the gory details.

During Vitale's testimony, he admitted to eleven murders. In October 2010, Vitale was sentenced to time served and disappeared, entering the witness protection program.

Attansio was sentenced to fifteen years. Two others who had helped clean up the Tall Guy crime scene were sent to the fed pen for ten years.

Joseph Massino, who orchestrated the hit on Galante, has the notoriety of being the first mob boss to turn rat. After orchestrating hits on any Bonannos who might tend to get in Phil Rastelli's way, Massino found himself in the upper echelons of the family.

Massino went to prison in 1986 for labor racketeering and was away when Rastelli died. Massino took charge of the family from his prison cell. In 1987, Massino was released from jail and ran the Bonannos in person, restoring order to the ranks, which had been fluctuating erratically for a whole generation. By the early 1990s, Massino was the only don of the Five Families who was not in prison.

That lasted until 2004 when that RICO bullshit caught up with him and he went down based on the testimony of his brother-in-law

Sal Vitale. Massino was looking at the death penalty when he agreed to turn federal witness and dish out the dirt on the Bonanno Family. If Massino had gone to the chair, he would have been the first mob boss to sizzle since Murder Inc.'s Louis "Lepke" Buchalter took the hot seat in 1944.

Massino kept himself off death row but was convicted on the conspiracy charges and sentenced to life in prison. In 2011, Massino helped the government again, this time testifying against alleged acting Bonanno boss Vincent Basciano.

During his testimony the government asked Massino about his first kill—everybody remembers their first time, right?—and Massino said it was a hit on Bonanno soldier Tommy Zummo, which was kind of a funny story because he was a friend of Phil Rastelli's and Rastelli would have offed Massino if he'd known he was in on icing Zummo, instead of making Massino his protégé the way he did.

The testimony against Basciano did the trick, a judge changed Massino's sentence to time served, and Massino became a free, although closely supervised, man in 2013.

Roy Cohn, Galante's last lawyer, remained a high-profile showman for the rest of his life, representing future president Donald Trump, New York Yankees owner George Steinbrenner, publisher Rupert Murdoch, Greek ship magnate Aristotle Onassis, and brand-name hoods like John Gotti and Fat Tony Salerno. Cohn was disbarred in 1986 for unprofessional conduct, i.e., perjury and witness tampering. He died of AIDS in 1986.

During the autumn of 2004, a tip regarding the "mob burial ground"— off Ruby Street in Howard Beach, Queens—sent a team of diggers, composed of FBI evidence-collection teams and NYPD detectives, to the swampy lot. Like ghouls with badges, they unearthed mob secrets that went back more than twenty years.

At first, they didn't find any bones, but they did dig up evidence that assured them they were in the right place—namely, artifacts belonging to Phil Lucky and Big Trin, both in on the Galante hit. The diggers pulled up a pair of glasses and a glasses case belonging to Lucky, a Piaget watch belonging to Lucky's wife, and a credit card and car keys belonging to Big Trin.

As expected, not far away were two sets of bones, which had been disassembled and intermingled. Figuring out which bone belonged to who might turn out to be impossible, but the bones were all there, two sets complete.

It took weeks, but forensic scientists eventually ID'd the remains as those of Phil Lucky and Big Trin, who had been gunned down inside a Brooklyn social club in 1981. Also whacked at that time was Sonny Red Indelicato, but his stiff wasn't found until weeks later.

Santo Giordano, the Bonanno mechanic/pilot who stood guard outside Joe and Mary's with a rifle in his hand while Carmine Galante was being iced, himself died a sudden and violent death.

Giordano, you'll recall, was a pilot who'd been paralyzed with a bullet pressing on his spine after he was shot on a Brooklyn street in 1981 as part of, he claimed, a road-rage incident. He was told that he'd never fly a plane again, but he was determined to get back in the air.

Making money by operating a gas station in Queens, he purchased a dark red Aero Commander at JFK Airport, cheap because it had been damaged in an on-ground collision with a cement truck. Giordano modified the plane in two ways, first so that it was a replica of a 1950 model plane and second so that it could be fully operated by a paraplegic.

At the end of July 1983, the forty-year-old Giordano was ready to take the plane on its maiden flight. With him was pilot Ralph Wheeler, who Giordano had agreed would pilot the takeoff and landing. Once aloft, Giordano would take the stick.

But the plane wasn't ready.

The plane was taken from its hangar and the men got in, Giordano with some difficulty because he couldn't use his legs. They were at Edwards Airport in Bayport, New York. According to the Federal Aviation Administration, the destination was Long Island MacArthur Airport in Ronkonkoma, New York. The purpose of the flight was, one, to test the plane, and two, to get it to MacArthur, where it could undergo still-necessary repairs on its radio.

With Giordano in the co-pilot seat, Wheeler rolled the plane nicely down a smooth, grassy runway. He got the plane off the ground, but only briefly. The plane immediately went into a steep climb and then plunged nose first into the ground, sending debris in all directions.

One witness recalled, "As he took off, it was like a stall. After lift-off he just rolled over and came down hard. It took all of three seconds, maybe four. It happened so fast. They didn't stand a chance."

The wreck caused a conflagration on the airport grounds. Witnesses ran to try to save Wheeler and Giordano but were driven back by flames and smoke.

Leader of the Zips Salvatore "Toto" Catalano went on to become the so-called King of Bushwick. This was the end of the 1970s. Joe Bonanno was in exile; the Bonanno Family was in disarray. There is an argument that Catalano, more than any other, was well served by the hit on Galante.

Catalano's power lasted until the mid-1980s, when he went down in the Pizza Connection trial, aka *United States v. Badalamenti et al.* Catalano was one of seventeen defendants accused of using pizza parlors to distribute heroin to the tune of $1.65 billion. The trial lasted seventeen months, making it the longest in U.S. history. Opium was brought from Turkey and Southeast Asia to Sicily, where it was processed into heroin. To a lesser extent, the same distribution system was used to bring cocaine up from South America. The feds' case against Catalano consisted of Salvatore Contorno, who said he had a 1980 meeting in Bagheria, Sicily, about heroin and Catalano had been there. Also in attendance were other heroin distributors, Gaetano Mazzara, and Salvatore Greco. Mazzara was a co-defendant at the trial but didn't survive till the conclusion. He was whacked on March 2, 1987, three months before he would have been sentenced to prison.

Anthony Mirra, Galante's co-defendant at his two drug conspiracy trials, the wiseguy whose misbehavior in the courtroom contributed to a mistrial being declared in their first trial and who threw a chair during their second, had a target on his back when he got out of prison. Mirra narrowly escaped several attempts on his life, but eventually his luck ran out. He was found shot to death in a Manhattan parking garage on February 18, 1982. He'd been lured to his death by members of his own family, men with whom he'd lived in the same house when he was a kid. The hood pulling the trigger was Joseph D'Amico, Mirra's cousin, who had pledged during a sacred ceremony that he would kill members of his blood family to defend his crime family and proved it here by blowing Cousin Tony's brains out. Mirra's uncle Alfred Embarrato and his cousin Richard Cantarella were waiting in the getaway car. In 2004, D'Amico testified, "I shot him several times on the side of the head."

Bill Bonanno, Joe's son, who was born a year after his dad became an official boss of one of the Five Families, knew nothing but the existence of mob royalty. It's heady stuff when your dad is getting his ring kissed by grown men. But Bill's career couldn't match his dad's. We left him in California, in prison. He served out his four years during the 1970s for mail fraud. In 1981, he was indicted in Oakland for defrauding senior citizens in a home-improvement scam. He turned rat and went so far as to co-author a book with Donnie Brasco himself, Joseph Pistone. Bill died at the age of seventy-five of a heart attack on January 1, 2008, and is buried in Holy Hope Cemetery in Tucson, Arizona.

*   *   *

And with that, we turn the final page on the Carmine Galante story, a tale of ruthlessness and grandeur, the tale of a man who never betrayed his pledge of omerta, whose ruthlessness and ambition raced him at a rate of twenty-four hours a day, seven days a week, toward a violent end under the hot July sun.

ACKNOWLEDGMENTS

The authors wish to thank the following persons and organizations, without whose help the writing of this book would have been impossible. Our editor Gary Goldstein; our literary agent Doug Grad; the Cemetery of the Evergeens; Christine Green; Jennifer Maloney; St. John Cemetery, Middle Village, Queens; St. Michael's Cemetery, East Elmhurst, Queens; Sergeant Edward Riley, spokesperson at the office of the Deputy Commissioner of Public Information, New York Police Department, and Deb Sperling.

SOURCES

BOOKS

Alexander, Shana. *The Pizza Connection*. Collingdale, PA: Diane, 1988.

Bonanno, Joseph. *A Man of Honor*. New York: Simon & Schuster, 1983.

Davis, John H. *Mafia Dynasty: The Rise and Fall of the Gambino Crime Family*. New York: HarperCollins, 1993.

DeStefano, Anthony. *The Last Godfather: Joey Massino & the Fall of the Bonanno Crime Family*. New York: Citadel, 2006.

Gallagher, Dorothy. *All the Right Enemies: The Life and Murder of Carlo Tresca*. New Brunswick, NJ: Rutgers University Press, 1989.

Heap, Chad. *Slumming: Sexual and Racial Encounters in American Nightlife, 1885–1940*. Chicago: University of Chicago Press, 2008.

Morton, Susan. *At Odds: Gambling and Canadians, 1919–1969*. Toronto: University of Toronto Press, 2003.

Pernicone, Nunzio. *Carlo Tresca: Portrait of a Rebel*. London: Palgrave Macmillan, 2005.

Petepiece, Andy. *The Bonanno Family: A History of New York's Bonanno Mafia Family*. Middletown, DE: TellWell Talent, 2021.

Pistone, Joseph. *Donnie Brasco: My Undercover Life in the Mafia*. New York: Random House, 1990.

Raab, Selwyn. *Five Families*. New York: Macmillan, 2005.

Saggio, Frankie, and Fred Rosen. *Born to the Mob*. New York: Running Press, 2004.

Schneider, Stephen. *Iced: The Story of Organized Crime in Canada*. Mississauga, ON: Wiley, 2009.

Vankin, Jonathan, and John Whalen. *The World's Greatest Conspiracies*. New York: Citadel, 2010.

NEWSPAPERS AND MAGAZINES

The Bay Ridge Paper
Brooklyn Daily Eagle
Brooklyn Times-Union
Chattanooga Daily Times
Fort Worth Star-Telegram
Gettysburg Times
Glens Falls Post-Star
The Independent
Knickerbocker News (Albany, N.Y.)
Montreal Gazette
National Post
Newark Evening News
Newark Star-Ledger
Newsday
[New York] Daily News
New York Evening World
New York Journal-American
New York Mirror
New York Review
New York Times
New York World-Telegram and Sun
The New Yorker
Ottawa Journal
Rome (Italy) News-Tribune
Soil of Liberty
Time
Tucson Daily Citizen
Tyler Morning Telegram (Tyler, Texas)
Washington Post

WEBSITES

Ballotpedia.org
Fifthestate.org
Fordham.edu
Gangstersinc.org
Narratively.com
Nationalcrimesyndicate.com
NYsun.com
Openjurist.org
Themobmuseum.org
Torontosun.com
Upi.com
Vault.fbi.gov

LEGAL BRIEFS

United States of America, Appellee, v. Carmine Galante, Defendant-appellant, 308 F.2d 63 (2d Cir. 1962).

United States of America, Appellee, v. Carmine Galante and Anthony Mirra, Appellants, 298 F.2d 72 (2d Cir. 1962).

United States v. Badalamenti, 614 F. Supp. 194 (Southern District New York, 1985).

INDEX

ABOUT THE AUTHORS

Frank Dimatteo's book *President Street Boys: Growing Up Mafia* is listed by culturetrip.com as the number-one Mafia book that "you need to read." He is also, with Michael Benson, the co-author of the Kensington True Crime books *Lord High Executioner, Carmine the Snake,* and *Mafia Hit Man,* as well as the publisher of *Mob Candy* magazine. He was born in Red Hook, Brooklyn, New York, in 1956. His father, Rick Dimatteo, was a key member of Joey Gallo's crew.

Michael Benson is the author of *Gangsters vs. Nazis.* He was Frank's co-author of *Lord High Executioner, Carmine the Snake,* and *Mafia Hit Man* and was also an editor of Frank's memoir, *President Street Boys: Growing Up Mafia.* His other books include *Escape from Dannemora, The Devil at Genesee Junction, Betrayal in Blood, Murder in Connecticut, Killer Twins, The Burn Farm, Mommy Deadliest, Watch Mommy Die, A Killer's Touch,* and *Evil Season.* He was a regular commentator on the Investigation Discovery true-crime series *Evil Twins* and *Evil Kin* and has made guest appearances on *20/20, Killer Couples, Evil Stepmothers, Deadly Sins, Southern Fried Homicide, Someone You Thought You Knew, Killer Affair, On the Case with Paula Zahn, Inside Evil with Chris Cuomo,* and *Murder in the Family.*